OCT   2016

Advance Praise for
The Marine Corps Way to Win on Wall Street

"Ken Marlin is a real player in the roller-coaster world of M&A and Wall Street. His formula for success in business is simple, and a great life lesson: understand the people you are doing a deal with and what they are trying to accomplish. Helping them get what they want gets you what you want—success!"
—Larry Kramer, President and Publisher of *USA Today*

"In *The Marine Corps Way to Win on Wall Street*, Ken Marlin lays out a compelling vision to improve Wall Street by returning to solid core values like taking the long view, behaving with honor, delivering excellence, and working for a cause greater than money. Ken is one of the most knowledgeable and trustworthy investment bankers I know. He lives up to the standards in this book." —Joe Mansueto, Founder, Chief Executive Officer, Morningstar; owner of *Inc.* and *Fast Company* magazines

"The attributes and virtues that have brought success to the Marine Corps since 1775—honor, commitment, sacrifice, adherence to standards, striving to achieve a common purpose, unparalleled individual and organizational expertise, and teamwork—are not exclusive to Marines. They will work in almost any endeavor and especially on Wall Street. Ken Marlin hit a home run in describing just how that can and should be done."
—Lt. General Robert R. Blackman, Jr.,
CEO of the Marine Corps Heritage Foundation

"Ken Marlin helped me sell my company iSuppli for $100 million. Forget all those other books on Wall Street. Ken Marlin's *The Marine Corps Way to Win on Wall Street* is the best book I've ever read on how to make money and win the right way."
—Derek Lidow, Professor in Entrepreneurship,
Princeton University, and author of *Startup Leadership*

"Ken Marlin's *The Marine Corps Way to Win on Wall Street* offers a fascinating rethink on how Wall Street ought to operate. This book resonates with practical insights from Ken's years as a Marine officer and as a Wall Street financier. I kept finding myself nodding my head in agreement!"
—Royce Yudkoff, cofounder ABRY Partners;
senior lecturer, Harvard Business School

"The reputations of almost all institutions have suffered in recent years, certainly including the reputation of Wall Street. Ken Marlin, a rare Marine-turned-investment banker, shows how financial professionals can learn from the values of the highly regarded Marines to earn back the respect Wall Street needs from Main Street. America's return to confident, growing markets depends on it." —L. Gordon Crovitz, columnist;
former publisher of *The Wall Street Journal*

"Few bankers are in Ken Marlin's league. And rarely does one of Wall Street's best take the time to explain the intersection of psychology, morality, and experience that goes into a hard-won reputation as a "trusted advisor" and "honest broker." This book is a must-read for those seeking to up their business game, as well as for everyone else striving to achieve more in the game of life."   —Barbara Yastine, Co-CEO, Lebethal Holdings LLC; former chair, CEO and president of Ally Bank

"A refreshingly frank, logical, and concise critique of Wall Street by Ken Marlin, who has both the moral courage and the credentials—a Marine who became a successful Wall Street insider—to challenge the venerable Wall Street institution/culture. *The Marine Corps Way to Win on Wall Street* is a compelling must-read."
—Colonel Paul F. Pugh (USMC retired), Dean of Students at Villanova University; coordinator of relief efforts in Bosnia-Herzegovina

"Ken Marlin is an innovative and deeply experienced adviser. His clarion call for new standards of behavior in the capital markets is a fresh breeze. Ken applies the Marine Corps Way to the markets in a manner that challenges all of us. His ideas are worth reading and debating."
—Jules Kroll, CEO of Kroll Bond Ratings; founder and former CEO of Kroll Inc.

"Ken Marlin is well known for his straight-up Marine Corps approach to problem solving. I've observed his techniques personally, and they work. Every CEO would be well advised to read *The Marine Corps Way to Win on Wall Street*—whether or not they are contemplating dealing with Wall Street bankers."
—Ed Miller, Chairman of American Express Bank and former CEO of AXA Financial

"Ken Marlin's book *The Marine Corps Way to Win on Wall Street* is right on target. And he is the real deal. As a banker with a successful m&a practice, an entrepreneur, a former tech company CEO and a Marine, he brings a unique perspective to achieving success that resonates with practical insight that is rarely seen in practice. I've seen Ken's approach. It works."
—Sanjay Swani, General Partner, Welsh, Carson, Anderson & Stowe

"Ken Marlin's book *The Marine Corps Way to Win on Wall Street* should be required reading by CEOs on Main Street as well as bankers on Wall Street—and those who would do business with them. He has been there—as a Marine, CEO, and a banker. The parallels between the Marine Corps teaching and success in the competitive financial sector are real. I've seen it first-hand."   —Michael Geltzeiler, CFO, ADT, and former CFO of the New York Stock Exchange

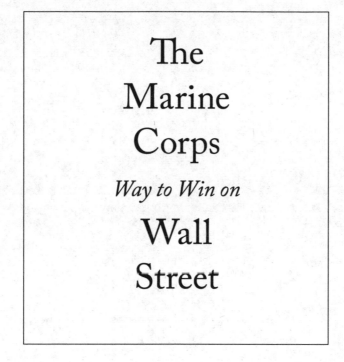

The
Marine
Corps
Way to Win on
Wall
Street

The Marine Corps

Way to Win on

Wall

Street

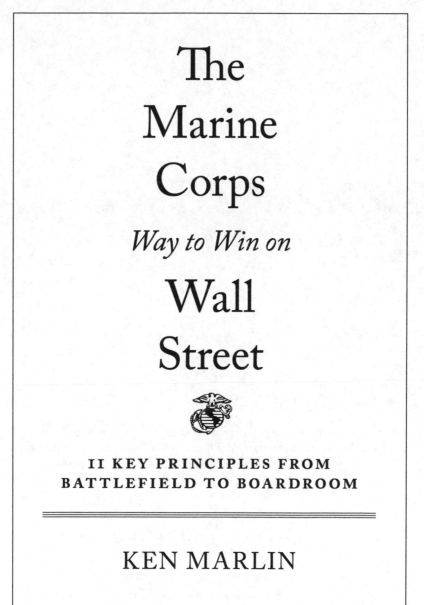

11 KEY PRINCIPLES FROM
BATTLEFIELD TO BOARDROOM

KEN MARLIN

ST. MARTIN'S PRESS ≋ NEW YORK

www.stmartins.com

The Library of Congress Cataloging-in-Publication Data
is available upon request.

ISBN 978-1-250-06666-4 (hardcover)
ISBN 978-1-4668-7686-6 (e-book)

Our books may be purchased in bulk for promotional, educational, or
business use. Please contact your local bookseller or the Macmillan
Corporate and Premium Sales Department at 1-800-221-7945, extension
5442, or by e-mail at MacmillanSpecialMarkets@macmillan.com.

First Edition: August 2016

10 9 8 7 6 5 4 3 2 1

This book is dedicated to:

Colonel Chuck Barstow, Colonel Joe O'Brien—and all the other leaders who showed me by example what the Marine Corps Way really is.

Captains Paul Pugh, Greg Von Wald, Chris Covert, and Jim McClain—my fellow company commanders—who showed me every day how it should be done in the field.

Bob Weissman, Dick Schmidt, Dave McBride, Bill Jacobi, Tom Wendel, and others who encouraged me to apply the Marine Corps Way to leading Main Street companies.

John Suhler and John Veronis, who first allowed me to apply the Marine Corps Way on Wall Street.

And Max, Paul, and Jason—who have been with me for the journey—still are—and who help me implement the Marine Corps Way every day.

Contents

Preface

In late 1985, the chairman and CEO of Dun & Bradstreet, Charles Moritz ("Charlie" to his friends; "Mr. Moritz" to me), summoned me to his office. I had been working for D&B for a little over four years, having joined the company after serving for a decade in the US Marines. I had never before been summoned specifically to see Mr. Moritz, and I had no idea what he wanted to talk about. I wouldn't call the scene intimidating; I'm not easily intimidated. But it was unusual and I was curious.

In those days, the D&B corporate headquarters, of which I was a part, operated largely as the center of a sector-focused private equity firm. It bought portfolio companies, supported the heads of those companies financially, provided capital, ensured that financial reporting was done well, and encouraged growth through acquisitions that could be "tucked under" their umbrella where they could share expenses and perhaps find some product or revenue synergies. As in many PE firms, D&B would subject budgets, acquisitions, and expansion plans to a thorough review, even selling companies when they were deemed to no longer fit the corporate strategy or were performing below D&B's standards. D&B then owned something like twenty-three different major businesses worldwide, each of which operated independently, and most of which had absolutely nothing to do with each other. They included Moody's Investors Service, Interactive Data Corporation, Reuben H. Donnelley, Donnelly Marketing, McCormack & Dodge, AC Nielsen, and the Dun & Bradstreet credit information business for which D&B is now best known.

D&B had been around for more than 140 years when I joined. It was a highly respected brand, and I was happy to be there. The chairman and CEO then was Harrington "Duke" Drake, a super salesman who had worked his way up through the Reuben H. Donnelley Corporation (a big marketing services firm best known as a publisher of classified phone directories) to become the head of that firm—and then, after it merged with D&B, to become our CEO. When I joined, Duke was in the midst of putting his imprint on the company. Over the next few years D&B invested billions of dollars in thirty-three major acquisitions and dozens of other smaller ones.

Moritz had been Duke's protégé. Both had attended elite private East Coast colleges (Yale for Moritz; Colgate for Drake); and both had come up similar routes through sales and then executive leadership.

Moritz certainly looked the part of the top New York executive. *The New York Times* had captured his essence in a piece announcing his ascension to CEO, describing him as "personifying the conservative businessman":

> He lives in Darien, Conn., he's 48 years old, and he has three children. He plays golf and reads spy novels. His neatly trimmed hair is gray; his suit, pinstriped; and his reading glasses, half frames that sit on the edge of his nose.

The last time I had been in a room with Moritz, he had rejected a proposed acquisition. In the past, the target company had been accused of paying bribes to local government officials. He wanted no risk to D&B's reputation. We had discussed this company's questionable past internally before bringing the deal to Moritz, and we had flagged the issue as a potential risk. The executive vice president (EVP) sponsoring the deal had concluded that the company fit his strategy, the price was right, the company had learned from its mistake, and that we could neutralize the potential fallout by bringing them into our culture and values. The EVP believed the risk of the company's repeating the bad behavior was low. But Moritz just hadn't been willing to take the risk; it wasn't just about potential damage to the one company, but about potential reputational risk to the other trusted D&B brands. In his view, if one D&B firm was caught in a scandal, it could tarnish others, including our flagship business-information company and Moody's, our bond-rating agency—and that could be expensive. Even though I was on the team advocating the acquisition, I respected Moritz's decision. It made sense; and I respect executives who assess a situation and take a stand, rather than deliberate forever.

Afterward, however, I overheard the EVP who had championed the deal screaming at one of his subordinates. He was worried that its demise would be a blemish on his career. Why had she let him take a deal to the chairman that would be turned down?! (As if it were her decision.) How could she have put him in this position? (As if he had no responsibility.) There was even talk of people losing their jobs. I didn't get it. We had done our homework, identified the opportunity as well as the threat (reputational risk), come up with a plan to neutralize it, and run the plan up the chain. The deal was a "nice-to-have"—not critical to D&B's long-term strategic mission—and we may well have avoided a later problem. (A few years later, the firm was indeed involved in another bribery scandal.)

The panic in that executive's voice was, for me, odd to hear from a leader. Marines take particular pride in how they handle adversity. Our whole institutional identity is wrapped up in the notion that you don't panic when things don't go as planned; you just push forward and calmly find another way to achieve the objective. No drama. Further, one of the first leadership principles Marines are taught is to "take responsibility for your actions." Own it. Blaming subordinates for a decision you made is about the quickest way to signal panic—and lose the respect of those subordinates.

The EVP described above was smart. He had an MBA from a top school; he'd been a management consultant at a top firm; and he had risen quickly within D&B. He was analytical and cerebral and had some pretty good ideas—notwithstanding the latest debacle. But he also was a caricature of a political manager with no clue how to lead, symptomatic of what to me at the time felt like an obvious disjuncture between the world I'd known in the Marines and that world I was now occupying—a world in which an individual's compensation and place of power in a hierarchy is enhanced by who your parents are, where you went to school, where you live, and who your friends are; and harmed by perceived judgmental failures (witness the failed attempted acquisition). On the rare occasion that success is measured by any objective criterion, the standard is likely to be the individual's achieving some short-term objective, without regard to the organization's long-term goals.

The Marine Corps had allowed me to complete my undergraduate degree and go on to get my MBA at UCLA. Three years later, in 1981, I left the Marines to join D&B as one of a small handful of

relatively young MBAs that D&B called financial management associates—or FMAs. We worked directly for the CFO, and our job
was to fight fires—to solve problems that had vexed (or been ignored
by) others. I found my fellow FMAs to be smart and hardworking.
Most had attended elite universities; many had worked at banks or
consulting companies before getting their MBAs. They all were more
politically aware than I. None had ever served in uniform. Most would
never dream of it. I might as well have been from Mars. I recall one of
them approaching me a few months after I had joined D&B and giving me some advice. Others might well have been intimidated by him.
He lived in the right suburb and played golf on the weekends with the
senior executives. He was always properly dressed, always had the
right tie, and he was never controversial. But, as I said, I don't intimi-
date easily—besides, I think he was trying to be helpful. He suggested
that I step back from trying to lead and just "execute"—learn to do
what I was asked to do and be more like him. I understood the com-
ment; Marines often ask young recruits to learn to follow before they
try to lead. But I wasn't a young recruit and it wasn't in my nature to
simply execute tasks others assigned to me without understanding
the context and how the task fit with our longer-term strategic objectives. Besides, as near as I could tell, the bosses appreciated my approach. I wasn't about to change.

One example was the question of what D&B should do with its
operations in South Africa, and this question had brought me to
Moritz's office that day in 1985. At that time, D&B had three separate
profitable businesses operating in South Africa: D&B Credit Services;
AC Nielsen, the global market-research firm best known for its television viewership measurement ratings; and the software company
McCormack & Dodge. One of the issues in the news and in conversations at D&B during that time was apartheid, South Africa's policy
of systematic and legal segregation of its black population, which effectively forced blacks to live in second-class communities, condemned
them to menial jobs, and largely denied them education or the opportunity for betterment. The policy had been simmering for years and
eventually made South Africa a pariah. In the mid-1960s, some British
universities had called for a political, economic, cultural, and sports
boycott of South Africa as well as of companies, such as Coca-Cola,
IBM, and Xerox, that did business there. In December 1980, the
United Nations passed resolutions condemning South Africa's policies.

Now D&B faced increasing pressure to adopt the Sullivan Principles, which would effectively prevent us from doing business in South Africa. Eventually, more than one hundred companies would adopt these principles. Legislation had even been introduced in Congress to promote the same outcome, although the bills had failed to become law, in part because President Ronald Reagan insisted that "constructive engagement" was the better approach, and that divestment, sanctions, or embargoes would cause economic harm that would fall hardest on the very people we were trying to help, without changing the behavior of the ruling whites. This view was echoed at the time by an influential African-American, former US ambassador to the United Nations, and then mayor of Atlanta, Andrew Young. However, on college campuses, students rallied and called on their universities to support divestment and sanctions. In 1984, more than fifty US universities had adopted some form of sanctions, as did a growing chorus of US cities and states.

Moritz (the CEO) and Bob Weissman (D&B's president and COO), along with the former chairman and CEO Duke Drake before them, had resisted adopting the Sullivan Principles. Their view was that, until divestment became the law of the land, we would heed the words of the US president and continue as an example of the right way to do business in South Africa. Moreover, plenty of companies from other nations were clearly willing and eager to do business there.

D&B's position was a bit self-serving, as its operations in South Africa were quite profitable. But it also was the embodiment of the conservative culture at the company that started at the top: it was not in the nature of Moritz or Weissman to get out in front of political issues.

Moritz's and Weismann's corner offices were on opposite ends of D&B's office, which ran the length of a full city block on Park Avenue just north of Grand Central Terminal. Each office took up nearly a quarter of the block, overlooking the avenue. Many of my colleagues— including some who were much more senior than I—were reluctant to enter either office unless summoned, and to most the COO, Bob Weissman, was the more intimidating. His quick intelligence, short attention span, hot temper, and lack of tolerance for fools were well-known.

I can't tell you today exactly what had prompted me a few weeks earlier to walk into Weissman's office to argue that D&B should get out of South Africa now. No one had asked for my opinion. But, by that time, I had become something of an expert in international divestitures as well as D&B's global strategy. Weissman and I had built some rapport—based in large part, I believe, on my willingness to take stands on controversial issues.

It was a short meeting. I had found a hole in his calendar and knew that I had the briefest of windows. I took the long walk to his large mahogany desk at the far end of his big corner office and, without taking a seat, launched into my pitch. I may have been sweating just a little. It was time to sell our three businesses in South Africa. I understood that neither he nor Charles Moritz wanted to be too far ahead of the political process and that our operations were integrated and an example for others, but selling our three businesses in South Africa now was the right thing to do from a moral as well as a business standpoint (taking the long view). The timing was not going to get any better by waiting; a political tidal wave was coming at us. We needed to get ahead of it before we were overwhelmed—before Congress mandated divestiture, before shareholders pushed us to adopt the Sullivan Principles, before we were harmed from a PR perspective as well as a financial one. I told him that while he and Moritz might not want to be among the first US corporations to divest, we should not wait until we were forced to do the right thing—and possibly wind up being among the last. Better to get on the offensive and control the timing.

I was prepared for counterarguments, in particular that the black South Africans who worked for us stood to lose their jobs. But that could be managed by controlling who we sold to. We also had an economic rationale to remain in that country as long as possible, but I argued that the economic rationale was largely upside down: over the long term the economic risk to the rest of our businesses of not divesting could dwarf any lost profits in South Africa (and even these could at least partially be offset by a sale). Moreover, the price we would receive from a sale was likely to decrease as time passed—some prospective buyers would likely flee, and other potential buyers would sense our need to sell.

It would take time to divest the three businesses, I argued. We needed to start the process now. Weissman asked few questions, but he clearly understood. He thanked me for coming but gave no hint as to his thinking other than to say that this would be a topic at the next board meeting.

A few weeks passed before that day when I was summoned to see the chairman and CEO. Again I stood—this time facing Moritz's desk, looking occasionally toward Weissman, who was sitting on a nearby couch. Moritz quickly got to the point. Could I find a way for us to sell all three of D&B's South African businesses quickly, and at a fair price, while at the same time preserving both our employees' jobs and negotiating some way for D&B to reenter the market should apartheid end?

Selling three companies at once, in a foreign country, for a decent price is challenging. It's tougher still when the potential buyers all know that you are under pressure to do it fast. And Moritz wanted me to preserve jobs and have a reentry plan! But I was a Marine. I knew how to plan and prepare for battle; I knew how to assemble a team of experts; and I knew how to execute. I knew how to negotiate international deals. I said yes, of course.

Over the next several months, I spoke with the heads of the three business units in the United States and the country heads in South Africa; coordinated with our internal legal counsel for recommendations of local attorneys; worked with our internal accounting and financial staffs for on-call help when needed; and worked with my bosses on priorities: Would price be more important than having a buyback provision? (No, we decided, the buyback was more important.) Did we have a minimum price? (No, we decided to run an auction and take the highest price the market revealed.) How important was speed? (Very.) What was our precise target for completion? (By year's-end 1986 if possible.) Should we use an investment bank? (No. "Marlin, you can lead it.") And what did we think about selling to employee-led teams versus outsiders? (We liked employee-led teams, but our real focus had to be on finding the best way to ensure continued employment for our people.)

In early May 1986, I flew to South Africa. We were ahead of the wave, but just barely. In late May the "Comprehensive Anti-Apartheid Act" was introduced by the US Congress. It was passed by the House in June and by the Senate in August. While President Reagan vetoed the bill in September, it became law on October 2, 1986, when Congress overrode President Reagan's veto. This marked the first time in the twentieth century an American president's veto of a foreign policy bill had been overridden.

Selling the businesses wasn't easy and required quite a lot of time in South Africa while I was, at the same time, working on deals in Japan and Europe. Once Congress acted, all prospective buyers knew that we were under pressure to sell. But we had signaled to the management of all three companies what was to come, and all three teams had themselves been fielding calls from potential suitors. In September 1986, Coca-Cola, one of the largest US employers in South Africa, announced its intention to sell its operations in the country—so we wouldn't be the first company, but we were still ahead of the tidal wave. We got two of the deals completed by year's-end and the third in January 1987. We sold two of the companies to firms that were led by former employees of our companies, and all three to firms that planned to continue employing our people. We obtained repurchase rights for all three. A few years later, well after apartheid had ended and after I had left D&B, AC Nielsen bought back a stake in its South African business.

My experience in pitching and then leading the divestment in South Africa revealed something that would repeatedly be demonstrated as I progressed in my career: my Marine Corps training had given me a set of skills that seemed completely suited to working on Wall Street.

How I Got Here

I enlisted in the Marines in 1970, right after my sophomore year in college; a year after President Nixon had pledged to end US involvement in the Vietnam War; and months after US forces had crossed the Mekong River from Vietnam into Cambodia, in a two-month operation that reportedly killed some ten thousand North Vietnamese forces. It was a confusing time. I was young, restless, and unfulfilled, and while I had no doubt that I would someday graduate from a university, I wanted to be somewhere else. I had worked summers at several jobs, and none of them had any appeal. Further, a war was going on and I was missing it.

My parents were not happy with my decision. More than four hundred thousand Americans were fighting in Vietnam. My parents thought that I would be sent there immediately after boot camp. (So did I.)

Marine boot camp is legendary for its physical and mental challenges. But I had been a runner and an ice hockey player in high school and college, so I started with a decent physical base; and for me the academic portions of our training were not particularly challenging. The hardest part was psychological. The drill instructors looked for ways to weed out the weak. They would work us to exhaustion, deprive us of sleep, work us some more, and yell at us if we made the slightest mistake or hesitation. Marines washed out daily: Some simply couldn't keep up physically—they dropped out of exercises and refused to continue. One recruit in the bunk next to me cried every night from the mental strain—until one day, he was gone. But soon it was over, and those of us who graduated did so with tremendous pride. Now, finally, we were Marines.

After boot camp all Marines go to infantry training school. Mine was at Camp Pendleton, California (a beautiful place), where we learned the Marine Corps Way to plan for battle, prepare, communicate, maneuver, and survive. We got to fire all kinds of weapons, including rifles, pistols, machine guns, and mortars; we got to toss hand grenades; we learned hand-to-hand combat and rudimentary martial arts; we detonated explosives, rode on tanks, assaulted beaches, climbed mountains—and rappelled down them; and so much more. For me it was great fun—until I got shot.

During a live-fire training exercise, I was crawling under barbed wire while machine guns fired overhead. I was later told that one of the guns had a bad lot of ammunition. Bullets fragmented and one hit me in my biceps—exiting through my triceps. It hurt. Another fragment hit the Marine next to me. I was told that he died.

Luckily, the bullet missed the bone. I spent a few days in the base hospital. A Marine lawyer offered me the opportunity for a medical discharge. I declined. Why would I quit now, just when it was getting to be fun? I spent another sixty days or so on "limited duty," working as a clerk in the company office at the infantry training school. After I returned and finished my infantry training. I was sent to San Diego to qualify as a combat radio operator (the job with the second-shortest life expectancy in combat, right behind second lieutenant platoon commander).

While I'd been working as an office clerk, my boss asked if I would like to be considered for Officer Candidate School. Few Marines were sent from the enlisted ranks to OCS; fewer still who had not completed a college degree. I was thrilled. I said yes, submitted the application, and then . . . heard nothing. While at combat radio operator school, one day I was suddenly called out of class: I had been selected for OCS! Within days, I packed up and moved to Quantico, Virginia, where I went through yet another form of boot camp. But this time, I knew what to expect. Twelve weeks later I was commissioned as one of those second lieutenant infantry officers, graduating as platoon Honor Man. (I tied for top of my class with another former enlisted Marine.)

Boot camp is where I began to learn to be a Marine. It's where I began to appreciate the virtues of honor, courage, competence, commitment, teamwork, and loyalty, as well as the related values of discipline, respect, and persevering in the face of adversity. Those were lessons that continued and were built upon through my time as an enlisted Marine; reinforced in OCS and during the six months I spent after OCS training to be an infantry platoon commander at a place that Marines simply call The Basic School, or TBS; and later as a platoon commander, a company commander, a battalion staff officer with the Seventh Marines (one of the most storied regiments in the Marine Corps); and as a member of the commanding general's staff.

Later in this book, I will relay a few of the many lessons learned during these times as I began to appreciate the level of competence expected of a Marine officer: the need to be a true domain expert—not just a generalist—and to respect and leverage others who are experts in their own domains. The Marine Corps is where I began to understand the challenges, obligations, and responsibilities of leadership and to realize that leaders must lead—not just "manage." They must "seek responsibility" and be willing to "take a stand" on positions of importance; not simply follow the crowd (or polls); not just be an "executor"—and then they must take responsibility for their actions, including their failures. The Marine Corps taught me the importance of knowing your long-term strategic objective before deciding on tactics (sometimes it's okay to skip battles); communicating with your team; and having a sober assessment of your own strengths and weaknesses as well as those of the other side before entering into a fight. Lives are in your hands. Lives depend on your judgments.

I'll write about a few of the lessons I learned when I deployed to the Far East as the senior Marine aboard the USS *Tripoli*, an amphibious assault ship (an aircraft carrier designed to carry Marines and their helicopters) as we cruised the South China Sea. That's where I lived the value of something Marines call disciplined "backward" planning; and then using repeatable processes to achieve predictable results. That's also where I learned a lot about dealing with people from foreign cultures. Later I found that it all applied on Wall Street as well.

Fast-Forward

There is a saying that there are no ex-Marines: once a Marine, always a Marine. That saying was brought home to me one bright, beautiful September morning in 2001, some twenty years after I left the Marine Corps. That beautiful morning I was sitting in my own big private office overlooking Park Avenue in New York City—about a block from the offices that Bob Weissman and Charlie Moritz had occupied when I was at D&B, fresh out of the Marine Corps.

The year 2001 was a tough time to be a banker on Wall Street: the nation was in a recession, stock markets had crashed around the world, and deal flow had died. I was preparing for an important meeting with Barry Diller, the media titan who created Fox Broadcasting and the USA Network and assembled properties such as the Home Shopping Network, Match.com, and Expedia. A few weeks earlier, along with several colleagues at Veronis, Suhler & Associates—the Wall Street merchant bank for which I was working at the time—I had met with Diller and proposed a wide range of potential areas for his firm to look for acquisitions. He had rejected most of them, but he liked a few of the areas that I had championed and had invited us to come back for a follow-up meeting to explore specific opportunities. This was an important meeting for me—and for the firm. It was so important that my boss and his boss, John Veronis, the firm's cofounder, were all going to attend. It was important enough that I had canceled my attendance at an annual breakfast conference that I had been going to for several years—a conference that was filled with potential clients and friends, at Windows on the World, the restaurant on top of the North Tower of the World Trade Center.

As I was going over the details of our presentation to Diller, one of my colleagues rushed into my office and called me into a conference room, where a small group faced a television screen showing the

North Tower of the World Trade Center burning. It was September 11. I couldn't turn away.

The morning grew more surreal. As we were trying to comprehend what had happened amid reports that an airplane of some sort had slammed into the tower, we witnessed the second plane slamming into the South Tower—where many of my former colleagues were working. The buildings were both burning; people were jumping from the high floors; and then both towers collapsed. It was stunning. I was thinking about friends who worked in the towers; thinking about the people I knew at the breakfast conference; thinking about my Marines, who would be getting ready for war. A thousand thoughts ran through my brain—including calling my local Marine recruiter.

Suddenly, my boss, the career Wall Streeter, appeared at the conference room door. His hands shook visibly; I assumed he was overwhelmed by the events downtown. But as he started to speak, his voice filling with something verging on panic, it became clear his only concern was that we might be late to meet with Mr. Diller. Why wasn't I at the elevator? he asked. We had to leave—now, he asserted. Where were the presentation materials? he asked, somewhat annoyed. No mention of what was happening on the screen in front of me. Just a strained tone and a quasi-order that it was time to go. He told me to grab the presentation material and meet him at the elevator "immediately."

I was immediately annoyed—probably more than that. I asked him if he fully realized that we were witnessing what might well be the most serious attack on the United States since Pearl Harbor. (He said that he did.) I told him that Mr. Diller would undoubtedly think we were fools if we did show up. But whether Diller expected a meeting or not, I certainly wasn't going to it or to any other meeting right now. There were more important matters to figure out.

To my surprise my boss still didn't get it. He asserted that since we had not received a call from Diller's office canceling or rescheduling the meeting, we should proceed. He looked me in the eye—while on the television the dust rose from towers that had burned and crumbled—and insisted that it was time to leave. He would not be late for this meeting no matter what was happening.

Sure, business was slow. But at some point there have to be priorities ahead of money. Did he have no perspective on where we and our deals fit into the larger scheme? Then it struck me: no, he didn't, and neither did at least some of the others around me—he wasn't the only one who seemed insistent on conducting business as usual.

It wasn't the first time I had been frustrated with the priorities of some of my Wall Street colleagues. I don't mean to tar everyone—most of my fellow investment bankers did get it, including John Veronis, who had his assistant call Mr. Diller's office to cancel the meeting. (Diller's assistant was surprised that we had even bothered to call. Of course it was off.) But the ones such as my boss who didn't get it bothered me. The whole thing was one giant wake-up call. For years I had contemplated starting my own boutique investment bank. I concluded then and there that if I was ever to do so, now was the time. I knew that I could build a better bank—one that would leverage traditional investment banking skills (e.g., analytical, financial, interpersonal) and experience (e.g., structuring, negotiating, valuing) and augment those with skills, values, and principles that I'd learned in the Marine Corps (e.g., honor, courage, competence, commitment, teamwork, loyalty, and persevering in the face of adversity).

We would avoid the worst habits of our competitors (short-term thinking, self-aggrandizement, prioritizing the individual ahead of the team, putting profit ahead of the client; rushing into battle without being fully prepared; pretending to have expertise where they had little). Instead we would take the long view in advising clients, making sure that we fully understood their strengths, weaknesses, capabilities, and constraints; be the domain experts; make careful, detailed plans and execute them with discipline. We would work as a team and always put the client's interest ahead of our own.

It has worked. For fifteen years, we have been winning mandates from clients and helping them to close deals. We have advised scores of companies in the United States and at least twenty-five other countries on successful acquisitions and divestitures; we've won dozens of professional awards from the top industry associations; and we've gone from three employees to a couple of dozen professional dealmakers at our headquarters in midtown Manhattan and at our offices in San Francisco, Washington, DC, and Toronto.

I'm writing this book for a couple of reasons. One is simply that I believe that the approach that we have taken with our firm is a better, smarter, more effective, and more efficient way to run many Wall

Street firms. It's not always easy. But the approach is fully conducive to and compatible with the very normal desire by bankers (and many others) to make lots of money over the longer term. In fact, for some Wall Street firms, over time, as they attract more repeat business (and pay fewer fines), it should increase their profitability—and as an added bonus, this approach may just allow bankers and their clients to approach Wall Street transactions, and other important strategic decisions, with more confidence that they are doing the right things for the right reasons. And isn't that something that we all should be aspiring to do?

A second reason for writing this book is that many of the eleven principles that I use leading my Wall Street firm are the same ones that I used in successfully running my non–Wall Street companies. I believe that they are equally applicable to a broader business and political environment. The principal reason that this book focuses most on Wall Street is because that is where I have been for the past twenty years. But I have led real Main Street companies, and every day I work with CEOs.

Finally, I am writing this book because I believe it is important to our economy as a whole that we find a way to better align the priorities and sensibilities of Wall Street with those of Main Street. If we can do that, we can start working together again toward common objectives that make sense. If we can't, than we run the risks of bureaucrats exercising more and more centralized control of our economy, and that will not be a good thing. Building a firm around these eleven principles is the best way that I know to help align our priorities.

Add it all up and you get some pretty powerful reasons to try the Marine Corps Way. I did. It works.

Introduction

MARINES ARE AN INTERESTING BREED. WE'RE BY FAR THE SMALLEST OF the military services, and despite that (or perhaps because of it) we excel. We value such things as honor, courage, competence, commitment, and teamwork. We believe in being always faithful—we sometimes call it loyalty. We value discipline, and yet, at the same time, we encourage independent thinking. We train Marines to be leaders, yet insist that they learn to follow. We value integrity, humanity, and empathy; and we teach people to kill.

Marines learn skills that are not taught in most business schools. Some of them are military-specific—such as hand-to-hand combat, field first aid, fire and maneuver tactics, and how to call in air strikes. But many of them are about such things as leadership, planning complex operations, perseverance in the face of adversity, dealing with foreign cultures, and honor. We then marry those skills with a set of principles, practices, and values that, together, help us to materially increase the probability of success on the battlefield. It's not an academic exercise. It's an approach that has been proven time after time to save lives. It's serious business.

Over the past few decades I have observed that the combination of those Marine Corps skills, values, practices, and principles can be quite relevant and quite effective in a wide range of environments, most certainly including but not limited to Wall Street. In many cases they result in a much more perfect solution than we often see in today's world. That's what this book is all about.

The focus of this book is on Wall Street because that's where I have worked for the past twenty years. However, I also spent fourteen years as a corporate executive, and I now work with corporate CEOs every day. The skills, values, practices, and principles that I write about in this book are just as applicable in the boardroom—and in my opinion just as applicable in political caucus rooms as well.

For ten years I was an active-duty Marine. I began as an enlisted Marine—a buck private at time when over four hundred thousand Americans were fighting in Vietnam—down from more than half a million not long before that. The communists had just taken over Cambodia. The year before I enlisted, US combat deaths were more than eleven thousand. The year I joined, as American involvement began to be reduced, still more than six thousand Americans were killed. Antiwar protests occurred on college campuses and in Washington, DC.

I was promoted through the enlisted ranks, sent to Officer Candidate School, and then became a platoon commander in a Marine infantry battalion. Later, I was promoted to captain and became a company commander, and then a battalion staff officer. I held several other leadership roles. Along the way, the Marines allowed me to complete my college degree and obtain an MBA from UCLA. I ended my career as a member of the staff of the commanding general of the First Marine Division, a storied unit that I'll touch on in a few of the chapters that follow. After a decade of active service, I left the Corps and moved to Manhattan, where I started a new life. But you never stop being a Marine.

For the first five or six years of my civilian career, most New Yorkers I met—most civilians—didn't know how to react to my military service. This was the early 1980s, and they hadn't served—nor, in most cases, had most of their friends and associates. The wounds of Vietnam were still fresh. Marines were a curiosity to many—baby killers to a few; simply brutes to others. The subtleties were lost on them. Marine MBAs anywhere near Wall Street were an anomaly. Paradoxically—at least to me—those same people generally reacted quite positively when I told them I worked in Manhattan in mergers and acquisitions. That was a place and a profession that they knew and respected. Most of my Marine buddies were impressed too. It wasn't a common transition. A few years later though, in the mid-1980s, that positive view of Wall Street and those who worked there would change. For many it started with the arrests of such people as Ivan Boesky and Michael Milken.

At first, and for years, Boesky, Milken, and others like them were admired. They were feted as prime examples of how Wall Street could help Main Street. Milken found creative ways to bring much-needed capital to midsize privately held firms and smaller public companies that had been virtually shut out of the capital markets. His junk bonds, combined with his network of buyers for those bonds, allowed those firms to raise money, expand, and create jobs.

"Ivan the Terrible," as Boesky was sometimes called, was originally seen as a smart stock trader who brought efficiency to many markets and made money for his investors. He also was a philanthropist. As his fortune and fame grew, he and his wife became fixtures in the society pages of New York newspapers. He was the epitome of the American success story: the son of Russian immigrants, he had started on Wall Street as a stock researcher, married the daughter of a wealthy real estate investor, and had, over time, amassed something like $200 million by buying shares in companies that were possible takeover candidates in the hopes that the stock would rise once a takeover was announced. For example, Boesky bought ten thousand shares of Pacific Lumber three days before Maxxam Group announced that they had received an offer to buy the company. Good timing!

Boesky attributed this uncanny ability to predict takeover candidates to superior company research—he asserted that his group was smarter and worked harder than anyone else, and he laid out his approach in a 1985 book called *Merger Mania,* which he billed as "the first comprehensive presentation of the fundamental theory of merger arbitrage."

Then it all came crashing down. In November 1986, nearly every evening news program opened with the story that the US government had charged Boesky with illegally profiting on mergers and acquisitions by paying to obtain nonpublic information (insider trading). Boesky's prescience was apparently derived mostly from paying bribes to insiders. It wasn't pretty. Then he wore a wire and took down Michael Milken. Among many of my friends and acquaintances, the news introduced a sense that Wall Street was filled with greedy crooks.

To me, Boesky was a trader, not an investment banker, and Milken was a bond salesman—but my friends didn't see the difference. To them, we were all part of the same crooked system. Oliver Stone's iconic 1987 movie, *Wall Street,* further cemented this view in the character of Gordon Gekko, an unethical corporate raider (possibly partly based on Boesky and partly on Milken) willing to sacrifice others for his own enrichment, who traded on inside information provided by a

Wall Street broker/sycophant. (The movie introduced the phrase *greed is good* to the lexicon.) As with Boesky and Milken, the characters in the movie also weren't investment bankers. They were unscrupulous arbitrageurs, stockbrokers, and corporate raiders—but, again, most of my friends didn't see any distinction. To them, it was all "Wall Street."

It took me a while to accept that my friends were picking up on something real. The entire financial world was changing in ways that incentivized less-than-stellar behavior, even at investment banks and in boardrooms. Wall Street firms were shifting from a partnership model in which top executives owned their firms—and focused on providing unbiased advice and playing with their own money—to public ownership. With the change, many Wall Street executives quickly realized that they could reap huge personal rewards by taking much bigger risks than they had been willing to take when they and their partners owned the firm. Their upside was huge—with little downside risk, since outside shareholders bore the brunt of any gambles gone bad. At the same time a growing number of corporations were incentivizing their top managers with stock and stock options that could be worth millions. They too became motivated to take large risks with few downside consequences for themselves.

Combine that dynamic with lenders willing to provide virtually unlimited cash to risky endeavors, and add Congress's slow loosening of many of the restrictions on Wall Street that had been imposed in the wake of the 1929 stock market crash. Add similar deregulatory moves in Europe, and you had a recipe and an environment for extreme risk-taking. Greed was in fact looking very good (for some).

Over the thirty-plus years since I left the Marines and moved to Manhattan, a never-ending and perhaps ever-increasing series of both corporate and Wall Street–related scandals have seemingly occurred—more so than during any other similar period that I am aware of. There have been far too many to list—especially since most don't get quite the media attention or the prosecutorial attention as did Ivan Boesky, who agreed to pay $100 million and was sentenced to three years in jail, or Michael Milken, who was accused of ninety-eight counts of securities fraud and racketeering and ultimately agreed to (personally!) pay $600 million in fines and restitution and served two years in jail. Many others were involved in the irregularities and eventual collapse of junk bond financing soon after, just as in the 1990s many were involved in irregularities at the nearly one thousand US savings and loans (S&Ls) that failed (at a cost to the taxpayers of nearly $150 billion) after their regulators loosened restrictions, and owners and managers began offering large, complex commercial loans they didn't understand—instead of the home mortgage loans they were chartered to provide.

Neither the junk bond collapse in the 1980s nor the S&L fiasco of the 1990s had anything to do with my m&a investment banking world. But it certainly contributed to the idea that "bankers" were a corrupt bunch, and investment bankers certainly weren't immune. In 1991, a UK bank, Bank of Credit and Commerce International (BCCI), went under in spectacular fashion—costing shareholders and debt holders billions; and costing thousands of people their jobs. BCCI had courted the rich and powerful, including US president Jimmy Carter and UN ambassador Andrew Young. With US government consent, the bank acquired three American banks before it was accused of fraud, tax evasion, money laundering, arms trafficking, smuggling, bribery, and the support of terrorism.

In 1995, Barings Bank, the queen of England's bank, founded in 1762, collapsed after an undersupervised trader amassed about $1.3 billion in trading losses. Shareholders were effectively wiped out. The Dutch bank ING bought Barings for one British pound plus assumption of liabilities. Hundreds lost their jobs.

In late 1997, prosecutors charged a former compliance officer at Salomon Brothers with getting paid for tipping off a network of brokers and traders to deals at the investment bank.

In 1998, a hedge fund based in Greenwich, Connecticut, called Long-Term Capital Management managed to borrow billions to bet on complex derivative securities. The company was led by some of the brightest minds in the country. But it seemed as if they didn't understand the risks they were taking. When markets turned against them, not only did the firm collapse, it nearly wiped out some of the largest financial institutions on the planet. Reportedly the secretary of the US Treasury as well as the head of the Federal Reserve concluded that unless the government stepped in to force a rescue, the result could be global financial crisis unlike any seen since the Great Depression. So that's what they did.

In 1998 another Salomon Brothers employee was charged with insider trading; in 1999, yet another. In 2000, the former chairman and CEO of the investment bank boutique Keefe, Bruyette & Woods Inc. was arrested and charged with leaking secrets about pending bank mergers to his mistress, a Canadian exotic dancer, escort, and porn actress, who used the information to buy stock in advance of those deals. And the list goes on.

In 2000, Enron, the Houston-based energy, commodities, and services company was worth $68 billion; by 2002, it was bankrupt. The accusation was that, with the connivance of its bankers and accountants, Enron's executives had engaged in massive accounting fraud. Thousands of shareholders were wiped out. Thousands more lost their jobs and their retirement accounts disappeared.

And then the tech markets crashed; NASDAQ crashed; the world entered yet another recession; more people saw large parts of their savings wiped out, and hundreds of thousands lost jobs. Many people were sure that Wall Street had created yet another financial disaster. In 2002 it was WorldCom—another company built on mergers and acquisitions—that collapsed, amid accusations that it had overstated assets by some $11 billion. More money and jobs lost. And then in 2007–8 came the subprime mortgage crisis.

For years, the US Congress and Wall Street worked together to help Americans get loans to buy homes, and as they did so, home prices rose. Wall Street and others contributed to campaigns, and congressmen created government-sponsored enterprises (GSEs) such as Fannie Mae (Federal National Mortgage Association) and Freddie Mac (Federal Home Loan Mortgage Corporation) to spur home ownership. The GSEs would buy mortgages from banks, savings and loans, and other mortgage lenders. That way the mortgage "originators" would have more liquidity to offer more mortgages. Freddie and Fannie would package the loans into securities backed by bundles of mortgages and sell these securities to investors. Wall Street helped by buying and selling these securities and by creating their own securities based on subprime mortgages that were below the standards set by Fannie Mae and Freddie Mac. It worked—until people started getting greedy. Some banks and other mortgage providers began to issue "liar loans" and engage in outright fraud. People who should never have received loans (based on their income) got them anyway; mortgages were issued based on over-inflated home values. Then borrowers began to default; home prices declined; more borrowers defaulted; and it all came tumbling down. For more on this subject, see the Oscar-winning movie *The Big Short*.

Not long ago, *The New York Times* ran a story about RBC Capital Markets, a part of Royal Bank of Canada that was ordered to pay $76 million in damages for advising the board of Rural/Metro, an ambulance company based in Scottsdale, Arizona, to accept a $438 million all-cash sale to the private equity firm Warburg Pincus. According to *The Times,* "RBC persuaded Rural/Metro's board to accept the offer from Warburg without telling the board it was trying to win a role in Warburg's financing of the transaction."

Over the past half dozen years, global financial firms have paid out more than $235 billion in fines to various US and international government agencies for bad acts, including ignoring obvious conflicts of interest, manipulating currency and interest rate markets, and selling fraudulent mortgages and asset-backed securities—yet they still managed to generate huge profits. No CEO went to jail. Mark Taylor, dean of the business school at the University of Warwick in central England and an adviser to the Bank of England's Fair and Effective Markets Review, said, "The problem is the incentives for cheating markets is massive. If you can shift a rate fractionally, you can make millions and millions of dollars for your bank and then for bonuses."

Did I mention Bernard Madoff—an icon of Wall Street, founder of Bernard L. Madoff Investment Securities LLC; philanthropist; former chairman of the board of directors for the NASDAQ; and a significant contributor to politicians—who was convicted of masterminding a massive $65 billion Ponzi scheme?

Ugh! This can't be my world.

I work on Wall Street. I know Wall Street. Most bankers are not crooks, and most Wall Street deals work out fine—otherwise there would be no Wall Street. To focus on the all-too-frequent ethical lapses in corporate executive suites, in Washington, DC, or on Wall Street misses the larger points of what has changed in the past thirty years. Sure, lack of individual ethics on Wall Street and in corporate boardrooms contributed mightily to many of these scandals. But these alone can't be blamed for the savings and loan crisis of the late 1980s and the NASDAQ and tech market crashes; or the rise and subsequent crash of the residential housing market and the ensuing global financial meltdown of 2008. These came as a result of a confluence of factors—many of which were political, and a few of which were macroeconomic.

Still, the *culture* on Wall Street (and increasingly in corporate executive offices and in Washington) has undoubtedly continued: it
still disproportionately rewards a few individuals over teams, encour-
ages completion over cooperation and compromise, fosters short-term
thinking over long-term horizons, measures companies by stock market value or profit, and too often respects people only in proportion to
their wealth or power. One has only to look at the recent ignition-key
debacle at General Motors or the Volkswagen diesel-engine emissions
scandal to see the same forces at work. What else, besides these kinds
of warped priorities, allowed GM executives to ignore repeated
warnings that ignition switches could shut off engines and thereby
create life-threatening accidents while simultaneously preventing air-
bags from inflating? (As of this writing GM has compensated families for more than fifty deaths and thousands of injuries as a result of
the failures. More than 2 million vehicles were recalled, and fifteen
GM employees were eventually fired.)

What else could have been driving VW corporate executives when
they knowingly created and installed sophisticated software that
would detect when diesel engines were being tested for emissions—
and trigger pollution controls that would help the engines pass those
tests—but shut the controls off during normal driving (thus allowing
health-threatening pollution at up to forty times higher than that allowed)? Volkswagen chairman Hans Dieter Pötsch said the scandal
arose from "a mind-set in some areas of the company that tolerated
breaches of the rules."

The values, habits, and repeatable processes that I'll outline in the
pages to come ought to be useful for anyone running an organization,
but my central goal today is to help my current profession, Wall Street,
break out of its cycle of tolerating breaches of the rules and other bad
acts and regain the trust of the American people.

In October 2014, a Harris Interactive survey found that 57 percent
of Americans trust Wall Street less than a few years before; 72 percent
trusted Congress less. Another Harris Interactive poll indicated
that two-thirds of Americans think that those who work on Wall
Street "are not as honest and moral as other people," and 64 percent
think Wall Street bankers don't deserve the money they earn. Seven
out of ten said everyone on Wall Street is willing to break the law for
bigger profits. Again, only our politicians fare worse.

As for my friends, I notice that they still don't find enough difference between various Wall Street types to bother distinguishing among them. And in this book, in fact, I will use the terms *Wall Street* and *bankers* the way most laypeople now use them: as shorthand for all of the traders, brokers, investment bankers, hedge fund managers, private equity partners, venture capitalists, financial executives, and everyone else who makes a living in today's financial community. We all operate in this environment. As William Dudley, president of the New York Fed, acknowledged in a 2013 speech:

"There is evidence of deep-seated cultural and ethical failures at many large financial institutions. . . . [Wall Street banks] really do have a serious issue with the public, and I think that trust issue is of their own doing. They have done it to themselves."

Don't get me wrong. I'm no socialist; I'm an entrepreneur and an investment banker. I like to earn money, and I have no problem with bankers, corporate executives, or others who do too—as long as it is done honestly, and in accordance with the basic values of honor, courage, competence, commitment, teamwork, loyalty, and persever-ance in the face of adversity. It is certainly not my intention to lecture people about ethics—other than to note that whether you are a banker, an executive, or a politician, lack of ethics is a surefire way to lose the support of clients (or constituents) and risk long-term business (and personal) disaster. That's the opposite of what most of us want. Ask the executives of Enron, or WorldCom; Washington Mutual or Countrywide; Drexel Burnham, or Madoff Securities; GM or Volks-wagen. That kind of behavior may catch up to you.

In spite of all this, most Americans recognize that they need Wall Street. The same Harris Interactive survey noted that, for all that mis-trust, nearly two-thirds of those polled said they still believe that "Wall Street is absolutely essential" to our way of life. If we want to save and invest, create jobs and opportunities, and build houses, roads, and schools, most people on Main Street realize that they are tied at the wallet to Wall Street.

Some critics believe that the solution to many of the problems in corporate America or in Washington or on Wall Street is increased regulation. I support the idea of reasonable regulation and oversight of Wall Street, corporate America, and politicians. (It would be nice if politicians had to follow the same rules and restrictions as the rest of us.) But it's a pipe dream to think that regulation alone will change a culture that sees opportunities to obtain wealth or power beyond the dreams of most and that, along the way, condones and rewards price gouging, system gaming, and other unscrupulous practices. Corporations, as well as the highest levels of politics and Wall Street banks, are highly competitive places. The financial rewards can be substantial. In that environment, a lot of businesspeople, politicians, and Wall Street bankers will find ways around the rules—or find ways to change the rules—if they believe the risk of doing so is low. (Give a professional race-car driver a choice between a fast car that is potentially unsafe and a safer but slower car and guess which one he will take?)

As a result, I am focused on an even more important, if quixotic, goal than simply changing the rules; I want to change a culture. I hope to show those on Wall Street another way to win, a better way—both for their clients and for themselves. The book that follows lays out the eleven key strategic principles and practices that I first learned and practiced as a Marine, and that I have applied to the businesses I have led—and around which I have built my own companies.

Applying any one of these principles can increase the probability of long-term success in business and on Wall Street—but, alone, none of them are unique or particularly powerful. It is the combination of all eleven that can not only help materially improve your odds of success, but also help to change a culture that needs changing on Wall Street—and beyond. It works. I've built successful companies around these values and practices, and I now lead a successful investment bank that employs these practices. It's what I call the Marine Corps Way.

It all starts in chapter 1 with a practice I call "Take the Long View." In the Marines, short-term thinking leads to shortsighted results. It's all about understanding what is in your long-term best interest as well as in the long-term best interest of those around you. It's not only about a Marine's responsibility to formulate clear long-term strategic objectives—although that's certainly part of it; but it's also about the responsibility of Marines as well as corporate executives and their advisers (including bankers) to figure out which battles need to be fought and which can be skipped over. It's about keeping those objectives the focus of strategic thinking, and avoiding the temptation to take an action (or to advise a client to take an action) that may serve short-term interests (or generate a fee) but may not be the best way for the client to achieve its long-term strategic goal.

Whether the issue at hand is to encourage a set-piece battle at a remote outpost near the Laotian border called Khe Sanh, or to withdraw forces from Iraq before the country has been fully stabilized—these are serious questions with serious potential long-term consequences. Whether it's smart to ignore the warnings about financial institutions that are overleveraged or about dot-com or housing bubbles, or to downplay the risk of acquiring some firm or of ignition-switch problems, may not always be issues of life and death, but they are serious too—as the wrong action can cost thousands of people their jobs and their life savings, and sometimes more. (Ignoring ignition-switch failures at GM may cost the company billions of dollars in fines, legal settlements, repair costs, and lost revenue, but it may also have cost more than 124 people their lives.) Short-term thinking can have serious consequences. What's more, it is possible to make this long-term thinking part of your personal habits—and your company's culture. It's also the foundation of trust between banker and client; executive and shareholder; politician and constituent. It's important.

Chapter 2 is called "Take a Stand." It has two connotations. The first is simply about being decisive. Decisiveness is one of fourteen leadership "traits" that all Marines are taught. You have to work with the data that you have at hand, make a clear, firm decision, and accept responsibility for the result. That way of thinking informs the way every Marine officer carries out his or her daily routine. It's ingrained. The second connotation is about doing the right thing—including taking a stand as an adviser—even when it's not what the client wants to hear. It's one thing to know what to do, it's something else to push your client to do the right thing—even at the risk of self-interest.

Bob Weissman, who was president of D&B and then became chairman and CEO at the end of my days working for that company, once told me that a key part of his long-term strategy was to be around in the long term—to keep his job. I understand well the desire for self-preservation, and I do not advocate taking actions that are highly likely to shorten your career—unless moral, ethical, or legal issues are at stake. But the Marine Corps Way is that leaders and their advisers both should not be afraid to take clear, unambiguous positions on the long-term merits of an action. We don't prevaricate to see what polls say or which way the wind might blow or blindly execute the actions that someone else has mandated as if we have no individual responsibility for our actions. Those are the excuses that too many business executives, politicians, and bankers give when they unquestioningly take a course of action that they know—or should know—is not in the best long-term interests of the organization, without at least taking a stand, speaking up about what should be.

Had some senior software engineers at Volkswagen taken a stand on the software that was being used to defeat emissions testing, VW would not now be looking at billions of dollars in losses—and a serious dent in their reputation. Had some senior mechanical engineers at GM taken a stand on faulty ignition switches, 124 people would be alive and GM would not be now paying compensation to the families of hundreds of victims. Had some US politicians taken a stand, fifty-eight thousand Americans (and more than a million civilians) might not have died in the Vietnam War; and we would probably never have invaded Iraq, where about forty-five hundred Americans died (in addition to about half a million Iraqis).

Taking a stand requires senior people at all organizational levels, including their advisers, to weigh inputs and make hard decisions or at least tough recommendations—even when short-term self-interest may indicate that the smarter move is to shut up or just go along. It's also about creating a culture where it's everyone's job to take stands—to stop bad ideas from becoming reality. I love Ross Perot's quote on the difference between the culture at EDS and that of GM: "An EDS employee who sees a snake kills it. At GM, they form a committee on snakes, hire a consultant who knows about snakes, and talk about it for a year."

Kill snakes. Take a stand. Over time the Marine Corps Way can result in more respect and more success.

In chapter 3 we'll discuss the need for senior executives and senior bankers to "Be the Expert (or Use One)" in some clearly defined field. I'm tired of generalists. My father, who is a retired mechanical engineer from the Cummins Engine Company, used to bemoan that senior executives at the company knew all about general management techniques but didn't know a crankshaft from a piston rod. I can relate. I see too many bankers who are good at financial analysis and managing process but know too little about the industry that they serve.

Marines are required to be "technically and tactically proficient"—

experts on multiple dimensions. To begin, every Marine is a rifleman, and every Marine officer is, at the core, a rifle platoon commander. Lawyers and clerks, tankers and truck drivers, supply clerks and jet pilots—all must be available to fight on the ground, in the trenches, at any time. But that base-level training doesn't make any of these Marines experts at infantry combat; it just means that they have a common starting point—a base on top of which they may start to build true expertise in some field. That happens by building on the base of knowledge through a combination of education and extensive real-world experience in the assigned area of specialization, in specific environments (desert, mountains, jungle, tundra, etc.) and under specific conditions. That field experience allows us to learn from our own mistakes and those of others. It helps us to anticipate what the other side will do—not just react. It helps us to know how best to act when life throws unexpected obstacles in our path. It gives us the edge over others in combat and in life. It allows us to survive where others perish.

Most bankers have decent financial-modeling skills. They can read a balance sheet. Most can manage parts of a transaction. Some have pretty good interpersonal skills. But it can't end there. The Marine Corps philosophy is that each individual must build on the common base to become a domain expert in a clearly defined field—and being a good pilot or an artilleryman is not specific enough, just as being a good generalist manager, banker, or politician is not good enough to be an expert. To win in combat, Marines must be experts at their jobs in the specific combat environment at hand.

Wall Street, like our corporate boardrooms and political capitols, used to be filled with true experts. These people not only knew how to get a deal done (or a bill passed), but also actually knew quite a lot about the industries they served—insurance, aviation, agriculture, energy, or any of a thousand other clearly defined areas. That's what made them successful. That's how we got good legislation passed. That's how we built great corporations; that's the approach of the best of Wall Street. True domain expertise allows leadership at firms such as Google, Apple, and Airbnb to quickly assess a situation and know what to do, what not to do, when and how to do the right thing. It may not be the only key to winning—but it's certainly one of them.

Chapter 4 is about the need to "Know the Enemy"—to study and understand the history, culture, and motivations of the parties on the other side of the conflict or the negotiating table. It's not an academic exercise. It's another key practice that increases the probability of coming up with a long-term strategy that will lead to success.

While many people agree in principle with this concept, few spend more than a few minutes studying the other side. Some believe that all parties are basically alike; some believe they can figure it out in five minutes; some believe that they negotiate from a position of such strength that they can dictate terms. That kind of hubris leads to failed deals and failed strategies—that kind of hubris led HP to buy Compaq, and led the United States into a quagmire in Vietnam, and to some extent in Iraq, Libya, and Syria.

The person on the other side of a business deal isn't typically an enemy. However, your odds of success in any business or political endeavor are significantly enhanced if you make an effort to understand the other side in depth—their strengths and weaknesses, capabilities and constraints, ambitions and motivations. It would be so nice if those on Wall Street as well as business executives and maybe even a few of our politicians would actually listen to those on the other side of the table—or their arguments—really listen. Just maybe they could work out a mutually winning strategy. With that knowledge and understanding you are much more likely to be able to pick your battles and sometimes avoid battles completely by creating win-win scenarios. When that is not possible, at least the knowledge gained from understanding the other side will help you anticipate how the other side will act and react to your moves—and that leads to success.

We'll follow that with a chapter on the need to "Know What the Objective Is Worth," a brief primer on the basics of *valuation* from a perspective that also is foreign to many bankers—the value that a Marine would put on seizing, occupying, and defending hostile terrain.

Marines value territory based on a clear-eyed understanding of the interrelationships among four critical factors: (1) the importance of the objective to achieving the larger mission at hand; (2) the appropriateness and necessities of the timing involved; (3) the affordability of the price required to attain the objective; and (4) the risk/reward trade-offs. Now you won't find those four factors in any Marine Corps manual. I've derived them from many teachings and my own observations. But what is interesting to me is that valuing companies or even valuing strategic political moves—such as bailing out a company or an industry—can be premised on these same four factors. Yet, MBA programs teach future corporate executives and bankers alike to assess value based solely on fairly simplistic quantitative metrics. They use discounted cash flow models and measure internal rates of return. They also use the one that I like least—they derive values by looking at "comparable" transactions. Don't get me wrong, these approaches have merit. They can help as a sanity check. But no Marine would say that because we paid for Iwo Jima with sixty-three hundred American lives (and twenty-five thousand casualties), plus two US Navy aircraft carriers, that this price somehow defines the price (lives, casualties, ships) we would pay to take Guadalcanal. It would be absurd. These naïve approaches to valuation are how Yahoo! wound up paying $5.7 billion for Broadcast.com and $3.6 billion for Geocities, and how Time Warner agreed to a $164 billion deal with AOL.

In chapter 6, we'll talk about why bankers, like business leaders and Marines, also need to adopt the mantra "Know Yourself"—to see their unit's strengths, weaknesses, capabilities, and constraints in cold, harsh objective reality and to understand how the other side is likely to perceive them. This is not only about understanding where you and your organization may have negotiating leverage—although it certainly helps. It's also critically important to understand your institutional strengths and weaknesses in order to formulate your strategic objectives as well as your tactics to achieve those objectives. General Custer should have better understood his regiment's capabilities before he refused the offer of a battery of Gatling guns and an additional battalion of soldiers before going after Indians at Little Big Horn. Daimler-Benz would have been much better served if it had better understood its own strengths and weaknesses before it decided to spend $38 billion to acquire Chrysler in 1992. (They were fortunate to sell it for $7.4 billion in 2007.) Americans would have been better served if we had understood our capabilities more clearly before we attempted the invasion of Cuba's Bay of Pigs in 1961—and before we disbanded the Iraqi Army in 2003.

Marine general James Mattis, the leader of Marines in Iraq, once famously said, "You cannot allow any of your people to avoid the brutal facts. If they start living in a dream world, it's going to be bad."

In battle and in business, lack of critical self-awareness can lead to disaster.

I worry about potential clients who cannot clearly tell me what makes their firm special; why that uniqueness matters; and why we should expect it to continue in the future. I want clients to be able to articulate what they do that is better than anyone else on the planet. (I can for our firm.) I simply don't understand the me-too company or the investment banker that is *almost* as good as the competition but less expensive; or the Wall Street investment bank that is pretty good at managing price and process but not much more. How do they differentiate themselves from the crowd? By their Rolodex? Bad idea.

In chapter 7, we'll talk about the need to "Control the Timing" of your strategic actions. It's about control—not necessarily about surprise. In the 1990s, Saddam Hussein could not have been surprised at the assault by US-led coalition forces in the first Gulf War. He probably watched the buildup on CNN. It took more than five months. But the coalition controlled the timing of that assault, and it made all the difference.

In 1973 a coalition led by the Syrian and Egyptian armies surprised the Israelis with a full attack on Yom Kippur, the holiest day of the year for Jews. It was a surprise. But they still lost the war. Controlling the timing is not about surprise; it's about moving with conviction when you have the resources in place to win—and not sooner. For too many corporate executives, the timing of major strategic moves is purely reactive—when an acquisition opportunity is presented or when a suitor has approached you. For too many bankers, the best time to enter into a deal is whenever they have someone willing to pay fees. For too many military buffs, the word *timing* is associated with the word *surprise*.

Chapter 8 is called "Negotiate from the High Ground." There are plenty of books on "how to negotiate," and this will not be another. Instead, this chapter is about the philosophy of negotiating in an environment where we want to win but are not—or at least we should not be—trying to completely destroy the other side. The *high ground* has two connotations in the Marine Corps. From a tactical perspective, it's the physical place you often want to be, since it's usually both more defensible than the low ground and a better place from which to launch assaults. Clearly, the *high ground* has a second, ethical connotation too. It involves doing the right thing. Ask any Marine about Marine Corps values, and several words will invariably come up in the conversation: *honor, courage, commitment, competence, loyalty,* and *teamwork.* These combine to form an ethos that is also about the high ground. It is instructive to remember that a transaction may be the end of the process for the bankers—but just as peace usually follows war, for most participants the transaction, like an armistice, is just a phase point. It's useful if on the way to signing it, the parties have contemplated what will come next. I'll set forth nine negotiating rules that I developed while a Marine and that have guided me in negotiating successful transactions for a long time.

In chapter 9 we'll talk about the benefits, and the nuances, of international dealmaking, and another philosophy that I evolved while a Marine—and refined during my early career days—that I call "Seek Foreign Entanglements." While it may make sense for some businesses and some bankers to retreat behind national borders, in most cases isolationism is self-defeating. Your competitors will think more broadly, your constituents and clients need to think more broadly—and you should too. A common thread throughout my career has therefore been the recognition that trying to build a world-class business by staying safely at your home port usually doesn't work. World class requires a truly global perspective. There is a big world out there beyond our borders, and many smart business leaders are trying to figure out how to take advantage of that. Clients seeking to hire an investment banking adviser would be well served to consider one that understands this concept. Again, this chapter won't tell bankers, executives, or politicians how to manage these complex transactions. I could write an entire book on that subject alone. Instead, it will lay out another set of eight rules that I have developed for increasing the probability of successful cross-border transactions.

Next, chapter 10 is about the due diligence review process and a philosophy I refer to as "Trust *and* Verify." Ronald Reagan didn't coin the phrase *trust but verify,* but he put it into the popular lexicon—and it's an apt description of the sometimes painful but always necessary practice of verifying critical assumptions before you take irreversible steps. It seems reasonable, I know. But I can't tell you how many times people buy used cars without having them inspected or buy companies without first doing their homework or start a process to sell their business without anticipating the due diligence review process that most buyers will want to pursue. There are no perfectly clear crystal balls, but gaining intelligence and carefully vetting your assumptions can go a long way to ensuring victory. It's something that Marines do nearly every day. This chapter is about the need for buyer, seller, and their respective advisers to anticipate the due diligence review process and manage it so that we increase the odds of winning the battle. I'll include a short list of the undesired consequences of a few due diligence reviews that could perhaps have been done better.

The final chapter calls for bankers and business leaders to "Be Disciplined." It may be my favorite chapter. Marines like winning. We don't like drama. As a result, we try to remove as many variables as possible before heading into action—and that takes discipline. We take the long view, we establish long-term strategic objectives, and then we plan using a rigorous detailed approach. When we are ready, when we have all the resources in place, when the timing is right, then we commit; we act in accordance with that well-developed plan. Discipline may be a hallmark of the Marine Corps, but we don't have a monopoly on it. General Electric has long been known for its disciplined approach to business; so is, for that matter, Warren Buffett. It's not always easy, but it is a critical practice to achieve long-term success, and it can be taught.

Discipline is not about blind obedience to orders. It is about more than the ability to get up at 4:00 a.m. after four hours of sleep or hike all through the night with fifty pounds of equipment on your back. That's grit as well as mental and physical toughness. Discipline is about doing the right things the right way—every time. Discipline requires that you not only know how to plan to win the battle but also about why you want to win it, and what you are going to do afterward. It requires courage, competence, commitment, and teamwork, and if done the Marine Corps Way, it requires honor too.

The Marine Corps Way requires us to conduct our business with honor. It requires us to persevere in the face of adversity in service to a cause that is greater than ourselves. It's not always easy, but I have seen firsthand that applying these principles leads to success on many fronts. It works for Marines, it has worked for me in the companies that I have led, and I believe it can work for others as well—for Wall Street bankers and for the corporate executives who engage them, and perhaps a broader world too. There will be resistance to change, but changing can help these organizations earn back America's trust and restore the fundamental faith that Main Street must have in board-rooms, Wall Street, and Washington for our economy to function effectively and efficiently.

When I relayed to a friend the premise of this book, he called it "tilting at windmills." He said that my expectations for change were "unrealistic and unreasonable." I agreed—on all counts.

When Marine Corps colonel Lewis "Chesty" Puller found his First Marine Division surrounded by thirteen enemy Chinese Army divisions plus another three divisions of North Koreans at the Chosin Reservoir in Korea, he is reported to have said, "They are in front of us, behind us, and we are flanked on both sides by an enemy that outnumbers us twenty-nine to one. They can't get away from us now!" And he led his men to the sea—destroying seven enemy divisions. Persevering in the face of adversity is a long-held Marine tradition.

George Bernard Shaw, the Nobel Prize–winning Irish playwright once said, "The reasonable man adapts himself to the world; the un-reasonable one persists to adapt the world to himself. Therefore all progress depends on the unreasonable man."

The US Marine Corps is filled with "unreasonable" people who boldly go where others fear to tread . . . in an effort to make the world a better, safer place than we found it—for all of us. Perhaps that is the reason why we who have served as Marines seem to take so much pride in our service to the Corps. Perhaps that is why every November 10, all around the planet, Marines of all ages and experience toast the birthday of our beloved Corps. When the "Marine Corps Hymn" plays, watch us stand tall.

It would be impossible to maintain such sustained pride in an organization were it not based on something very real. Marines know that we have achieved victory precisely because we have put into prac-tice the skills, values, and principles that I talk about in this book. We have succeeded "in every clime and place where we could take a gun," according to the lyrics of the "Marine Corps Hymn." These are the action-oriented principles that brand-new recruits begin to learn in basic training, and that we strive to live every day we serve, and beyond.

The same friend asked another question—why you? What makes you the one to set forward eleven principles to change the way Wall

Street works? You're not famous; you never ran a bulge bracket firm. Why you? To this, I can only say—why not me? Someone should. As Ronald Reagan said in his second inaugural address, "If not you, who? If not now, when?" I now turn that question around to readers: "If not you, who? If not now, when?"

I

Take the Long View

In 1972, I was in training at The Basic School (TBS), the six-month-long course of instruction after OCS that is designed to give newly minted Marine officers the skills needed to lead Marines in ground combat. This was weighty business. Even though American involvement in the Vietnam War looked to be winding down, we lived with the real possibility that it could reescalate or that we might be sent to war elsewhere. And the instructors were deadly serious about having us develop both the hard skills we would need to survive (hand-to-hand combat, marksmanship, field first aid, physical fitness, land navigation, skills to call in artillery and air support, communication, etc.) as well as (particularly) the leadership skills we would need to lead Marines to success in battle. They wanted us to know how to fight, and they wanted us to know how to win. These are separate. As part of this effort, they wanted us to understand not only what to do in various situations and how to do those things, but also why Marines do things a certain way. After all, once we were in the field, we would often be on our own—and we would have to lead our Marines. Failure to apply these lessons properly could result in our own deaths and those of our men.

Our instructors were all combat veterans. They used their real-life experiences in Vietnam to punctuate our daily lessons. Several of them had been involved in a battle in Vietnam near a small village called Khe Sanh, astride a key North Vietnamese Army (NVA) supply route a few miles from the Laotian border.

The battle at Khe Sanh was fought in 1968—and has already entered Marine lore every bit as much as those battles fought in World

War I at Belleau Wood, World War II on Guadalcanal, Tarawa, or Iwo Jima—or for that matter the 1847 battle at Chapultepec (the "Halls of Montezuma" that is celebrated in the opening lines to the "Marine Corps Hymn").

Most battles in Vietnam were measured in minutes—or at most in a few hours. The siege at Khe Sanh lasted more than seventy-seven days—and we weren't even fighting over any particularly important territory. Whenever the subject of Khe Sanh came up in conversation, our Marine instructors who had fought there would physically tighten. Their manner would become more serious. For them, Khe Sanh was the embodiment of two almost diametrically opposite feelings: One feeling was that of pride that Marines had fought valiantly and defeated the enemy. But the one that came through most to me was a feeling of anger: anger that our political and military leaders had put us in a position to incur more than twenty-five hundred Americans and allies killed and more than nine thousand wounded, for what they saw as no particularly good reason. For them Khe Sanh was both vindication of our military prowess—and a painful example of the complete failure of the senior leaders to have a clear sense of how to win a war.

More than that, they taught us that this had been a failure to understand that any individual action (or battle) that puts men and matériel at risk must support and advance us toward achieving the larger mission—or it should not be fought. Sure, at times when overwhelming forces dictate a need to act quickly without regard to the long term—when survival is at stake. But, time permitting, you need to take the long view, or you are more likely to fail at achieving the larger mission. You may also get people killed for no good reason.

To understand Khe Sanh, you first have to understand something about two of the top American generals in the war: US Army general William Westmoreland (four stars), and US Marine Corps lieutenant general Lewis Walt (three stars). Both were legends. By the time I made it to TBS, Westmoreland had gone on to become the chief of staff of the entire US Army. A distinguished artillery officer, he had graduated at the top of his West Point class in 1936, attended Harvard Business School, and had his first taste of combat in World War II, in Tunisia, Sicily, France, and Germany. He had been superintendent of the US Military Academy at West Point and had led the Army's storied 101st Airborne Division. He looked the part of the military hero: he was tall and fit, with short hair and flawless military bearing, and he'd been in Vietnam nearly since the start of American military involvement there, rising to command of all allied forces in the country—including both Army troops and Marines. The Battle of Khe Sanh was *his* battle, and for many, Vietnam had become identified as Westmoreland's war.

Walt was the other general involved. He was a Marine's Marine, and his background was very different from Westmoreland's. If Westmoreland was the epitome of the aristocratic and politically astute general, Walt was the down-in-the-mud-with-the-grunts general—sometimes known as Uncle Lew. Westmoreland briefed presidents. He was on the cover of magazines. It was said by some that he might someday seek to follow in the footsteps of General Eisenhower and himself run for president. Walt would never be in that category. He was a warrior.

At seventeen, Walt had enlisted in the Colorado National Guard, earned a commission in the Army Reserve, and then resigned it in order to pursue a commission in the Marines. He'd fought in the Pacific in World War II with the First Marine Division (later to be my division) in such places as Guadalcanal and Cape Gloucester and had *twice* been awarded the Navy Cross (second only to the Medal of Honor as a recognition of extreme valor in combat). Twice! That doesn't happen often. He also fought and was decorated for actions in Korea. In 1968, General Walt was commander of all US Marines in Vietnam, and he reported to General Westmoreland. After his return from Vietnam, Walt would be promoted to four-star rank and become the assistant commandant of the entire US Marine Corps.

My instructors had little good to say about General Westmoreland. Walt, on the other hand, they loved. Now, you may think this would come down to institutional loyalty (Army vs. Marines), but in fact, as they told it, it came down to their approach to winning the war. One leader took a long view that they understood, agreed with, and embraced; the other did not.

Like all US military leaders of that time, General Westmoreland and Walt both operated within political constraints in Vietnam. They were not free to expand the ground war beyond South Vietnam by seizing the North Vietnamese capital of Hanoi, for example, and they were not free (at least until late in the war) to cross national borders into Laos or Cambodia to interdict the enemy's supply routes.

This allowed the enemy fairly free passage for their soldiers, supplies, and weapons just out of our reach along what was known as the Ho Chi Minh Trail. It was frustrating for all and made it much more difficult for the Americans to achieve our stated national goal of protecting the south from being taken over by the communists of the north. They would need another approach.

As my instructors described it, General Westmoreland's long-term strategic objective was to demoralize the NVA and their irregular compatriots (the Vietcong) by a combination of killing as many of them as possible and bombing their industrial capacity to rubble. He was a big believer in the use of artillery and air power. It was sometimes called a war of attrition.

General Walt was a warrior who was more than willing to engage with and kill the enemy, but according to my instructors, he simply didn't believe that a war of attrition would work in Vietnam given the realities of the situation, in which, among other things, we were prohibited from having ground forces cross into neighboring countries, much less into North Vietnam. Further, they pointed out, killing masses of people hadn't resulted in victory for the Nazis in Russia or for the German air force bombing London in World War II. It just made the survivors angry. And even when it did work—such as when the Germans took Poland and Czechoslovakia, or when the Russians themselves later occupied Poland and Czechoslovakia, the resentment of the people ensured that success didn't last. Further still, in Vietnam, limiting the killing to those you could bomb from the air or soldiers you could find in a jungle environment—where the enemy could often just melt away—was even more challenging. Walt believed that defeating the North was a very different task from defeating the Nazis or the Japanese, and that a long-term strategy to win this war meant finding a way to do so that would result in a lasting peace.

A big part of Walt's long-term strategy was to convince the non-combatant Vietnamese in the South that they would be better off with the stability and prosperity of the market-driven, democratically elected government that the United States supported, as opposed to the dictatorship and centrally controlled communist economy that North Vietnam wanted to impose. For the people to reach that conclusion, they would need to see the benefits of our approach personally in every hamlet and village. They would need to be protected, to be free to pursue their livelihoods, and to feel safe. They would need to believe that their children would be better off if the regime that we were supporting prevailed. Conversely, if they perceived that their personal lives and the lives of their children would be better, safer, and more prosperous under the communists of the North, that's whom they would support.

Pursing this strategy, Walt greatly expanded the concept of "combined action platoons" that included medical personnel as well as forces of the South Vietnamese Army. Their mission was more than just to kill the soldiers on the other side who dared venture near the villages; their mission was also to protect locals (which they did with vigor) and to thereby enlist them to our side. Meantime, they worked with local South Vietnamese forces to open health clinics and improve water quality. Marines patrolled like cops, protecting regular people. In some cases they patrolled on foot, greeting the locals at farms, homes, villages, and markets, trying to win hearts and minds one at a time. It was a "pacification and protection" strategy to complement a "search and destroy" tactic. Walt wanted to deny refuge to the interlopers from the North and at the same time win over the villagers for the long term. In 1967, *Life* magazine put Walt and his combined action platoons on its cover.

General Walt's strategy may seem obvious after recent experiences in Iraq and Afghanistan, but at the time it was anything but. General Westmoreland, for one, had serious doubts about the long-term efficacy of Walt's pacification and protection strategy. It is possible that he simply believed that it wouldn't work—and that even if it did, for a time, it wouldn't last. Certainly, he had seen what had happened when the Americans left these villages. The communists moved in, killed the leaders who had been friendly to the Americans, and left others in their place who were friendlier to the North. He may also have been skeptical that the rampant corruption of South Vietnamese politicians would ever cease. My instructors weren't too keen on those government officials either. But they could see that Westmoreland's strategy was to win by attrition—by killing so many of the enemy forces that they would withdraw behind their borders—and Walt didn't believe that strategy alone would work. But General Westmoreland was in charge.

In 1966, Westmoreland made the village of Khe Sanh near the Laotian border and its surrounding area a focal point of his plan to

wipe out large numbers of the enemy. US Army Special Forces had
established an airstrip and a small combat outpost there, and if
Westmoreland couldn't yet cross into Laos to interdict the NVA supply lines, his idea was to at least interdict them near Khe Sanh—and
perhaps draw the NVA into large-scale combat. He began building
up a small base there from which US ground forces could patrol and
air forces could conduct reconnaissance. He may also have hoped that
someday Khe Sanh could be a jumping off point, if permission was
granted, to cross into Laos and cut off the North's supply routes along
the Ho Chi Minh Trail. (Media reports said that in 1967, Westmoreland petitioned President Johnson for permission to conduct
combat operations in Laos. But that permission was denied.) Westmoreland ordered Walt to send a battalion of Marines—about a
thousand people—to protect the base at Khe Sanh.

My TBS instructors said that, for at least two reasons, General
Walt hated the idea of having his Marines tied to a base. First, as his
strategy suggests, he felt the Marines were better used in the villages—
patrolling and protecting the people. And second, to engage in a
large-scale battle with the North from a fixed defensive position near
one small village was counter to the Marine ethos. Or as Sun Tzu, the
famed Chinese general and author of *The Art of War*, once said, "One
defends when his strength is inadequate; he attacks when it is abun-
dant."

"Winning" (killing a lot of the enemy at Khe Sanh and causing
them to withdraw) would do little to advance us toward accomplish-
ing our long-term mission. But Westmoreland was spoiling for a fight.
As he would soon learn, the North Vietnamese commander, General
Võ Nguyên Giáp, was happy to oblige.

General Giáp was the third player in this dynamic, as we studied
at TBS. A confidant of North Vietnam's president, Ho Chi Minh,
thirteen years earlier, in 1954, the Vietnamese general had led about
forty thousand soldiers to a decisive victory over the French, who had
established their own fixed defensive position in a valley near the village of Dien Bien Phu. That victory was credited with leading the
French to withdraw from Indochina altogether. Giáp wanted to drive
the Americans from Vietnam, and he knew he could not do so with
military might alone. Giáp coveted the opportunity to try to replicate
his success against the French—this time, with the Americans. At
Khe Sanh, he saw the Americans making the same foolish mistake as

the French: underestimating the communist forces of the North; setting themselves up in a fixed base and just waiting to be attacked.

His tour of duty over, in late 1967 General Walt returned to the United States, where he was soon promoted to four-star rank and made the assistant commandant of the US Marine Corps. He was replaced in Vietnam by Marine lieutenant general Robert E. Cushman Jr. (who was later to become the commandant of the Marine Corps). In January of 1968, Giáp's force, estimated at seventy thousand NVA soldiers, attacked the Marines at Khe Sanh. Over the next seventy-seven days, television, newspapers, and magazines around the world followed the battle daily—and nightly. It is said that no single battle in history had ever been viewed by so many, over such a prolonged period. Taking his cue from Westmoreland, President Lyndon Johnson ordered that the base be held at all costs. Westmoreland ordered General Cushman to send four thousand more Marines as reinforcements, and Westmoreland sent thousands more soldiers from the Army's First Cavalry Division. US Air Force B-52s from Guam reportedly dropped nearly one hundred thousand tons of bombs during this battle. (This compares to about nineteen thousand tons of bombs that the Nazis rained on Britain over seven months of the London Blitz.) General Westmoreland was said to have requested permission to use low-yield tactical nuclear weapons, if required—a request that was denied.

Despite many differences militarily between Khe Sanh and Dien Bien Phu, politically they were cousins. Khe Sanh was perhaps as influential in ending American involvement in Vietnam as Dien Bien Phu had been for the French. Months of continuous media coverage exposed Americans to the truth of the war. Westmoreland's attrition strategy may have been to kill a lot of North Vietnamese, but their willingness and ability to continue their quest seemed unabated. Giáp's strategy was not only succeeding militarily but also politically, as American support for the war waned.

Eventually, the NVA largely withdrew from the fighting at Khe Sanh, and Westmoreland asserted that the United States had won. He also asserted that the NVA had suffered more than fifteen thousand soldiers killed, a number that was impossible to verify as the NVA generally took their dead with them. But the cost to the United States had undoubtedly been high. Further, while the NVA did draw back, they did so only after their larger Tet Offensive had successfully been launched. Their attack on Khe Sanh had diverted critical American military resources that left cities and towns across South Vietnam vulnerable. In short order the NVA captured many of these cities and towns, but the real victory by the North was that no battle more clearly demonstrated to the American public that America's strategy was failing. Further, the NVA never really completely left the area around Khe Sanh; they continued to shell the base sporadically.

Shortly after the most intense period of fighting ended, Westmoreland's tour of duty as the top general in Vietnam came to an end. He returned to the United States and was made chief of staff of the entire US Army. More than a half million Americans were then fighting in Vietnam.

Soon Westmoreland's replacement in Vietnam, Army general Creighton Abrams, ordered the Marine base at Khe Sanh evacuated and destroyed. Shortly after that, on July 9, 1968, NVA soldiers raised their flag above what was left of the airfield at Khe Sanh. General Giáp congratulated his troops on their victory.

The Long View

My TBS instructors were angry about Khe Sanh. Friends had died there. We had "won" the battle—and yet we had achieved nothing. And by 1972, we were clearly losing the war. As we listened to their lectures, President Nixon's national security adviser, Henry Kissinger, was in Paris trying to negotiate "peace with honor" with the North Vietnamese. Our instructors rhetorically asked us, Where had we gone wrong? How had the most powerful military in the world been so roundly trounced? To them it was all about a failure to take an appropriatly long view.

At a minimum, they asserted, there should have been a more robust debate at the highest levels of government about our long-term objectives and the viability of our strategy to achieve those objectives. Someone should have forced a debate with General Westmoreland over the alternatives to a strategy that assumed that if we killed enough North Vietnamese and bombed enough of their industrial capacity, they would run home never to return. Perhaps someone should have forced a similar debate over the long-term viability of General Walt's

Combined Action Program approach. And if neither was deemed achievable, perhaps there should have been a wider debate about the constraints on the military and the feasibility of achieving our long-term objectives in Vietnam. It could have saved lives.

The Lesson

The lesson of Khe Sanh was that debate about our long-term goals in Vietnam and the best strategy and actions required to achieve those goals should have been conducted a lot more vigorously at the nation's highest levels. The failure to do so was extremely costly to many that I knew personally. There are dozens of similar examples of failure to take the long view in military lore—how about Napoléon's attempt to conquer Russia? Or the British at Gallipoli in World War I? The Russians in Afghanistan? And then there are positive examples: Admiral Chester Nimitz's island-hopping strategy of World War II, for example. Or we can take lessons from a long list of politically motivated decisions that fixed short-term problems and created longer-term ones in now-troubled cities such as Camden, New Jersey; Detroit, Michigan; and Oakland, California.

Most Wall Street bankers I know don't think a lot about the long view. They see their role as short-term by its very nature. They help their clients execute actions that the client has defined. But, in my view, we serve our clients best if we are also in the business of helping them to define their strategic objectives first—and then, at a minimum, fostering a robust conversation as to what actions are best taken to achieve those long-term strategic objectives. It is one reason that the Securities and Exchange Commission (SEC) requires stockbrokers to certify that the investments they put some clients into are "suitable." But, unfortunately, that requirement only extends to smaller investors whom the SEC has defined to be not "accredited." The Marine approach requires us to take the long view for all of our clients—not just the less sophisticated ones—and for ourselves.

It never ceases to surprise me how many CEOs can't clearly articulate their long-term strategic objective, much less clearly articulate how taking some action—winning a particular battle—will advance them toward achieving that objective. They just keep pushing forward along some path, such as reducing costs, improving profit margins, or growing the company 15 percent. Or perhaps they want to be the best, greatest, largest, most highly respected corporation in some narrowly defined field of endeavor. These are fine aspirations, but they are not strategic. It's sort of like aspiring to kill more Vietnamese; or trying to keep South Vietnam democratic and allied with the United States: these are worthy goals, perhaps, but not particularly useful from a strategic perspective.

The stories are many of Wall Street bankers who did what the client asked them to do—or worse, encouraged the client to take actions that were potentially counter to the best long-term strategy. The stories are, unfortunately, nearly as legion as those of CEOs who led their companies to disaster through their own short-term thinking—without any help from bankers.

In the introduction to this book I referenced the $235 billion (and rising) in fines and restitution that Wall Street banks have paid over the past half dozen years for bad acts, including ignoring obvious conflict of interest and allegedly misleading investors (and in some cases defrauding investors) about the safety of mortgages and mortgage-backed securities the investors bought in 2007 and 2008—the period leading up to the recent home-mortgage crisis. One federal agency alleged that seventeen banks "repeatedly made false claims to Fannie Mae and Freddie Mac about the very nature of the loans that these banks were pawning off on these agencies . . . [selling] the shoddy loans even after a third-party analysis company informed the banks that billions of dollars' worth of mortgages did not meet the specifications that the banks made in legal filings and in statements to Fannie and Freddie, which are still owned by U.S. taxpayers."

"Make no mistake: fraud is a business model," said Janet Tavakoli, president of the Chicago-based consulting firm Tavakoli Structured Finance. Later, US Senator Bernie Sanders (I-Vermont) repeated the mantra saying, "I think that the business model of Wall Street is fraud. And I think these guys drove us into the worst economic downturn in the modern history of America."

I don't believe that the business of Wall Street is fraud, but it certainly seems to me that many of these transgressions could have been avoided with a different culture. That fact alone should cause some banks to think twice about the business values, principles, and practices that they are allowing to flourish. As I am writing, several large financial institutions have been forced to pay hundreds of millions of dollars in fines for allegedly rigging benchmark interest rates and foreign exchange prices and separately to settle charges that they willfully continued to do business with countries and entities on the US sanctions list. To go on:

The New York State attorney general recently sued Barclays—maintaining that the company failed to protect clients from aggressive or predatory high-frequency trading in its dark pool.

The City of Los Angeles has sued Wells Fargo & Co. for allegedly pressuring employees of its retail bank to commit fraudulent acts, such as opening customer accounts without their approval, in order to meet management's sales goals.

It's all about culture.

At around the time of the mortgage crisis, Jefferson County, Alabama (which includes Birmingham), was forced into Chapter 9 municipal bankruptcy. I can't blame it all on their bankers, even if the county did sue and allege malfeasance by Wall Street banks. A wide raft of unsavory characters combined in graft, greed, incompetence, and malfeasance. But bankers and their culture didn't help. It all started with a need to replace an antiquated sewer system at a cost that was first estimated to be about $250 million. By the time they had it built, it cost the county closer to $3 billion. Birmingham's mayor was convicted of fraud and money laundering for taking bribes funneled to him by Wall Street. A major Wall Street bank agreed to cancel $647 million in termination fees, pay a $25 million fine, and pay an additional $50 million to the county. It was just ugly.

The Alabama fiasco was reminiscent of the bankruptcy of Orange County, California, in the 1990s when, with the advice of Wall Street bankers, the county swapped $14 billion of fixed-interest debt for complex derivatives contracts. When interest rates rose, the county lost $1.5 billion of its total investment funds and couldn't make its loan payments. That county too was forced to file for bankruptcy.

Procter & Gamble once sued a big Wall Street bank asserting that a group of bankers had encouraged it to swap $200 million in low-interest debt for a complex instrument that ultimately cost the company more than $100 million in losses.

How were these actions in the best long-term interests of the Wall Street banks or of their clients? To me, they feel mostly like ways for banks to make a lot of fast money. How can the advice that these banks gave to their clients be in anyone's long-term best interest—their own or the client's? This is a culture and a mind-set that needs changing.

D&B

In the preface to this book I commented on my first job after leaving the Marines—helping to lead international strategy as well as mergers and acquisitions at Dun & Bradstreet in the days when that firm was more of a holding company than a unified business. Over many years, D&B had acquired a series of vaguely related information service businesses with no particular long-term strategy that I could discern, other than to get bigger and make more money. The catch-as-catch-can nature of its acquisitions strategy became clear: this large, publicly traded multinational company known for its Dun & Bradstreet credit information and Moody's bond rating businesses wound up owning broadcast-television stations, a company that sold ads in the yellow pages, another that distributed direct-mail discount coupons, a company that sold inexpensive consumer goods through the mail to US customers and another that sold discounted cosmetics to German customers, a commercial bill collector, a publisher of trade magazines, a UK company that put advertisements on the side of private autos, a US firm that sold flowers by phone, and a half dozen others.

The bankers who called on D&B loved this approach because it meant that practically every service- or information- or marketing-related acquisition opportunity was fair game. Okay, I understand that most companies want to get bigger and make more money. But did it matter how we got bigger? Would we buy a movie studio? An amusement park? Was there any battle we would not fight if we thought we could win? Was there any deal we would not chase, any acquisition candidate we would walk away from if it was in a service business, growing, and the price seemed fair? For me, the problem with this approach was that I couldn't figure out how to prioritize or even know if we were winning, other than by the amorphous standard of whether we were getting bigger and making more money. And I couldn't understand how top management could lead. There was no domain expertise at the top. I recall a budget meeting in which the head of D&B's broadcast-television stations group put forward a budget that called for a sizable investment in new technology. After the meeting I realized that top management had no idea how to react. They had no basis to know whether that technology was needed, whether a better technology might exist to consider, etc. They were totally at the mercy of the group head. (They approved it—and later sold the group.)

Many private equity firms work that way. They look to buy under-valued assets, find strong managers to lead them, and manage them purely from a financial perspective—encouraging their portfolio companies to grow through both organic and inorganic means (acquisitions), employ debt leverage to increase their returns, and then sell them at a big profit, returning profit to investors. Warren Buffett's Berkshire Hathaway seems to work that way too—at least in the sense that it is a pure conglomerate. But D&B wasn't supposed to be a private equity firm. It rarely sold companies, and then only if they didn't "fit" someone's concept of what was needed. D&B didn't return funds to shareholders beyond its quarterly dividend. We never sold any firm of significant size while I was there. (Later D&B sold off everything, but that is another story.) Nor was it Berkshire Hathaway. The chairman and CEO of D&B told the investment community that we were "strategic," that we added value beyond smart buying, selling, acquiring, and effective tax planning. But if that was the case, what was our long view—other than to grow and make money? And how can the leaders lead?

The good news, at least for me, was that by the time I arrived on the scene, the leadership of D&B had reached a similar conclusion—that D&B needed to become a lot more sector-focused. At a minimum, the leadership realized that to add real value, they should stick with owning companies that top management had some real ability to understand the impact of and alternatives to major decisions.

D&B's then CEO and board chairman, Harrington "Duke" Drake, worked together with his chief strategist (my boss's boss), Richard "Dick" Schmidt, to take a longer view on where we were heading—and how we would get there. They formulated a long-term goal—of sorts. They still wanted to be a holding company with a bunch of portfolio companies that they could help grow; but now they wanted a unifying vision. They wanted businesses that provided business-to-business information and tools that marketers, corporate executives, bankers, and insurance companies could use to make better-informed business decisions. It wasn't about "one company"; it was about "one vision." At least that made sense to me.

Dick Schmidt knew how to take the long view. He wasn't a Marine, but he looked as if he could have been one—tall, fit, tight haircut, and erect Germanic bearing. (He had been born and raised in East Germany.) Dick was a former McKinsey consultant, a disciplined practitioner of the idea of developing a clear long-term objective and then working with his team (including internal and external bankers, lawyers, and consultants) to develop plans to achieve that objective. He preached that each transaction was simply a single battle—a phase point—along our path to the larger goal. He focused on a new objective that I had not thought much about since the stories of General Walt's pacification strategy. Dick talked about the need to win hearts and minds—to look beyond the immediate transaction to the peace that follows war, to life with the people on the other side of the table. I understood immediately. It resonated. As my TBS instructors would have put it, it's not about fighting battles for their own sake—even if you can win. It's about patient, focused, long-term strategy to achieve your ultimate mission.

In later chapters I'll talk about some of the many steps D&B took in those days to refocus the company. I was tasked with selling many of the firms that didn't fit the new mold, didn't advance us toward our goal (TV stations, flowers by phone, cosmetics by mail, etc.), and for building on those that did: adding business-information firms in the United States as well as in Germany, Switzerland, Denmark, Australia, and Hong Kong, and trying hard in Brazil, Hungary, Japan, and other places. It was a process. It took time.

Applying the Lessons

As a CEO and now as a banker, I try to learn from the lessons of Khe Sanh and of D&B as well as the negative and positive examples of my fellow investment bankers. Among other things, I encourage my team to take the long view and to help our clients take the long view within their own organizations. When we are approached by a client that wants us to advise them on a strategic move, we often ask a series of questions such as Why do you want to do this? What's your long-term objective? How achievable is it? What are the forces arrayed against you? Is this a battle you need to fight now? Do you have the resources to win? Should you wait? What are the alternatives?

It is easy to support whatever course of action the client espouses. Lots of bankers take the approach that by doing so we won't get blamed if it's wrong, and in any event it shouldn't be our problem if that course of action does the firm more harm than good. It's just not our way, however. On occasion a client brushes off our questions—they've made up their mind and want to get down to business. But more often than not, they like the approach and produce answers that help us to advise them. Not infrequently we help the client articulate their long view in ways they may not previously have done. Sometimes the process causes them to confirm—or reject—the reason to fight this particular battle at this particular time.

SWIFT 1

Shortly after I launched my own investment bank, I was approached by Leonard "Lenny" Schrank, then the CEO of a well-regarded financial services company based in Belgium called SWIFT. Among other things, SWIFT manages the computer network that moves money between most of the banks in Europe. Lenny and I had worked together fifteen years earlier. It started when I led D&B's acquisition of Interactive Data Corporation* from Chase. Lenny, an American and a graduate of MIT, led IDC's international operations and was based in London. Later, he and I worked on melding those international operations with those of another London-based firm that D&B had acquired, and later still we worked together on creating a joint venture with the Japanese company NTT Data. I had let Lenny know about my new investment bank, and now he asked if my firm could help SWIFT pull off an international acquisition.

My firm hadn't been around long at the time, and we needed business. Moreover, SWIFT is a name brand in financial circles, and helping them achieve their goal would be great for marketing. So I

---

* In 2010, Interactive Data was sold to a couple of PE firms for more than $3 billion, and in late 2015 they sold it to the Intercontinental Exchange for about $5.2 billion.

had strong short-term incentives, to say the least, to help them with their potential deal.

This was SWIFT's first attempt at an acquisition in anyone's memory. Their target was a small, privately owned data and software firm that I will call Objectivo.* I enlisted two of my team members to help: Paul Friday and Byron Raco. Paul was the more senior of the two—with ten years of relevant experience. He had led deals before. Byron was younger but extremely valuable. He was fresh out of JP Morgan and knew how to analyze a company. He was also good with clients.

Lenny had appointed three senior executives to lead his deal team: his CFO, Francis Vanbever; his head of products and marketing, Gottfried Leibbrandt; and the champion of the deal, Johan Kestens, the head of SWIFT's banking and insurance data business. They knew their business and their industry well. So, we started with a long phone call with the team at SWIFT.

We began with our basic questions about the long view: Why do you want to do this? What do you know about them? What's the long-term objective? How achievable is it? Do you have the resources to win? What are the alternatives? It soon became clear that the deal was an opportunistic experiment for SWIFT. They saw that SWIFT and Objectivo had common customers—companies that used Objectivo's data and technology to supplement a bank-reference-data service provided by SWIFT. Also, SWIFT's midlevel managers knew Objectivo's founder, whom I will call Antonio, an Englishman who had been a SWIFT customer when he worked at a big European bank. He had purposely built his service to run in conjunction with SWIFT. They believed that acquiring Objectivo could help them in their long-term quest to improve on their bank reference–data product. They said that they could internally build much of what Objectivo offered, but building it would take time and money and had execution risk. Further, if they didn't buy Objectivo, they would have to compete against it—possibly together with whoever else might acquire the firm. They saw the acquisition and integration of Objectivo

---

* In this book, I will need to give some companies and their people pseudonyms and to disguise other details to protect their confidences; I'll let you know when I'm doing that.

products into theirs as a way to achieve their long-term goal faster and with less risk. It all made sense to us.

After we understood the long-term goal as well as the tactical situation, we agreed to advise SWIFT (and they agreed to engage us). Since we were advising a company that wanted to make an acquisition (as opposed to one that wanted to be acquired), I recommended moving forward with the next level of investigation quietly and quickly, before the seller could entice others to bid up the price. The next step was to have preliminary informal discussions with Antonio and his financial backer and gather more information. Since one of the members of the SWIFT team, Johan, already had some dealings with Objectivo's CEO, Antonio, we suggested that Johan set up the meeting. A few days later, Johan, Gottfried, and Francis, together with Paul and me, flew to London to meet with Antonio and his main financial backer.

Antonio was excited about the potential to join with SWIFT. He had big plans: to build a sales force (he had none); establish an international presence in a half dozen countries; and obtain data and expertise from SWIFT to enhance his products. (He had given little thought to melding his products into those of SWIFT. He wanted SWIFT to help him grow—that was what excited him.) He told us that much of Objectivo's workforce was based in Italy, where, he asserted, the availability of educated people, wages, and employee turnover all were better than in the UK. His financial backer was clearly eager to see the company sold (albeit at a high price). Neither had thought a lot beyond the point of the transaction. We had a good meeting, asked for follow-up information, and returned to our respective home bases. A few days later, after reviewing the information, getting clarification on some points from Antonio and his financial backer, and chatting a few times with the team in Belgium, we had another long phone call with SWIFT to decide our way forward.

Most investment bankers I have worked with would have been strongly tempted simply to analyze the data, form an opinion on value, and help SWIFT execute. After all, Objectivo was growing nicely, its customers seemed to like its products, and the strategic fit with SWIFT seemed clear. Further, my firm needed the business—and the money. SWIFT had hired us to help them buy the company, not to question their overall strategy. But that's not the Marine Corps Way. We suggested that SWIFT take a large step back and consider alternatives to acquiring Objectivo in order to achieve their larger mission. They were surprised.

Price was one issue—Objectivo's financial backer had signaled a price that we considered quite high; but you can always try to negotiate price. The bigger issue was that we did not believe that this deal was the best way to advance SWIFT toward its long-term goal. Or at a minimum, a robust debate was required.

After delving deeper into the product line, we had concluded (and SWIFT's middle managers agreed) that Objectivo's principal product was less fully formed than we had at first believed. More investment would certainly be required. Only SWIFT could estimate the order of magnitude of that additional investment.

The Italian workforce was another potential stumbling block. Sure, SWIFT could leave them in place and slowly, over time, build up a workforce in Belgium to take over—which is where SWIFT had earlier told us that they wanted all product efforts centralized. But that approach too required extra costs and added risks.

Senior management commitment and backup was yet another open question and potential risk area. In one conversation with Antonio, he had told us that he had hated working for a big bank and loved being an entrepreneur. We asked, why would he stay with SWIFT? What was their plan to motivate him to stay—and what was their backup plan if he left?

We also discussed SWIFT's lack of experience in integrating acquired firms.

We told SWIFT that we could help them win the immediate battle—form an opinion on value and structure, complete due diligence reviews, negotiate, and get a deal done—that's what most bankers strive to do—but then what? We suggested that they needed to take the long view. Before they moved any further on this deal they should begin to formulate a clear plan about what would happen in the weeks and months after the transaction was completed and be confident that this deal was the best way to put them on the path to achieving their long-term mission.

In the end, Lenny and his senior managers concluded that this was a single battle that SWIFT did not need to fight. With our complete concurrence, SWIFT walked away from the deal. We lost the success fee, and that hurt. We also lost the chance to be involved in an important visible transaction. But, we gained credibility and respect from the team at SWIFT. In the years that followed, that goodwill would pay off.

The Payoffs—for SWIFT and for Us

Two years after we parted company over Objectivo, SWIFT's CFO, Francis Vanbever, and Gottfried Leibbrandt reached out to us again. They wanted us to attend an off-site strategic retreat in Virginia with their company's senior management to talk about what makes a successful acquisition. (By then, Lenny Schrank had retired, replaced by a new CEO, Lázaro Campos.)

We spent a long day educating SWIFT managers on the philosophy and practice of mergers and acquisitions. We talked about the need to take the long view—to establish clear strategic objectives and to formulate plans to achieve those objectives. We talked about the need to ask hard questions up front: What's the long-term objective? How does this deal fit? How achievable is it? Do you have the resources to win? What are the risks? What are the alternatives? And we talked about Objectivo and the lessons it had imparted. (Clearly the word had spread and we got credit for not being one of those firms that push deals at any cost.)

A few months passed, and Gottfried called again. This time, some of SWIFT's midlevel people thought that a big American company called SunGard might be open to selling a business that provided software that facilitated currency transfers between banks and their corporate clients. SWIFT was a powerhouse in bank-to-bank transfers and had long been looking for a way to move into this bank-to-corporation space. They saw this as a unique opportunity to buy a business that they would be challenged to develop internally. It would be a perfect fit into SWIFT's long-term strategy. Would we help them evaluate and possibly help structure, negotiate, and complete a deal?

The long view was clear. We went through an initial process that was similar to the one we had used with Objectivo. Soon it became clear that this deal might have as many challenges as with Objectivo. The asking price was high, the business had software development teams in Israel that were not going to move; SunGard wanted to keep using the software for their own corporate-to-corporate product line, which meant that complex cross-licensing and noncompetition agreements would be needed; and some key management would not be joining SWIFT but would stay with the seller. But after looking carefully at the opportunities and the challenges and working with the SWIFT team, we concluded that the hurdles could be overcome and that this transaction could advance SWIFT toward its long-term strategic goal better than any other alternative. We then helped SWIFT negotiate a fair price and buy the business. It fit with the long view.

I call the Objectivo deal that we didn't do SWIFT 1, and the successful SunGard deal SWIFT 2. Another successful later deal I call SWIFT 3, and I recently heard from the company that there may be a SWIFT 4. Not doing SWIFT 1 cost us. But it ultimately led to more revenue, and a long-term relationship that I am quite proud of. That's part of taking the long view too.

The Bottom Line

Not every contemplated action is strategic (cleaning windows?). And not all contemplated actions put at risk lives, limbs, or meaningful amounts of money, leadership time, or matériel. Not all actions distract leadership from other important duties. And sometimes, when overwhelming superior forces are bearing down upon you, there is time only to fight the battle at hand in order to survive. But when there is time, those actions that do put at risk lives, limbs, or meaningful amounts of money, leadership time, or matériel shouldn't be fought unless they must be fought—in order to advance the organization toward its long-term goals. And those battles should be fought only when you have the courage, commitment, and resources to win. To ensure success you must take the long view.

General Giáp understood that principle when he attacked the French at Dien Bien Phu and the Americans at Khe Sanh. General Westmoreland said he understood that too, so perhaps we just have different perspectives as to the long-term viability of his tactics. Duke Drake and Dick Schmidt embraced taking the long view when they began to reshape Dun & Bradstreet. Too many on Wall Street, however, along with too many politicians and too many in corporate executive suites, forget about the importance of taking the long view. So they just try to muddle ahead—fighting fires or, at best, trying to be good executors of strategies that someone else has determined. Taking the long view is rarely expedient—it is so much easier to just be reactive. And sometimes taking the long view may start a debate that alienates important clients or constituents. But when lives or important strategic matters are at stake, taking the long view is the best way I know to preserve precious assets and increase the probability of long-term success. That's the Marine Corps Way.

2

Take a Stand

EARLY IN MY DAYS AS A MARINE CORPS OFFICER, WHEN I WAS STILL IN training at TBS, we had a series of leadership lessons, each of which began with a film showing some situation that led to an unresolved crisis and ended with the phrase "What now, Lieutenant?"

I would hear this phrase again and again in the Marine Corps. It became a bit of an inside joke when we were confronted with a challenging situation—even when I was no longer a lieutenant. I think of the phrase still when I'm confronted with a complex situation that requires a clear, calm, quick resolution. Often the best answer isn't clear, all avenues have risk, and sometimes you don't have much time to decide.

When your sergeants ask "What now, Lieutenant?" you can't say, "Well, on the one hand . . . but then again, on the other hand . . ." You can't vacillate; you can't prevaricate; you can't form a committee. If there is time, you can get input from others, and if there is time, in many cases you should. But at some point, you must be decisive. (Decisiveness is one of fourteen leadership "traits" that all Marines are taught.) You have to work with the data that you have at hand, make a clear, firm decision, and accept responsibility for the result. That way of thinking informs the way every Marine officer carries out his or her daily routine. It's ingrained.

The best CEOs are decisive. They live the Marine Corps leadership principle of: "seek responsibility and take responsibility for your actions." However, the people in the middle—the managers, the politicians, and especially the consultants, bankers, and other advisers— surprise me with their aversion to making tough recommendations.

They may talk a good game about seeking or taking responsibility, but they don't really want to take the risk. It's too bad.

When I was fresh out of the Marines and working at Dun & Bradstreet, I observed a series of managers, consultants, and bankers who would seemingly go to any length to avoid making hard calls out loud. I remember one midlevel manager who was tasked with evaluating and recommending an account-receivables accounting software package for the company. From my perspective, it wasn't that big a deal. The choices were all among reputable vendors—none would have been horrible. He had months to gather data; talk to users and vendors; get references; compare and contrast. He told me that he did have a favorite—one that had more functionality that was appropriate for our firm than the others and was more cost-effective. But when it came time to make a recommendation, he just couldn't do it. He just wanted to list the features, functionalities, and price trade-offs on a detailed spreadsheet and let someone else decide. I get it. Taking a stand on issues means accepting responsibility, and that can mean putting your job on the line. Taking a stand can have real-world consequences—especially in jobs where people are fired for failure. I don't take that risk lightly. I suppose that manager could live with himself if D&B put in an inferior A/R system when he knew of a better option. The consequences weren't all that big. (D&B did eventually go with the smart choice.) But how do you live with yourself if you are the GM engineer that watched more than 100 people die as a result of faulty ignition switches when you knew that they were faulty and were afraid to take a stand?

I recall another more senior D&B manager—he reported directly to the chairman—waffling endlessly over a fairly straightforward recommendation (not even a decision) on whether D&B should hire a senior marketing executive. Like the more junior manager, he wanted a committee to decide. I saw the same thing from our consultants and our bankers. They refused to get out front on any issue. They waited to see which way the bosses were leaning, then wanted to be second or third jumping onto the bandwagon—never first.

At that time, D&B was working extensively with a number of Wall Street investment banks, as well as with a premier strategy consulting firm: Bain & Company. The similarities between the bankers and the consultants were striking in at least two ways: first, in both cases their key staff were smart, hardworking, and analytical; and second, they were virtually all what I call confrontation avoiders. One day I was in a meeting with the senior Bain manager who led several of the case teams working with us, along with Dave McBride (my boss and the EVP responsible for D&B's activities outside the United States), and Bob Weissman, then D&B's president. The purpose of the meeting was to review Bain's findings and recommendations regarding one of D&B's operating units. Because I had discussed it with the Bain manager before the meeting, I knew that he believed (and I agreed) that the head of that unit was in way over his head. He had been a finance manager before being promoted, and he still acted like a finance manager. His monthly and quarterly reports were always on time, detailed, and accurate; and he was a nice enough guy; but he simply did not have what it took to lead this unit. He had mediocre managers reporting to him that he refused to discipline or replace. When he wasn't on vacation (he took a lot of vacation), he was nearly always at his desk and rarely—if ever—out meeting customers or reviewing his remote branch locations. His unit was failing.

The Bain manager knew all this—we had talked about it. But when it came time to review results with Weissman and McBride, the manager waffled. He was not going to go out on a limb. He noted the tough economic environment the unit faced, the competitive challenges, etc.—and totally let the unit head off the hook. It was the direct opposite of what he had told me in person privately before the meeting.

I was dumbstruck. When we were finished, I confronted him. (My wife says that I am a confrontation seeker.) His response was that this was the way he was expected to fulfill his job. As he explained it, Bain consultants are taught to never be confrontational. Their goal is to observe and nudge gently in private. I get that too. Sometimes bad news is best delivered in private. He would not want to inadvertently embarrass the manager who should have long ago done something about this failing unit head. That's not how consultants do their job. Most of the investment bankers we worked with then must have gone to the same schools.

At D&B, at Telekurs, where I worked next, at Bridge, and at dozens of firms with which we have worked over the years, I have seen managers and advisers prevaricate endlessly. They seek others' opinions, try to build some sort of "consensus," and drag out the decision process as long as they can. I believe they called it self-preservation.

I get it. The problem—for me—is that this is not the way we make real progress. It's the difference between what these people called managing and Marines call leading.

At Veronis, Suhler, the private equity firm and merchant bank where I worked immediately before founding my current firm, I observed similar confrontation-avoiding behavior among many of the bankers. One day, for example, I observed one of my fellow managing directors dealing with a CEO who had approached us a few months earlier for help in selling his small, publicly traded company. The market was down, and the company's growth rate had slumped. Between the two, his stock price was down 30 percent from its peak less than a year before. Even with that decline, the market value of his company was still strong when measured against most common benchmarks.

My colleague and his team had worked hard and brought in several strong offers to buy the company, including one at a 100 percent premium to the company's current stock price. At the time, average premiums were in the 20 to 30 percent range. And this was on top of a healthy base-market valuation. The offer was from a strategic buyer with a compelling need for the company. It was well above what any of us had expected. I was impressed, but the CEO was not. He had decided that he should get a 200 percent premium to the current stock price. He was nuts. But what surprised me more was that my colleague did not push back. He knew that 200 percent was ludicrous, but he was not going to confront the client.

Later I talked with the banker. He had his logic: The client was paying us a big monthly retainer. If he fought with the client about what constituted a reasonable value, he would not only be putting that retainer at risk, he would also be risking a potential large transaction fee later. He would prefer to avoid the confrontation, and keep going—trying to get a higher price. If it didn't work, then perhaps, eventually, the client would figure out that his price expectation was ridiculously high and accept a more reasonable offer.

For me, the problem with this approach was that (a) it was intellectually dishonest (the banker knew well that 200 percent was not going to happen), and (b) declining the current offer might not be in the client's best interest. Neither the banker nor I believed that the company would come close to an offer that high from anyone else,

anytime soon. Like the Bain consultants, many of my fellow investment bankers seem to believe that confrontation with anyone—clients,
superiors, etc., should be avoided at all costs. They may make soft
recommendations—hints really—and then usually only after they see
which way the wind is blowing. Marines don't take that approach.

I'm not suggesting that advisers should poke their clients in the
eye with a sharp stick. I'm not suggesting rudeness or an attempt to
usurp the prerogatives of the CEO. But there are ways.

One of the best investment bankers D&B worked with was Goldman Sachs's Geoff Boisi. Now, this was a smart guy who could have
been a Marine. (He wasn't.) At thirty-three, Boisi had been named
head of Goldman's mergers department. He was the real deal—and
he wasn't afraid of confrontation. One day, when I was a relatively
junior member of the D&B planning and acquisitions staff, I was in
the back of the big D&B boardroom at a meeting to discuss strategy
regarding the largest acquisition that D&B had yet undertaken—the
merger with AC Nielsen. It was potentially transformative; it was
complicated; and it was risky. Several senior executives were not convinced that the risks were worth the potential reward. In fact they
had a hard time seeing the reward. All they could see was risk to the
value of their stock and stock options.

One of them confronted Boisi with a litany of potential downside risks to the deal. I waited for Boisi's "What now?" moment. He
took on the challenger calmly, firmly—and brilliantly. One by one
he explained how the risks could be mitigated and our fallback position in the event we were wrong. He also focused on the significant upside transformative potential of the transaction—including
the potential impact on the stock price. By the end of the conversation he certainly had me convinced, although a few risk avoiders
in the room were still, as always, most comfortable with the status quo. D&B did get the deal done—and it was transformative.
D&B's revenue growth and profitability rose to new levels. The
company was given significantly more respect by Wall Street analysts, investors, customers, and employees. And its stock price rose
accordingly. It all worked out as Boisi had predicted. (Later still,
he advised on dozens of the most prominent deals of the 1980s,
including KKR's $25 billion buyout of RJR Nabisco, which was
famously portrayed in the book and movie *Barbarians at the Gate*.)

He and others showed me in those early days that not all invest-ment bankers are confrontation avoiders.

Over the years I have had many "What now, Lieutenant?" moments—both in the Marines and after. So many that taking a stand—assessing the situation, making decisions, and taking action (almost always based on imperfect information)—has become a natu-ral instinct. And I believe that is a good thing, for leaders and also for their advisers. I'm not always right. One time I authorized blowing up a half dozen cases of hand grenades after I was denied permission to return them to the storage location where they belonged. The resulting explosion in a small valley sent shock waves several miles and broke windows in a nearby town. I heard from my battalion commander about that one. But taking a stand is what Marines, good leaders, and good advisers should do—including bankers. It's what our clients should expect of us. Even if sometimes we break windows.

NYSE—the Client Is Still the Commander

A few years ago, we were advising the New York Stock Exchange (NYSE) as they investigated buying a fast-growing (albeit unprofit-able) European technology business called Fixnetix. I liked the sector in which Fixnetix operated and the services they offered—essentially running large portions of the back office of trading floors for big se-curities trading firms. Also, I could see how acquiring Fixnetix could fit with NYSE's long-term goal to take over the back offices of secu-rities trading floors. The two companies' products complemented each other. This could be a straight merger of like businesses—taking out a competitor and achieving substantial cost synergies. Strategically it felt like a no-brainer.

Our principal client on the deal was Stanley Young, CEO of NYSE Technologies, the group that was responsible for a wide range of technology then owned by the NYSE and used by many big secu-rities traders. Stanley was a smart, outgoing Englishman, and he got along well with Fixnetix's CEO, Hugh Hughes. Stanley also was no confrontation avoider. Like most good CEOs he had strong opin-ions and was not afraid to go out on a limb. Stanley coveted Fixnetix's product line and customer base, and Hugh was flat out ready to sell.

Initially, the biggest single challenge was simply Hugh's asking price, which, after doing a fair amount of due diligence, my team and I concluded was too high by a factor of two at least. (In a later chapter we'll talk about how we approach valuing companies.)

I'd known Hugh Hughes for years. While I respected his acumen and the business that he had built, I didn't entirely believe his extremely optimistic views of the near-term revenue growth for his company. Entrepreneurs are supposed to be optimistic, and I am often suspicious of an entrepreneur who doesn't believe that his company will change the world, but I have learned to take their predictions with a grain of salt. Our not buying into his revenue projections was one of the reasons why our sense of value differed from his.

The company wasn't making money, and I thought one big reason was because they couldn't seem to focus. They were always chasing after some new expensive product or product enhancement—several of which I felt they had not thought through. Further, they had a bloated staff that Hugh seemed to have no interest in right-sizing.

If all the above were not enough, I also questioned the fit of Fixnetix's culture with that of the NYSE, which was far more bureaucratic than the much more opportunistic approach at Fixnetix. (It was an interesting reversal of stereotypes to have the UK firm be more entrepreneurial than the US firm.) In my view, the culture at Fixnetix was *too* entrepreneurial.

I believe clients retain investment bankers such as me to give them our considered advice. While I cannot force them to accept that advice, they can't stop me from giving it—unvarnished. I took a stand in this case, as I believe advisers are supposed to do. I told Stanley of my concerns and recommended that he not buy the company at this price. Largely, he agreed. But he and Hugh still very much wanted a deal.

Someone (not me) then suggested a compromise: What if NYSE were to buy only a small part of Fixnetix—say 25 percent? Stanley liked the idea. By buying a minority stake, he reasoned, NYSE would have access to the fast-growing business that they wanted to enter, without committing to the high price that Hugh and his backers wanted. If everything worked out, NYSE could buy more of the firm later. It reduced NYSE's cash commitment and in Stanley's mind would reduce his risk. He also posited that leaving Fixnetix as a stand-alone company for a while could be a good thing so that

NYSE's bureaucracy wouldn't smother Fixnetix's entrepreneurial spirit.

Hugh liked the idea too, as long as a minority investment from NYSE didn't get in the way of a full sale of the company at a high price in a few years. He would have preferred an outright sale now, but that wasn't happening. The minority deal would provide him with much-needed cash and the imprimatur of the NYSE—and he could continue to operate Fixnetix independently.

Just about everyone involved liked the idea—except for me. I believed that not only was the price still too high, but also, as important, that a minority deal would not do enough to advance the NYSE toward its long-term strategic objective of being the leader in this sector, eliminating a competitor, and achieving cost synergies. Certainly, it would be a management distraction.

At this point, most investment bankers would have shut up and executed. I had already taken one stand—but I took another. I told Stanley that I thought a minority deal was not smart. Fixnetix would still be out there competing. And the company would still be managed in an entrepreneurial way that was not likely to lead to profitability. Meanwhile Stanley or some other senior person from NYSE would have to pay attention to it—attend board meetings, review budgets, etc.—and yet they would have absolutely no control. They were not a private equity firm. In my view, the only way a deal with Fixnetix was going to advance NYSE toward its long-term strategic goal would be if NYSE bought the company outright and melded the two firms together. Anything short of that was doomed to failure. I strongly advised Stanley to either push for a full sale at a lower price or to walk away. How did he respond? He overruled me.

Stanley was no wimp. He was an operator, and as with other good CEOs he was more than willing to take a stand. I respect operating leaders willing to do so. He wanted to buy and Hugh wanted to sell. In his view, the price for 25 percent might seem high now, but if the company did perform, it would later seem like a bargain. And if he was wrong, NYSE could afford the mistake. The risk was low. "What now, Lieutenant?"

I had made clear that I didn't agree. I had taken my stands—twice. But now it was time to execute. Buying a piece of Fixnetix was not illegal, immoral, or unethical, and the client was the commanding officer. So after voicing my views, I saluted and moved forward. I worked hard to get my client the best deal we could—at the best price and with best protections possible. That's my job, and we got it done.

iSuppli

I could tell a dozen other stories about the advisability of accepting the inevitability of confrontation, and of being decisive, of taking a stand, in the face of opposition when you don't have time to gather all the facts. This applies to the business world in general, to politics, and especially to my Wall Street investment banking brethren. It's a critical part of the Marine Corps Way. One vignette that comes to mind involves a brilliant CEO who hired my firm a few years ago. When I first met Derek Lidow I was impressed. He was in his 50s, tall, slim, somewhat professorial-looking—and brilliant. Armed with a BS in engineering from Princeton and a PhD in applied physics from Stanford, he had gone on to become CEO of a well-regarded publicly traded company in the electronics industry. Following that stint, Lidow had founded the highly successful market-intelligence company that he was now leading, called iSuppli.

Lidow had originally launched iSuppli as a marketplace for semiconductors and other electronic parts. He raised growth capital from three venture funds. That plan hadn't worked out exactly as planned, but he'd pivoted and morphed his company into an information and research company that tracked everything about semiconductors and electronic components (who makes them, where, how much they cost, who uses them, what are the trends, etc.). When a company such as Apple comes out with a new iPhone or iPad, a lot of Apple's competitors, potential investors, and others want to know what exactly is in it and how much the components cost. Often, iSuppli can tell them. The firm also provided a lot of other market intelligence services around this same theme.

The new strategy was much more successful. The company added high-tech customers such as Intel and HP; consumer electronics companies such as Samsung, Nokia, and Sony; multinational industrial companies such as GE; hedge funds; and even some international government agencies. His company grew revenue and made a profit. He even bought and integrated four small companies. With success, Lidow raised more capital from an investment fund managed by Goldman Sachs. This was a sign of confidence from a sophisticated investor.

Now Lidow had an opportunity to acquire a European company that was bigger and more strategic than all of his previous acquisitions. It was strong in sectors of the economy that were adjacent to iSuppli's core business, and it had success in Europe and Asia—areas that had been challenging for iSuppli. It was highly complementary to iSuppli without overlapping.

A Clear Objective

Lidow wanted us to help him find a financial partner to provide the cash he'd need to finance the acquisition, and a bit more to take out some of his existing investors if possible and support his management team so they could grow the company for a few more years.

While the strategic objective was clear, we also clearly had more than a few challenges—most of which are not relevant to this chapter. In brief, we would have to move quickly. The European company's CEO liked Lidow, and the CEO's team liked the idea of teaming with iSuppli (which would require no layoffs—unlike the likely outcome if the company went to a competing bidder, a large European-based corporation). But the founder would not wait forever. We were told that we had four months—and no more. Normally these processes take much longer. Valuation would be another challenge. Because the profit margins of both iSuppli and the target were relatively thin, we would be seeking a valuation that we knew some financial investors would see as absurdly high. (Not us.) Further we would be asking investors to bet on a merger that hadn't yet happened. And finally we would have to explain away why none of iSuppli's four current institutional investors planned to put any more money into the company. Normally, when new investors come in to fund an expansion of a company or an acquisition, they expect to see the existing investors invest too. But with iSuppli, some of the current investors were even hoping that the new round would give them a chance to cash out.

There was a legitimate explanation. The newest investor, Goldman Sachs, had made its investment via a fund whose rules specifically prohibited it from making follow-on investments in any of its companies. The three other funds had invested in the company at a time when iSuppli had a completely different strategic plan, and further they were approaching—or had already exceeded—the end of their fund lives. They too were not allowed to make any further investments. These were all reasonable explanations; but it's never fun to start an assignment with so many things to explain away. Still, I liked the company, liked the deal that Lidow was trying to put together, and I liked Lidow. We reached terms with him and his board of directors and went to work.

A New Objective?

My instructors at TBS recognized that plans need to be adaptable, and tactical objectives may have to change because circumstances on the ground are almost never exactly what you thought they would be based on maps and intelligence reports.

Lidow had made it clear that he and his team wanted to raise capital to make their acquisition and keep the company going independently for a few years—and then exit. To my mind and his, that helped to define our tactics. We'd be helping him to attract professional investment firms—*financial investors*—firms that buy or invest with an explicit plan to sell in a few years and make a profit, as opposed to *strategics*—industry participants that buy with the intent to leverage the strengths of both companies to build a stronger whole and have no specific plan to sell what they have bought. So we started down Lidow's path and within thirty days had identified interest from several potential financial investors. Then, at Lidow's request, we met with the iSuppli board of directors to brief them on our progress. The board, which included Lidow and representatives of each of his company's four major investors, were happy to hear of the progress, but the outside board members wanted to know why we had not approached strategics.

We told the board that going after strategics wasn't the smart way to achieve the long-term objective that we had been assigned. We had recently advised another client in this same broad arena on a sale and had talked with many of the strategics. We were highly confident that several of them would buy into Lidow's vision, but we were just as sure that none of the strategics were likely to be happy with owning less than substantially all of the company, much less with spending money to strengthen iSuppli as an independent company that could compete with them. Further, they would not want to negotiate long-term strategy or budgets with other board members.

Now, however, the outside board members pushed back. They wanted us to pursue strategics anyway, in addition to financial investors, and it soon became clear why. They had a different long-term strategic goal in mind. As is typical of investments made by institutional investors such as private equity firms, these investors had made their investment by purchasing "preferred" shares in iSuppli, which gave them the right to take the first money off the table in the event of a sale of the company. Common shareholders (including the company's management) got nothing from a sale until the investors first got back their entire investment plus a return on that investment. After that, the common shareholders would receive a disproportionate share of the upside until an agreed level was reached. It was complex but clear that with an investment by another PE firm, some of the current investors might be able to cash out some of their shares, but not all, and in the most likely scenarios, the lion's share of any further upside would go to the new PE firm and management. A complete sale on the other hand, at a decent price, could allow them to cash out now and get a decent return on their investment. Clearly, among the stakeholders the long-term objectives diverged. "What now, Lieutenant?"

Now Lidow had to take a stand. He had hired us, and he had defined the strategic objective. And he did take a stand—sort of. He told the board that we would talk to strategics. This was not a battle that he wanted to fight—yet. I could tell that his heart wasn't in it. Nevertheless that's what we did.

Within two months we had indicative (nonbinding) offers from members of both groups. As predicted, we had found several financial investors who were excited about Lidow's dream and willing to provide the cash required to buy the European company, fund growth, and even partially buy out some of the investors—even at the high asking price. *And* we had identified several strategics eager and willing to buy the company outright. However, as we expected, none of the strategics had any interest in owning less than 100 percent. We pushed all parties to be sure that we had stretched them. We were now in a bind—a good bind, but a bind nonetheless—with several seriously interested suitors and no clear direction. That's the problem when you don't have a clear long-term goal!

Stalemate?

Lidow wanted to negotiate with one of the private equity firms. Their valuation was strong, he liked the firm, and he liked the lead partner. It met his objectives. We had done business with the firm before and trusted them. Lidow did reference checks, and the firm came back extremely strong. Further, in his view, the strategic option wouldn't take him to where he wanted to be. His management team (owners of common shares) would get almost nothing if the firm was sold at the price offered by the strategic, and Lidow had no interest in subjecting his team to that fate. (Lidow himself would receive a fair amount of money in this scenario because much of his ownership was in preferred shares.) Further, Lidow told us that he had no interest in working for a big public corporation. He'd been there and done that.

Meanwhile, Lidow's investors were increasingly interested only in selling iSuppli outright.

"What now, Lieutenant?"

Time was growing short. Neither option could go forward without Lidow's support and support from the rest of the board. This was looking like a stalemate. In the meantime, another party's vote counted: that of the founder of the European target company that was the original impetus for the deal. He had no idea that iSuppli and his firm might be sold to some big multinational corporation that would subsume both companies. How would he react? Yet, all the offers on the table assumed that the acquisition of the European company would go through.

Lidow was conflicted. We clearly didn't have the clarity of objectives I'd thought we had at the start. We now had less than sixty days before the option from the European company expired, which wasn't nearly enough time for most buyers or investors to conduct full due diligence reviews. Lidow didn't want to even introduce a potential strategic acquirer to the target company until a deal was on the table that both he and his board would accept.

Bankers Should Take a Stand

Most Wall Street bankers I know would now have punted. They would have said that this was in the hands of the CEO and the board of directors: it's above my pay grade. They might help lay out the options, but most would say that the company should decide and then they would execute. But abdication of the responsibility to take a stand is not the Marine Corps Way.

When we began working with Lidow and his management team, I thought that they had been clear on their long-term objective: they wanted to find a partner that would provide the money to buy the European company. Not until months later did I realize that finding a financial partner was *not* the long-term strategic objective—it was an intermediate tactical one. Lidow and his management team were not looking to stay forever; they clearly said that they wanted to sell the company outright—just not right now. This desire to wait a few years was not about achieving world domination for the firm, but instead about the management team's desire to reap greater rewards from a sale.

That explained why, when the board had pushed us to go talk to strategics, Lidow had not objected strenuously. In our private conversations, however, he clearly wasn't happy with the prospect of a sale to a strategic *at the price on the table.*

Lidow and I discussed the current stalemate. A wise former Army corporal (my father) once told me that life is about selecting from among real alternatives, not hypothetical ones. We had to figure out what those alternatives were and which among them would best lead to Lidow's long-term goal. And we had to do so with imperfect information. We hadn't yet talked to the CEO of the target company, nor did we know just how far we could push the buyers. This was no time for wimps!

I took my stand. I advised Lidow to tell his board that he absolutely would not support a sale to a strategic at the current prices on offer. However, he would enthusiastically support a sale at a higher price if his management team could get the deal that he wanted them to have. If not, he would push for a deal with the PE firm. While technically the board didn't need Lidow's acquiescence to sell the company, practically speaking, none of the strategics would be interested in buying the company unless it had a happy management team in place, so Lidow had a de facto veto. But this approach was risky. The board could simply fire him.

Lidow took a stand. He called a board meeting and laid out the situation and his recommendations essentially as above. Several board members grumbled, but agreed that we would go back and push the strategics for more—which we did. It didn't work. While two of the strategics increased their offers a bit, none came up enough to meet the needs of the management team. Lidow wanted to go with the PE firm; the board still wanted to sell. "What now, Lieutenant?"

In our dealings with potential partners for iSuppli, one potential strategic acquirer stood out from the others. They were strong financially and could afford to invest in the companies after a deal; the culture of the two firms seemed compatible; the key people seemed to get along; the products seemed to meld; and this strategic had a sterling reputation for integrity both during deals as well as in their actions with acquired companies and their management. While they were not active in iSuppli's sector, they had already acquired three firms providing analogous market intelligence. Lidow's company, when coupled together with the European target, was attractive to them. Their price was high enough for the investors. The problem was simply that it wasn't high enough for management—and they had made it clear that this was their "best and final" proposal.

So, we advised Lidow to make one last stand focused on closing the perceived value gap for management. With his board's consent, we would go back to the strategic; explain the situation; and tell them that we could close this deal if they would increase the purchase price by coming up with a package of restricted shares, stock options, and cash bonuses that would close half of the value gap for management. Lidow would do his best to keep his management team and the founder of the European company in the fold and get the deal done. We would tell them that this would work in part because the holders of preferred shares would divert a portion of their proceeds to management sufficient to close the rest of the gap. We would tell the strategic that if they would not agree, then we would go with the PE firm. Lidow agreed. That's what he told his board.

Several board members groused about giving up some of their proceeds, and they asked my opinion. I took my stand. I told them that this was their best opportunity to sell the entire company, which was their goal. Even after giving the extra piece to management, they would be getting a better deal than in most alternative scenarios, which left them with less in three to five years. They agreed: our new objective and the plan to accomplish it was set into motion.

The strategic and the investors both agreed with our approach and the deal got done. It was a tremendous win for everyone. It was made possible only once we stepped back, adjusted, and formulated a new smart, clear objective and a plan to achieve it, and only after we took a stand—several stands. That's the Marine Corps Way.

3

Be the Expert (or Use One)

THE MARINE CORPS TEACHES LEADERS TO BE "TECHNICALLY AND TACTI-cally proficient." We are each supposed to be the experts at what we do—and, most important, to accomplish the mission we are supposed to form teams of experts that take advantage of others whose domain knowledge extends beyond our own. It all sounds reasonable and logical—until you start to contemplate what makes someone an expert.

Every Marine, as I've noted earlier, whether male or female, old or young, regardless of rank or occupational specialty, is a rifleman. Every Marine officer is—at the core—a rifle platoon commander. Lawyers and clerks, tankers and truck drivers, supply clerks and jet pilots—all must be available to fight on the ground, in the trenches, at any time. That not only means that they all must go through infantry training and prove their proficiency in ground combat skills when they are new to the Corps. It also means that every year, all Marines must prove that they remain physically fit enough for combat and proficient with their assigned weapon. That effort doesn't make all of these Marines experts at infantry combat, but it means that they have a starting point—a base on top of which they may start to build true expertise in some field.

Marines become true experts first by building on their base of knowledge through a series of intensive schools, and then through practical experience in the field. Being a trained fighter pilot or artilleryman is good, but when we finish our training, we still aren't experts. Expertise comes from a combination of education and extensive real-world experience in the assigned area of specialization, in specific environments (desert, mountains, jungle, tundra, etc.) and under specific conditions. That field experience allows us to learn from our own mistakes and those of others. It helps us to anticipate what the other side will do—not just react. It helps us to know how best to act when life throws unexpected obstacles in our path. It gives us the edge over others in combat and in life. It allows us to survive where others perish.

My father, who is a retired mechanical engineer from the Cummins Engine Company, used to bemoan those senior executives at the company who were generalists. They knew a lot about structuring compensation plans and perhaps about managing difficult people. Many had spent some time working in sales or administration or finance or some other staff group at some other company, but in his words, most of them didn't understand much more than the rudimentary basics of an internal combustion engine. As a result, while they could "manage" existing operations, they were not capable of leading the company forward with innovative ideas and concepts. They could not even opine with any credibility beyond the financial on where the industry was heading; and they were at a distinct disadvantage when some self-proclaimed expert told them that they needed to redesign their core product. They could manage, but they couldn't lead.

Wall Street, like our corporate boardrooms and political capitols, contains a mix of true domain experts and others who seem a lot like the generalist corporate managers that my father complained about. The generalists are often smart and educated; and they have had the basic training. They may even have spent time in the field. But while there, did they develop true domain expertise? (Not everyone does.) Wall Street bankers for example usually have financial-modeling skills; most of them know how to read an income statement and a balance sheet; they all have taken and passed tests that certify their base knowledge in stocks, bonds, options, other securities, privacy rules, anti-money-laundering rules, insider-trading rules, and a thousand other rules. Many bankers are capable of managing a transaction. But all of the foregoing does not make them experts—at least not by my definition. They must also spend enough time in the trenches in specific industries to be able to opine credibly on whether a transaction should be entered into in the first place. To be an expert, they must have what I call both depth and breadth—and some length wouldn't hurt. (I'll reflect more on these dimensions later.) They should know what to do if things don't go as planned. They should be able to do more than manage; they should be able to lead.

Hire a banker who is a true domain expert, one who can lead; you will get better advice. Personally, I'm tired of working with people who are good at managing process—but don't know a piston rod from a crankshaft.

Tripoli

In 1974, I was assigned to be the senior Marine officer permanently assigned to the USS *Tripoli*, a Navy ship that looked a lot like a shorter version of a modern aircraft carrier. There, I got a small lesson on the value of practical experience on top of formal training. It wasn't a huge deal, but it was memorable. *Tripoli* was designed to deliver Marines into battle by helicopters, not to launch fighter jets. She had a crew of about seven hundred US Navy sailors and could carry as many as seventeen hundred members of a Marine Expeditionary Unit (MEU)—a fully equipped, air-ground quick-reaction combat force. Moreover, *Tripoli* was the centerpiece of an amphibious squadron that usually included at least three other ships that carried Marines into battle, plus destroyers and other ships that offered protection. *Tripoli* was the central ship in the squadron—the only one with a complete combat operations center for managing land, sea, and air battles and a fully equipped hospital.

My job was to manage the ship-end of *Tripoli*'s ship-to-shore movements and to act as the principal amphibious assault adviser to the ship's captain and the Marine colonel who commanded the MEU. It was a complex job, and I was expected to know every detail about where and how to get those Marines from the ship to the shore on time and without a hitch. I had been trained—had attended several schools—and I had a small team of experienced Marines that worked with me. I understood that our job began well before the MEU embarked. My gunnery sergeant—a grizzled, combat-experienced Marine who had been coordinating ship-to-shore logistics for the better part of fifteen years—and I worked with the MEU's logistics officer, the S-4 and the ship's deck officer. We planned where on the ship the Marines would live, where they would store their weapons, ammunition, vehicles, parts, food, shelter, and more—all the stuff they would need to conduct an amphibious assault—and prosecute the battle inland. We were to do so in such a way as to allow for the rapid retrieval of the people and their equipment so the units could be deployed quickly. When the time came to plan for an assault, I had to make sure that the Navy and the Marines were fully coordinated. We all had to know what people and what equipment had to be brought to the flight deck at what time, and then ensure it was embarked on the correct helicopter. At the appointed hour, the entire MEU had to flow off the ship in a fast, smooth, and coordinated process—for hours. Then we had to be able to get them back. The process was extremely intense for the first six hours or so and could easily go on for a few days, with almost always periods of insane stress.

When I started the job, it felt impossibly complicated. I knew that if anything at all didn't work on time and as expected, it would be my fault. I had to be an orchestra leader and a circus ringmaster. I had to improvise quickly when something went wrong, as often happened. I was expected to be the ship's expert on Marines and the Marines' expert on the ship. But at first, I wasn't yet qualified. I was still learning—still a generalist. Fortunately, I had a team.

One small incident stands out in my mind. It began around 3:30 a.m. as the Marines on board *Tripoli* were preparing for a predawn amphibious assault exercise in coordination with the Philippine Navy and Marines. We were simultaneously patrolling the East China Sea. While most American combat units had left Vietnam by that time, the war was not yet quite over. A few months earlier, our sister ship, the USS *Okinawa*, had supported forces of South Vietnam in an amphibious assault. On *Tripoli*'s previous deployment, her crew had supported several combat operations along the coast of Vietnam. We were all on edge. The Marines were finishing breakfast, cleaning weapons, checking gear, and generally preparing; the helicopters were warming up; the Navy was positioning the ship for the assault. And I had work to do.

I was in the office of the ship's executive officer (the second-ranking officer on the ship) coordinating with him, along with the Marine colonel who would lead the MEU, and the Navy air boss, who would control the flow of aircraft to, from, and near the ship. Meanwhile, five decks below the ship's main deck, in the ship's cargo holds, Navy personnel with forklifts were working with my gunnery sergeant and his team to load elevators to bring up pallets of ammunition and equipment to the staging area. Suddenly the ship's senior deck officer, out of breath and visibly sweating, rushed in to tell us that the ship's elevators had broken down, that it could not be fixed anytime soon, and that they had no alternative plan that could be implemented to get the Marines' equipment out of the ship's cargo holds in time for the assault. I had more than a thousand Marines waiting for their ammunition and equipment in preparation for an attack that was to launch in less than two hours. The ship's officers were nonplussed. As they huddled with the deck officer, I went to confer with my team. "What now, Lieutenant?" indeed!

Fortunately, my gunnery sergeant was an expert. He had been to all the schools and, as important, had spent more time at sea coordinating logistics than most of the sailors around us; certainly more than I. He had been to this rodeo before and knew exactly what to do. He suggested that we round up a company of Marines—about 150 people—and bring up the gear by hand. It may sound like common sense, but it's much more complex than it sounds. In fact, the Navy senior chief petty officer responsible for the deck and the holds of the ship didn't believe that it was possible to accomplish in the time allotted. The Navy senior chief, with twenty years of experience, argued that it would be a waste of time to try to move this much gear by hand in the allotted time. He pointed out that before we could start we would have to rearrange vehicles and equipment on the ship's full and busy hangar deck to create space to stage the gear once it came up—out of the way of the helicopters, vehicles, and people that were being prepared for the pending amphibious landing. It was already hectic and crowded there. We'd have room only for a small group inside the ship's holds, who would have to break down each pallet—and make sure they did so in the right order—inside tightly packed storage compartments. They'd have to hand each piece of equipment one at a time to a Marine, who would in turn hand it to the next Marine, who would be standing a step or two above—up five flights of steep stairs (or ladders, as the Navy calls them). Many of those pieces were quite heavy, weighing as much as seventy-five pounds. Then, when we got the gear up to the ship's busy and full hangar deck, the equipment would have to be repalletized, marked, and staged so as to ensure that it all was loaded onto the right helicopter at the right time. We didn't have the resources or the time. And don't forget that the Marines themselves needed time to prepare for their role in the amphibious landing. The Navy chief wanted no part of this effort, but my gunny was confident and eager. I felt that we had nothing to lose. There wasn't much time.

While the Navy worked on mechanical fixes to the elevator, and the senior chief stood aside and watched, I found the MEU executive officer. With his help we quickly got organized. We selected the last of the Marine units expected to assault the beach and briefed their leaders on the task. (That way we would not slow the flow of those slated to launch first.) Once the process was flowing, I left the gunny in charge and returned to the ship executive officer's office. The group there was still trying to work out what to do when I told them that we had a potential solution. To everyone's relief, it worked! Expertise comes from a combination of many factors, including both education and real-world experience. My gunny knew what to do and how to do it. It all works smoothly when you have experts in the job.

Domain Expertise in Banking

In 1981, I left the Marine Corps and joined Dun & Bradstreet, where I soon had the opportunity to watch people from many investment banks in action as they advised my D&B colleagues. Some of them were quite good. Some less so. One group of bankers stands out in my memory, those from the now-defunct Bear Stearns.

Back then, Bear Stearns was one of the nation's "bulge bracket" investment banks; i.e., they were among the biggest in the business. Bulge bracket banks provide m&a advice, but they also offer many other services, such as bond and equity underwriting, direct lending and investing, brokerage, and investor research, and they also trade financial instruments such as equities, bonds, commodities, credit rates, and insurance-linked products. They tend to advise large firms and to operate globally—at least in the sense of having clients who operate in the world's largest financial centers. They were the banking equivalent of the large, high-end department stores (think Saks Fifth Avenue or Bloomingdale's, Harrods or Galeries Lafayette). Bulge bracket banks are the ones that some now label "too big to fail."

Within their investment banking division, Bear Stearns and most other bulge bracket firms had both product groups and industry groups. Product groups were responsible for providing services such as mergers & acquisitions, equity capital markets, leveraged finance, and restructuring. Industry groups were focused on serving clients in defined areas such as agriculture, business services, consumer, health care, natural resources, financial institutions, financial sponsors, real estate, and industrials. As Bear Stearns (and others) defined the world, D&B fell within a group that they called TMT (technology, media, and telecommunications), and they were self-proclaimed experts in our industry.

One of the first things I realized, however, was that this group of smart, hardworking bankers had little of what I call depth in our business (more on depth below). It wasn't their fault. They had an awful lot of territory to cover. Could they really be domain experts in the newspaper industry, radio and TV broadcasters, radio and TV stations, movie studios, cable companies, theme parks, Internet service providers, advertisers, publishers, Web sites, digital consumer media and video game manufacturers, digital business-to-business content providers, and more? And that's just part of the *media* part of TMT. Could they really know the intricacies of the various companies within the broadly defined technology industry too? Could they know the strengths and weaknesses of companies that provided computer equipment, network equipment, IT outsourcing, semiconductors, payment processing, Web hosting, enterprise software, application software, and much more? Add to that those in the *telecommunications* part of TMT: phone companies and communications equipment providers and hosting services and more? Wow, they had to cover a lot! How could they possibly be "experts" about us and our industry?

To me, the Bear Stearns bankers were not true domain experts. However, the common wisdom at Bear Stearns and in many other firms on Wall Street is that bankers don't need to be domain experts at the level I describe. They just need a superficial understanding of the players in the industry and to know how to manage price and process. From their perspective it was not necessary for them to understand our strengths and weaknesses in any real depth, only to understand enough about our firm and our industry to be able to listen carefully to what we wanted to accomplish and to guide us to the right "product group" (m&a, debt financing, etc.), where we'd find product specialists who knew how to get transactions done. The Bear Stearns bankers did not see it as their job to have an opinion as to whether the battles they were suggesting that we fight (the companies that they were suggesting that we acquire or divest) made strategic sense. That was our job—as clients. They were there to help us execute—to manage price and process. They would help with valuing, structuring, financing, and communicating with the various parties involved in the m&a process. They had a big balance sheet that they were willing to use in conjunction with other lenders to finance the transaction. Also, once the deal was done, they offered (for an additional fee) to write a document called a fairness opinion, certifying that in their opinion the price we'd paid for the company was "fair" (which did not mean that it was the "best" price—just that it was not stupid).

They had opinions as to how much would be reasonable for D&B to pay—or for us to receive if we were selling. But those opinions were largely based on their sense of prices in the market—what we would have to pay to win—not on whether the market itself might be over- or undervalued. Much less did they have opinions as to how this particular deal would impact D&B strategically over the long term. Even their sense of market prices we should be using was derived from either (a) an analysis of the values of a few publicly traded firms that weren't all that comparable to the business that we were talking about, or (b) an analysis of the price that others had paid for some other business that also didn't seem particularly comparable.

Some bankers are more expert at giving strategic advice than others. Among the Wall Street banks that D&B dealt with in those days were a group that did have the domain expertise to give strategic advice in addition to advice on price and process. Many of them—not all—were "boutique" investment banks. To me these boutique banks were analogous to boutique luxury-goods stores, as compared with big department stores. Or, if you prefer, more like Ferrari than GM. They were experts who were highly focused on providing a limited number of high-quality services. These boutique banks relied on the expertise and industry knowledge of talented bankers. They couldn't offer underwriting or lending and didn't engage in proprietary trading. They generally didn't deal with the retail public. They couldn't rely on an enormous balance sheet or elaborate infrastructure. Their success reflected their domain expertise combined with a rejection by a growing number of US and international corporations of the idea that the size of a bank's balance sheet had anything at all to do with the quality of its advice.

The boutiques didn't seek to replace the bulge bracket firms—at least not on the largest transactions, when some sort of financing is required—and so they welcomed a client's hiring multiple banks for advice on a single transaction, pairing a boutique with industry expertise and a bulge bracket bank that could provide the financing.

In some ways, the boutique investment banks brought back a dimension to Wall Street that had been lost at many bulge bracket firms: unconflicted, well-considered strategic advice, combined with product-specific financial advice and high levels of personal attention. To many, the boutiques were a return to the trusted advisory role that firms such as Barclays, Bear Stearns, Credit Suisse, Goldman Sachs, Lehman Brothers, and Morgan Stanley had once had, before proprietary trading and market-making became their biggest moneymaking activities.

If the Bear Stearns bankers that were seeking to advise D&B exemplified generalist investment bankers who were expert at managing price and process, bankers such as John Suhler and John Veronis (who had formed an m&a advisory shop called Veronis, Suhler & Associates) were a different breed. They were bankers who were qualified to have an opinion as to whether a client should enter into a transaction to begin with, and then to guide the client through the process. They limited their practice to advising CEOs and boards of directors only in those industries in which they had true depth—domain expertise. (Years later I would join their firm.) They were not alone. Plenty of other bankers on Wall Street had similar levels of industry expertise combined with high levels of expert execution capabilities—for example, Felix Rohatyn of Lazard Frères, and Steve Rattner, who also spent time at Lazard before setting up his own boutique. Roger Altman, the former treasury secretary who later started his own boutique firm, Evercore; Eric Gleacher, a former Marine who also started his own boutique (Gleacher & Co.).

The boutique bankers were in no position to offer financing, but they could offer more than managing price and process. They could offer considered, relevant, on-target, unconflicted advice. They knew the industry, the players, the value drivers, and the hot buttons of every major executive within their sphere of interest. They understood the mission of their clients and could advise on the best battles to fight to achieve that mission. They were frequently more on point in their advice and suggestions than the generalists, which makes sense. They not only had transaction experience; they also had great "depth." (We'll talk about the importance of depth, breadth, and other important life dimensions in the second half of this chapter.) They could identify suitable companies that we should contemplate acquiring, and they knew *why* we should acquire them. They understood how one firm's strategy within their niche fit with the strategy of others; they knew the strengths and weaknesses of the various industry players (including many smaller, nonpublic niche players). They understood the drivers of value in the niches that they called their own—and those drivers went well beyond market comparables. (We will explore in depth drivers of value in another chapter.)

To me, this was the kind of expertise that I'd appreciated in the Marine Corps: experienced advisers who also saw the benefit of relying on other experts in other areas, so that the sum of their expert advice was greater than the whole of its parts.

Telekurs and Telesphere

In 1991, after ten years with D&B, I accepted an offer to lead the North American operations of a Swiss-based information-technology company called Telekurs. It was an exciting time to be in technology. The Internet was just about to find momentum, and computing power, network speeds, storage capacity, and the sophistication of software applications all were multiplying at dizzying rates. Customers desired what we offered and they had money. We had a strong base—even if the company wasn't profitable.

I held my role there for four years, during which we grew the company and made it profitable. Meanwhile, the Swiss drove me crazy with their rules and bureaucracy, and I undoubtedly drove them mad with my push to grow faster with products that were based around an interesting business that they had acquired before I had joined the firm and were not standardized to their liking. We began to battle over budgets and priorities, and to resolve their issues and mine, I suggested that they sell the business that they had acquired and around which I was focusing and simply license back the subsets that they wanted to use. After a year of discussions they agreed, and eventually, with financial backing from a private equity firm, I led a management buyout of that business—to form a new company called Telesphere. There's a longer story about that time and that transition, some of which I'll touch on in a later chapter, but the point here is the lesson that brought home to me about the limits of generalist m&a

expertise. In this case, I was the generalist, even if I didn't understand it that way at the time.

I had led scores of deal negotiations at D&B, and so I managed the buyout of Telesphere on my own, without the help of an investment banker. I negotiated with the Swiss and got a pretty good price and terms for the company. I was quite pleased. I still am. Separately, I had negotiated with our investors on terms for them to fund the transaction. That negotiation had been just as challenging, but in part because I had already secured a good price for the company, plus several firms were vying to back our deal, I had a fair amount of negotiating leverage. I'd gotten a good deal for the management team. I just didn't see a need to use an expert banker, even though I knew plenty of them from my days at D&B. But now, with the benefit of hindsight, I can see that I was naïve and perhaps a bit arrogant. It just took me a while to realize it.

Like the investment bank that I now lead, Telesphere was a "boutique." We focused on providing software, hardware, and real-time information on stocks, options, and other listed securities. We also provided the infrastructure required for high-frequency stock and derivative traders to connect and trade with market venues such as stock exchanges and futures exchanges. We were a much smaller company than the big full-service software firms like Oracle or IBM, and we were focused on meeting the needs of select group of clients—with a highly specialized "Ferrari-like" product line. Our service was blazing fast and technologically very advanced. Customers measured our latency in microseconds, and we always won the race against competitors like Reuters and S&P. Further, unlike Ferrari, we were less expensive than most viable alternatives. But we weren't perfect. Customers wanted features that we didn't yet have, and they wanted support in places where we had no presence, such as London and Tokyo. And the technology was ever changing. We wanted to meet customer needs and keep up with evolving technology. And that would cost money.

It was a heady time. I've never worked so hard. At the same time, I struggled with the outside investors who controlled our board. My main problem was that they had no experience with fast-growing technology businesses. Their previous investments had been in manufacturing companies and banks. This became particularly clear when I wanted to raise additional money in order to add products, expand geographically, and generally take advantage of our momentum and customer interest. They had veto power over any additional capital raises and they wanted to exercise it. At first they fought the whole concept. Why couldn't we just grow using internally generated cash flow, they wanted to know. Why couldn't we slow down—live within our means—and focus on selling our products in one location (the United States) and make profit. But, in the world of fast-growing technology companies, that strategy isn't always smart. If you don't meet customer needs for features and functionality, they go elsewhere. If you don't keep up with technology, your product capabilities will lag behind competitors. If their need includes servicing them in Tokyo, London, Sydney, Singapore, and Chicago, you need to be there for them. And if you don't meet their needs, the competition will. In this world, once you gain a customer you have a good chance of keeping them for a very long time, as it costs a lot of money to switch to a competitor. But the amount of money they have riding on this technology dwarfs that spend. At some point they will leave you, if you don't keep up. Once you lose a prospective customer—or worse a real customer—it's really hard to get them back. My philosophy was, if you are riding on a tiger's back, don't try to slow the tiger; keep up! Our product line may have been narrow, but we had top-level customers such as Credit Suisse, Nomura Securities, UBS, Goldman Sachs, Morgan Stanley, State Street Bank, Charles Schwab, Chase, Fidelity, and dozens of others practically begging us for what we had (plus a few logical extensions and expanded support). It didn't make sense to slow down—and I didn't know how to do so anyway, without putting the franchise at risk.

Once I convinced the investors of the uniqueness of the opportunity and its temporal nature, they only wanted to provide the money we needed in a way that would have significantly eviscerated my management team's equity stake. That led to the next fight. This one was even bigger. Lawsuits were threatened. It was not pretty.

Eventually, we worked out a compromise that got us our additional funding, but that cost the management team dearly in terms of dilution of our ownership stake. Over the next six months, Telesphere went on a roll: sales soared; we rolled out great products; we added subsidiaries in the UK and Asia; and we hired more people. Paradoxically, all of this success meant we were still in big trouble. The market wanted more of what we were selling, but to keep growing at the rates that I knew we were capable of, we would need still more capital.

Having won the battle with the investors the last time, I realized that it was highly unlikely I would win a second, similar fight. It was clear now that the investors would again fight us about the need for capital—or again force us to bring in the additional capital in a way that was likely to result in less equity for the managers (and more for the investors). I was not pleased.

My mistake, I now realized, was not having an expert at my side at the outset of my negotiations to buy the assets to form Telesphere—an expert with real-world experience negotiating these sorts of transactions. Among other things, an expert with more domain knowledge than I had at the time might have warned me off dealing with these particular investors at all. I mainly focused on that they seemed like nice people who had successfully invested before, and on the financial terms we could negotiate—not on the experience of the partners themselves in working with forms such as mine. A true professional who knew this industry might have guided me to other, more suitable potential backers. In fact we had had a terrific offer from an investor group controlled by Fidelity Investments, the big mutual fund company. We turned them down in favor of this group. In hindsight, that may have been a mistake.

I began to realize that I had made a few other mistakes—some of which stemmed from a simple (incorrect) assumption that the interests of the investor group would be perfectly aligned with the interests of my management team and me because eventually we both would want to sell Telesphere at the best possible price. But I had neither expected a need for more capital, nor had I fully understood the possible implications of that need. I certainly had not contemplated that the general partners of a private equity fund might have their own constraints and priorities. It's not their money; they have investors themselves—their "limited partners"—and the general partners' loyalty to me and to my management team worked only so long as that loyalty did not conflict with their greater loyalty to themselves and their limited partners. I had also not focused on how some situations could make them richer at our expense, or on how they might take advantage of that. I did not have an expert at my side who could have helped me to negotiate stronger protections against the sort of dilution of ownership that we now faced. I had accepted "standard" terms and conditions that the investors had insisted upon without appreciating the leverage that I had to modify those "standard" terms. I had not accepted the limits of my own experience. The Marine in me should have known better. I had never before negotiated exactly this kind of deal—a management buy-out with a private equity firm. I had never been on this side of the table. It wouldn't have been hard to find someone who had.

My lack of expertise could now cost us real money. If we took in more capital, it might well mean working hard for many more years, to make less—even if we made the company worth a lot more. This was untenable, and my fault because it could have been avoided had I used an expert at the outset. I had been arrogant. I'd thought I could do it all myself. Now, I had to fix it.

The best solution I could come up with now—the least bad option—was to sell Telesphere. I didn't want to sell; it was early. Besides, I liked being a CEO. Other than my fights with the investors, I believed that I was on the path to where I wanted to be—and that made me happy. I certainly didn't want to go back to being an employee at some big corporation. However, since the investors weren't likely to agree to recapitalize the company at values and terms that I believed were reasonable, or to renegotiate management's equity piece (we had little leverage), I thought selling now was the best way out of this dilemma. And that's what I did.

I'll save the detailed story of the sale of Telesphere for another time. What is important here is that we got it done—and that we were able to claw back some of the equity the managers had lost. The investors tripled their money on an investment they had made only a few years before. I got them out of my hair; and they got me out of theirs. There was mutual relief, I'm sure. My customers got a new owner with great technology, a worldwide presence, and the willingness and resources to invest in more product improvements. My employees got a new career path, my management team and I got a lot more money than we would have if we had simply been employees, and I relearned a lot of lessons about using true domain experts.

Expertise Requires Volume

A few years after I had left the Marines Corps and was working at D&B, I was invited to an award presentation at Marine Corps Base

Camp Pendleton. My former battalion commander in the Seventh
Marines, Colonel Joe O'Brien, was being awarded the Navy Cross—
our nation's second-highest decoration for valor in combat. He was
getting the medal some twenty years after his actions in Vietnam.
You hear about this kind of thing sometimes—the Pentagon fouled
up—but at least he was finally getting his due. I had great admiration
and respect for Colonel O'Brien; reading his citation gave me more
pride in having served with him. It began, "The President of the
United States of America takes pleasure in presenting the Navy Cross
to Captain Joseph J. O'Brien, United States Marine Corps, for ex-
traordinary heroism," and went on:

> . . . When three amphibious tractors were hit by enemy artillery fire, Cap-
> tain O'Brien exposed himself to a hail of enemy fire as he made repeated
> trips to move the wounded to a position of relative safety. Despite sustaining
> multiple burns to his hands and face, he refused to be evacuated. . . . [The
> next day] he launched a predawn assault with a reinforced rifle company. . . .
>
> Noticing enemy soldiers dragging wounded Marines away, he . . .
> engaged and killed numerous enemy soldiers with his pistol and an enemy
> rifle while he protected the wounded Marines . . .
>
> Although painfully wounded . . . he shunned medical treatment and
> urged the Marines on with their relentless actions against the disorga-
> nized enemy forces. When enemy automatic fire from a concealed position
> stalled the advance, he spearheaded an assault on the position with hand
> grenades. After overpowering and eliminating the enemy, he collapsed
> from his wounds and was medically evacuated.

Looking at it again now, as then, I get chills. What inspires someone to persevere like that, after being burned and wounded—to refuse
to be evacuated, "shun medical treatment," and continue the mission—to risk his own life to save and protect his wounded comrades?
What makes people like Colonel O'Brien such great leaders of
men? It must be more than simple bravery. It got me thinking. . . .
They are truly domain experts.

What separates leaders such as Joe O'Brien from others—at least to
me—is a multidimensional level of expertise. It has four specific
dimensions—length, breadth, depth, and honor. Together they add (or
perhaps multiply) to give certain leaders more "volume" than others.
Volume is what makes experts.

We didn't explicitly study the concept of volume at TBS or any-place else in the Marines. I invented it. But it came as an outgrowth and an extension of lessons that the Marines do teach. In some ways this revelation about volume and its dimensions has led me to believe that the very object of my life should be to maximize my volume. (Others may have their own object.) The people I respect most, Marines such as Colonel O'Brien as well as civilians such as D&B's Dick Schmidt, are those who have achieved significant volume in their lives and, as a result, have developed a rarely seen level of exper-tise. The dimensions of that volume, and thus the dimensions of ex-pertise, are more than academic for me. They help guide my daily decisions; they help me keep perspective and evaluate opportunities as they arise. When I contemplate engaging others to work with me, advise me, or guide me, such as accountants, lawyers, financial advis-ers, consultants, bankers, teachers, or race coaches, I find myself eval-uating them along these four dimensions. Volume is the best measure of expertise that I can derive.

I think a lot of problems on Wall Street, in Washington, and elsewhere could more easily be solved if other people adopted this long-term strategic objective of life. Unfortunately, many employ another long-term strategic objective that I have heard espoused on Wall Street and elsewhere: "He who dies with the most toys wins."

Having volume maximization as my long-term strategic objective of life is different from understanding the "meaning" of life. I have not yet figured that out; I'm still working on it. I'm also willing to ac-knowledge that life has other dimensions besides these four. I suppose that, for some, power, prestige, fun, and toy count could be dimen-sions, but my four are the ones that drive expertise, and that's impor-tant to me. Let me expand.

Length

The first dimension of life volume is *length*, which is more than sim-ply a measurement of how long you are on the planet—although that is important. It's largely (although not always) true that the thirty-five-year-old Marine or banker with ten years of relevant experience is—or at least ought to be—more knowledgeable than the twenty-two-year-old Marine or banker. The gunnery sergeant who worked

with me aboard *Tripoli* had length; but so did the senior chief petty
officer who refused to believe that there could be another way for us
to solve our broken elevator problem. A wise Marine once told me that
over twenty years some people get twenty years of experience, and
some have one year's worth repeated twenty times. The experience that
comes with learning what works and what doesn't—making mistakes,
having victories, seeing the successes and failures of others, and, most
important, learning from them all—leads to expertise. Length is important and can add expertise, but, at least in this formula, it is no more
(and no less) important than the other three dimensions.

Breadth

Next up is *breadth*: the variety of your life experiences. Learning to be
a rifleman adds breadth to the life of a pilot as well as the rifleman, and
vice versa. So does learning to windsurf, even if not quite as much in
my estimation. (Not all experiences are equal.) But even windsurfing
can teach you about wind and currents and vectors that a pilot or a land
navigator may find useful. To me, the most interesting breadth requires
you to get out of your comfort zone. It requires some degree of risk.
But all breadth adds some volume to life, and that is a good thing.

I once worked with a woman who spent years studying classical
violin—and then left her warm, safe cocoon to tour the world with
some famous rock groups before later going into the business world.
Her experiences dealing with different people under pressure in foreign lands make her a much better businessperson. Now she can relate much better to the people on the other side of the table than
many of her colleagues. She understands their constraints, and she is
a great negotiator. I have a friend who left the military to become a
full-fledged CIA undercover spy, then five years later moved to the
business world. His experiences have helped him rapidly rise above
peers with less breadth. I have another friend who spent years as a
journalist. She lived and worked in Moscow before the fall of the
Soviet Union and in Beijing before Tiananmen Square. She now runs
a nonprofit organization, and those broadening experiences have made
her a standout leader. Another friend climbed two of the world's tall-
est mountains and once drove the length of Africa from south to north
with his wife and two young kids, camping every night. (It took them

a year!) In each case, the breadth of these experiences of these friends of mine has made them more expert in their current, unrelated fields of endeavor.

For me, the breadth that adds the most to expertise has some relationship to the task at hand; a Marine infantry officer who spends a month with an artillery unit returns to his unit with a much greater understanding of and appreciation for how the infantry can work more effectively with artillery. It adds to his or her breadth and thereby to his or her expertise. Investment bankers who spend time working closely with the industry they advise can gain similar breadth and thus have more volume—more expertise than the bankers who do not have the same experience. My time on the *Tripoli* later made me a much better company commander and a much better battalion staff officer. But all those experiences have also made me a better investment banker. They have added a dimension to my expertise that others may not appreciate. But it's real.

Depth

The third dimension is *depth*. It's the dimension people most associate with expertise. Depth should not be confused with time in school—although the right training can certainly add to depth. Depth is about how much you have learned about an area, how intensely you have absorbed some aspect of life, how deeply you have gone into that dimension. In the first part of this chapter I mentioned several Wall Street bankers that had developed great depth—Felix Rohatyn, for example, or Roger Altman. Or, if you prefer, think of Martin Luther King Jr., who died at thirty-nine, or Amelia Earhart, also thirty-nine when she disappeared, or Mozart, who died at age thirty-five. Think about their depth. To me, largely because of their depth, these people amassed more volume—and had more expertise—in a short period than most of us could aspire to in a much longer lifetime.

Honor

The fourth dimension to volume, to building expertise and, for me, life, is *honor*. For some this dimension is a bit amorphous, perhaps a bit moralistic. But it all comes back to the Marine Corps motto: *semper fidelis*—"always faithful." Honor acts as both an amplifier and a check on the other three dimensions, and without it, any level of volume—of expertise—is simply wasted. Even if you think you still have that expertise, few will care.

I wrote earlier about Michael Milken, Ivan Boesky, and other Wall Street bankers who broke their covenant with the people of Main Street and saw their volume wiped out. There are so many other examples on Wall Street and in life. I recall reading with great disappointment about the fall of Rajat Gupta, the former head of McKinsey & Company, one of America's top strategy consulting firms. I had observed Gupta from afar for years with great admiration. Born, raised, and educated in India, orphaned at an early age, Gupta obtained a degree in mechanical engineering from a top Indian university, attended Harvard Business School, and by all accounts through his hard work, brilliance, and networking prowess rose to become the trusted consultant to some of the top business leaders in the world. He donated his time and his money to causes in both the United States and India, advised the Bill & Melinda Gates Foundation, the Global Fund to Fight AIDS, Tuberculosis and Malaria, and served on the board of the University of Chicago and as a member of Yale's President's Council. He cofounded a business school in India that became one of the leading business schools in the world. And then he was charged with leaking inside information to a business partner related to activities on two boards on which he sat: Goldman Sachs and Procter & Gamble. According to news reports, Gupta had reason to believe that the business partner, who ran a hedge fund, would trade on that information. Gupta was convicted on three counts of securities fraud and one count of conspiracy and sentenced to serve two years in prison and pay a $5 million fine—all for trying to either curry favor or make a few extra bucks. Ugh. (He is appealing.) Unlike Ivan Boesky, Gupta's success had not been based on a scam. He really was an expert in his field. He had huge breadth and depth. But if he really leaked that information, then in a few brief moments his lack of honor wiped out years of volume.

In my way of looking at life's volume, you can have tons of experience, have lived a long and varied life, and have substantial depth, but if you are not *always faithful*—if you don't honor your commitments—few will acknowledge or accept your expertise. It's all wasted. I think of Dennis Hastert, a former high school teacher and coach from a small farming town in Illinois, who rose to become Speaker of the US House of Representatives. He retired with dignity only to have all that volume wiped out when he was charged by federal prosecutors with trying to hide his payment of hush money over allegations that he had sexually abused three students more than thirty years earlier. This man was once third in line for the presidency of the United States. All that volume gone—wasted.

The Formula

The Marine Corps Way calls on Wall Street bankers, corporate executives, politicians, and others to do their best to maximize all four of these dimensions of life's volume. In so doing, they build domain expertise—and that's important. My theory does not exactly work like a mathematical equation. You can't quite come up with a single numeric volume measurement by multiplying L x B x D x H. But it is possible to appreciate lives lived that maximize volume.

We should expect more expertise from those who have built volume than from others. They are the Marines, executives, politicians, and bankers like Joe O'Brien, John Suhler, Eric Gleacher, and Steve Rattner. They have pursued their vocations with diligence and along the way also taken real risks. They left their warm cocoons for a while. They started and ran real businesses, dealt with angry customers, and managed people in scenarios in which failure had real consequences—and in which the time frame was longer than a six-month deal cycle. They systematically, over time (length), built breadth and depth and did so with honor. They have volume. They are experts. That's my way. That's the Marine Corps Way.

4

Know the Enemy

Two decades after I left the Marines, I was leading my current investment bank when a senior member of my team, Paul Friday, introduced me to the three founders of a Connecticut-based company called Triple Point Technology. TPT provided risk mitigation and software trading for businesses that buy or sell energy and physical commodities—such things as gasoline, heating oil, and natural gas, along with agricultural commodities (rice, corn, sugar, and wheat, for example) and other physical commodities such as gold, silver, and platinum. The company had customers in seventeen countries and served them from offices in Connecticut, Houston, London, and Pune, India.

For its first seven years, TPT had grown rapidly and prospered. The three TPT founders owned 100 percent of the company, having avoided using outside capital. That meant that they had poured almost everything the firm earned back into building their company, and things were going pretty well. They were growing and serviced almost all of the era's best-known commodities users, as well as many producers and traders.

It hadn't always been that way, however. A few years before we met the founders, TPT had suffered substantial losses when one of their largest customers, Enron, had collapsed in a scandal of historic proportions. That catastrophe was followed by a global economic slowdown, and TPT nearly went under. Suddenly the founders realized that all their hopes and dreams could easily come to naught.

For the next six years, TPT's founders fought their way back.

About a year before Paul and I met with them, the founders had been approached by an executive at a big publicly traded corporation that was interested in acquiring their firm. Over several months, they had several meetings with the suitor. Price was discussed and the founders became excited at the opportunity. They thought it was a done deal. But now, nearly a year later, the deal had died. The big corporation had moved on to other priorities.

The founders were still interested in selling their company to the right partner at the right price, but they were weary from the last effort and wary about trying again. The process had taken up a lot of their time, diverted their attention from running the business, and had not gotten them to where they wanted to be.

In chapter 1—"Take the Long View"—I relayed that before we take on an assignment for a client, we often ask questions such as Why do you want to do this? What's your long-term objective? How achievable is it? What are the forces arrayed against you? Is this a battle you really need to fight now? Do you have the resources to win? Should you wait? What are the alternatives?

We asked those same questions of the TPT founders and got some answers. The approach by the big publicly traded suitor had made them realize that they had climbed out of the big hole in which they had been operating after the Enron debacle. Now they owned a very salable company—potentially worth a lot of money. None of the founders had been able to take much money out of the company for years, and they were excited about that opportunity. Moreover, the big suitor seemed as if it could be a good partner. There hadn't been a whole lot of deep thought beyond that.

When clients want to sell their company, we ask an additional series of questions: Who would want to buy your firm? Why? What might be their primary motivation? Where would be their perception of the strategic fit? What do you see as the fit? What constraints do they have? In this case—as in other cases where a potential client has already had serious conversations with a potential buyer—we wanted to know the same sorts of things and more: Why did this particular company approach you? What was their primary motivation? Where was their perception of the strategic fit? What did you see as the fit? Were you excited about them as a partner? Why? What constraints did they have? And of course, why did the deal die?

The TPT founders were experienced businesspeople and knew

that the big company that wanted to acquire them was already in the business of selling market information about physical commodities to traders and other customers in the financial services industry. They reasonably assumed that the company wanted to extend their product range and customer base to include the services and the market that TPT addressed. But TPT had never had an explicit conversation with the other side on the subject.

Understanding the Opposing Force

In the summer of 2008, General David Petraeus, who was then leading all military forces of the US-led coalition in Iraq, disagreed with a number of US politicians, including then US senator and presidential candidate Barak Obama, about how best to fight al-Qaeda, the organization founded by Osama bin Laden that had repeatedly attacked US installations—including the September 11, 2001, airliner attacks on the Pentagon and the World Trade Center. Among other things, General Petraeus took issue with Obama's assertion that "Afghanistan has to be the central focus, the central front, [in] our battle against terrorism."

As recounted in *The General's War,* a book by *New York Times* reporter Michael Gordon and General Bernard Trainor, Petraeus knew the enemy; he had studied al-Qaeda in depth. Petraeus pointed out that the war was wherever al-Qaeda took it, and that ranged far beyond Afghanistan and Pakistan, where al-Qaeda's central leadership was based. Petraeus also pointed out the organization's increasingly decentralized strategy and the need to stop it in Iraq, Indonesia, Syria, Sudan, and other places where al-Qaeda was increasing its influence— as well as in Afghanistan and Pakistan. Some politicians asserted that al-Qaeda was no more than a terrorist group whose primary goal was to destroy Israel and the United States, but Petraeus noted that al-Qaeda's attacks were actually a means to well-defined long-term strategic objective. More than being motivated by America's support of Israel, or America's Judeo-Christian heritage, al-Qaeda's had a larger objective in attacking American institutions. Namely, they wanted to convince the American government to stop supporting the leadership of many Muslim-majority countries whose rulers encouraged—or at least tolerated—behavior that was contrary to al-Qaeda's interpretations of the Koran.

In 2012, Peter Bergen, the CNN National Security Analyst, said, "Historians will likely judge David Petraeus to be the most effective American military leader since Eisenhower." Bergen pointed out that Petraeus had brought back Iraq from the brink of disaster and he did it in part by using tactics that he had honed—writing the US Army's counterinsurgency doctrine years earlier.

Petraeus was a student of history and taught the subject at West Point. He recruited his own expert to help develop his doctrine: John Nagl, a Rhodes Scholar and Iraq war veteran with a PhD from Oxford who had written on counterinsurgency. They also referred to the writings of David Galula, the French soldier, author, and counterinsurgency expert who set forth the principle: "The population becomes the objective for the counterinsurgent as it was for the enemy." It is clear to me that Petraeus understood that, regardless of the way they were portrayed by Western politicians and Western media, al-Qaeda's leaders did not see themselves as terrorists any more than did the early American revolutionaries—or Ho Chi Minh. They saw themselves as political revolutionaries with a moral duty to try to overturn a corrupt existing order and establish a government that would be more in keeping with their fundamental religious beliefs. As with those American patriots, and as with North Vietnam's Ho Chi Minh, al-Qaeda's leaders saw themselves as the good guys, battling evil foreign interlopers using the only tactics available to them to achieve their goals, in the same vein as the American revolutionaries saw themselves when they used unconventional warfare to oust the British. Petraeus understood defeating al-Qaeda required not only killing or capturing their leaders, but, more important, countering their message. If not, they would just keep recruiting new members to replace the ones that we killed. A large, ready supply of unhappy, often unemployed, undereducated, disenfranchised, and unappreciated youth around the world were longing for adventure, a meaningful life, a worthy "cause" to fight for, and a group that would train them and embrace them. Petraeus also knew that if we were to defeat the enemy, we had to show them as well as local citizenry that we were the good guys—there to protect them and bring them freedoms that they had never before enjoyed. He understood that knowing the enemy is the key to defeating them.

"If you know the enemy and know yourself," the Chinese philosopher and general Sun Tzu wrote twenty-five hundred years ago, "you need not fear the result of a hundred battles. If you know yourself but not the enemy, for every victory gained you will also suffer a defeat. If you know neither the enemy nor yourself, you will succumb in every battle." General Petraeus got it.

The people on the other side of a Wall Street (or corporate) negotiating table are not "the enemy" in any military sense. None of us are trying to literally kill anyone or use violence to physically conquer territory. But in Wall Street transactions, and indeed in most corporate transactions and in political negotiations, the parties on the other side of the table are usually working hard for themselves and their constituents—not for some amorphous concept of the greater good for all. That's why negotiations can sometimes be analogous to a battle where each side is in a fight for domination. The odds of prevailing in these battles are materially enhanced if you know the enemy and understand his or her motivations.

Opposing Forces Come in Many Varieties

In the Wall Street world in which I work, many types of people and organizations may be on the other side of the negotiating table. Each type and each individual or firm within that type has a unique set of strengths, weaknesses, capabilities, constraints, and motivations. They include, for example, founders, entrepreneurs, venture capitalists, private equity firms, nonprofit companies, public corporations, private companies, pension funds, insurance companies, banks, high-net-worth individuals, long-term investors, "activist" investors, SPACs (special purpose acquisition companies), family offices (the investment vehicles of wealthy families), hedge fund operators, mezzanine capital funds, government agencies, and a dozen others.

Just as Marines tend to group the many types of potential military opposition that we may face into categories with common characteristics (nation-state military forces, paramilitary forces, insurgent and guerrilla forces, nonmilitary insurgents, etc.), I started thinking long ago about how to reasonably group transaction participants so as to make it easier to develop strategies when we negotiate with them, and to communicate. I came up with three distinct seller categories and three other distinct buyer categories, each based on its own combination of constraints, motivations, and consequent deal approaches.

The three seller groups are:

- individuals
- financial sponsors
- corporations

The three buyer groups are:

- strategics
- control investors
- minority investors

It's an imperfect segmentation, and I am well aware that there are many other potential groupings. Moreover, some firms may fit into multiple categories. (Warren Buffett's Berkshire Hathaway comes to mind, for example.) But this segmentation works for me. It helps me to begin to formulate strategy and it helps me communicate with clients.

The TPT founders were well aware of the existence of various types of buyers and investor firms. They just didn't see the relevance of those distinctions. Many people—including many Wall Street bankers—don't spend enough time thinking through the strengths, weaknesses, capabilities, constraints, and motivations of the people on the other side of the negotiating table. But failing to do so sends you into battle at less than full strength. There are good reasons to care.

Strategics

TPT had been approached by a "strategic"—an industry participant with a "strategic" reason for wanting to combine with another firm—and, most important, no plan to sell TPT or any of its pieces once a deal was completed. (Below, I'll talk about people and firms who buy with an explicit plan to sell.) Usually, strategics are motivated by one of two things: either they want to gain leverage in adding incremental revenue or else they are looking to reduce duplicated (or anticipated) expenses. While at one time some strategics (such as the old D&B) bought companies as part of a diversification strategy—to "smooth" earnings—those days have largely passed. (There are firms such as Warren Buffet's Berkshire Hathaway that buy promising companies with no intention of ever selling them, as part of an investment strategy. To some extent D&B operated in that manner when I worked there. But I consider firms like this to be essentially financial investors and not strategics. There will be more on those types of firms below.)

I know about strategics in part because I've worked at them: it may not be how D&B operated at the holding company level, but it is how our portfolio companies did—and that's how I started my career at D&B. Telekurs, the company I joined after D&B, was a strategic as well. It too made several acquisitions and at least one divestiture—to me. Bridge, the company that acquired my firm, Telesphere, was a strategic—albeit one that was backed by a financial investor. Bridge made nearly a dozen acquisitions. My investment banking advisory firm works with strategics all the time, both as clients and as the parties on the other sides of our clients' negotiating tables.

In chapter 2, I wrote about our experience advising the New York Stock Exchange as they looked at acquiring or investing in companies including UK-based Fixnetix. Clearly NYSE was a strategic. Revenue growth in their core exchange business was slowing, and their profit margins were under constant pressure. Their investors wanted them to find higher-growth, higher-margin proprietary businesses to enter, and that was their prime motivation for looking at acquisitions.

When I was working at D&B, I spent much of my time advising and working with D&B–owned companies that were contemplating strategic acquisitions. Investment bankers would pitch us all the time on potential "tuck-unders"—companies that might add to the capability of one of the firms we already owned. The bankers had many ideas, but the briefings often seemed facile. Most of the bankers seemed to have only a vague idea of what any of our companies did—and even less understanding in any detail of what the potential target did (much less knowing how it would add value to a specific part of our firm). They didn't seem to know anything about the target's decision-makers—their personalities or their motives (other than an assumed desire to make money). The bankers just wanted to talk about the numbers, but people make decisions based on more than just that.

I told the TPT founders the story of my experience at D&B and also with Telekurs, from which I had bought the assets to form my company Telesphere. Knowing what motivated Telekurs (another strategic) to buy those assets in the first place was as important as understanding what might motivate them to sell those assets to me. Telekurs bought those US assets to provide real-time market data on listed stocks, bonds, commodities, and their respective derivatives to bank clients around the world. Subsequent to buying those US assets, Telekurs had developed similar infrastructure capabilities in Switzerland, but lacked the data from US and Asian venues that customers required.

I also knew that the people who now led Telekurs were not the same people who had purchased the US assets, and they were not wedded to keeping them. Moreover, I knew that the US assets that I wanted to buy no longer fit the direction that the Swiss wanted to go. Further, I knew that offering what were similar—if not exactly competing—services in both the United States and in Europe complicated the message that they were sending to clients. Additionally, I understood that the clients in the United States were traders, but that the Swiss mostly wanted to serve the back office of banks, and I knew that the Telekurs board cared more about who the buyer might be than they did about the sales price, although they wanted to believe that they were selling for the best possible price.

I also understood their constraints. They needed data; they didn't want to sell to a competitor; and they also didn't want to assure any buyer that Telekurs wouldn't later become a competitor. In this complex set of factors, the purchase price was but one of many important considerations for the seller. Overall, my deep understanding of the seller's strengths, weaknesses, constraints, and motivations helped me to negotiate a deal that was acceptable to all sides.

A strategic might want to buy or sell for many reasons. In the preface, I wrote about D&B's moral motivation to sell its units in South Africa—and its desire to get a deal done before the US Congress or shareholders forced them to do so. Obtaining a high price was clearly of minor importance.

As another example, a few years ago my firm advised the big credit-rating agency S&P, which wanted to sell off a company that it had acquired only a few years earlier called Vista Research. Vista was founded in 2001 to connect clients to a network of well-vetted industry experts with relevant experience in industries such as aerospace and defense, basic materials, energy, financial services, health care, hospitality, retail/consumer, technology, telecom, and more. Its customers were hedge funds, private equity funds, corporations, and others who were usually looking to invest in a company that operated in one of the sectors in which Vista could provide access to experts. It was called an expert network. These experts didn't work for Vista—they had other jobs. Vista simply allowed subscribing customers to locate an appropriate expert. The client would pay the expert an additional fee, which Vista would administer.

S&P bought Vista in the first place to increase its revenue by leveraging the strength of the S&P brand and its reputation for expertise with the clients that Vista targeted. S&P's motivation later to sell was quite different. Vista had performed well, more than doubling its revenue in the few years S&P had owned it. The problem was that the New York State attorney general's office had begun probing the entire expert-network industry, suspecting that some participants within it had been facilitating illegal insider trading of stocks. Even though Vista had not been accused of anything, and even though Vista had taken strenuous precautions to ensure that no illegal or even unethical practices could take place, S&P realized that they were vulnerable to the *perception* of helping others to engage in such practices. As a result the S&P CEO wanted nothing to do with it. It was all about potential reputational risk. Yes, he wanted the best price possible, but he wanted Vista gone. Not selling was not an option—not unlike the situation when I led the divestiture of D&B's three South African businesses years earlier; I understood it well.

Whatever their motivation, strategics buy, merge, or combine without any specific plan to later sell the assets they have acquired, even though, as in the case of S&P and Telekurs, they may someday do so. (If at the time they buy acquirers already have plans to sell, than they are considered *financial* buyers or financial investors, not *strategics*.)

TPT's founders had been excited to talk to a strategic about being acquired, but they had apparently never focused on *why* the strategic would want to acquire their company. Thus, they never tailored their presentation or answers to questions in ways to give the potential buyer confidence that acquiring TPT would help them get where they wanted to be.

Many investment bankers assert that finding the strategic fit is not the seller's problem and may often not even be possible for the seller to divine. The bankers assert that only the buyer can figure out what he wants to buy—and why; it's not up to the other side to figure out the "fit." But that's not the Marine Corps Way.

We told TPT's founders that if we were to take them on as clients, their odds of getting a successful transaction with the right partner would materially be improved by understanding the motivations, constraints, and personalities of the people on the other side, and working with them to see how a deal would benefit both sides—if it would. If appropriate, we'd want to get all sides excited about it. We told TPT that each potential party on the other side is different; each strategic rationale is unique; and they may not all be right for you, even if the offered price is high. You can't count on the other side's figuring it out for themselves without your help.

Plenty of strategic deals were being done at the time. Google had been buying companies at a furious rate for years, including the purchases of multiple companies in mobile software (such as Android), mapping, advertising, and technology. It had also been lapping up small social-media players to fit with Google Plus. Why? Because Google's objective was to build a series of capabilities that could be fully integrated into the company's various offerings and keep their products competitive. Microsoft had been doing much the same, including purchases of multiple companies in security software, online music search and audio technology, Web conferencing, and mobile advertising technology—as well as a host of deals related to the MS Office suite.

Other corporations have different acquisition approaches. McLaren, the manufacturer of Formula 1 race cars, has tried to use its skills in remote data capture and telemetry to enter health-care management. Long ago, Apple moved from computer manufacturing to making consumer electronic devices and distributing consumer content for those devices. What the acquisitions all have in common is that focus and fit have become the rage. For all but the largest strategic buyers that we see, the acquisition rationale question is no longer "What can we [the buyer] do for the target company?" Instead, it's "What can the target do for us?" What product, technology, customer, or other strength will it bring to us? Thus, the vast majority of strategics that we talk with only buy or invest as part of a larger, long-term strategy designed to strengthen their overall organization—not the target.

Investors

If strategics emphasize acquiring companies with products or capabilities that will aid their firm's top and bottom lines—and have no specific intent to sell what they have bought—then investors have a very different approach. They buy without the opportunity for synergies often (not always) with the specific intent to later sell at a higher price. I break investors into two broad groups: control investors and those investors who are content with a minority ownership. I am well aware of the many other ways to divide investors and that some firms may fall into both camps, and I know that my having only two groups may seem simplistic to some. But in my world this grouping works and makes for a clear way to begin thinking about strategic negotiating approaches and about communicating with clients. We refine these strategies as we begin to learn more about the strengths, weaknesses, capabilities, constraints, and motivations of the specific party on the other side of the table.

With all this in mind, we asked the TPT founders if they had considered working with an investment firm as opposed to a strategic. Why limit the potential pool of acquirers? Paul and I knew the strengths, weaknesses, capabilities, constraints, and motivations of several control investors, and we believed that TPT was a prime candidate for them. We also knew that most of these firms have the ideal characteristics that they look for in a portfolio company, including industry type, size, and growth; product or service; market share; company revenue size, growth, composition, and profit potential; and management strength.

We believed that TPT would be ideal for several of these firms (but not all). Besides the fit on industry, revenue, and profit characteristics, TPT was an innovative market leader in a large and growing market, and it had a strong management team. It was also large enough to be a "platform" investment—a vehicle on top of which to add other acquisitions, which these PE firms like and which seemed to fit with the TPT founders' vision. PE firms are willing to have a significant portion of their money go to shareholders, which also fit the founders' desires. PE firms do worry about having key management stick around and manage the business, and they want those managers to be significantly invested in the company they are guiding. But that too fit the needs and desires of the three founders, two of whom wanted to stay and run the firm and were happy to allow the third to leave as he wished.

I know this world. When I bought the assets that formed Telesphere, we were backed by a family office that acted much like a private equity firm. Bridge, the company that later acquired Telesphere, was controlled by a private equity firm, Welsh, Carson, Anderson & Stowe (WCAS). I had worked for Veronis, Suhler & Associates, which controlled two PE funds and a mezzanine fund, which, together, managed nearly $2 billion. And my investment bank has advised many control investors including Bain Capital; Goldman Sachs; Welsh, Carson; Francisco Partners; Vista Equity; and other large funds as well as many smaller ones.

In our view, TPT was not a great candidate for most minority investors. We have worked with many of them over the years. While TPT had been doing quite well by most measures, the typical venture fund (managed by a venture capital firm) invests in younger companies than TPT and looks for higher growth rates. The venture funds have little opportunity to use debt, so their entire investment is equity. That means higher risk for the investor, so they look for opportunities to reap very high returns. In most cases, they want their investment to go into the company to fuel growth and not into the hands of selling shareholders.

Mezzanine capital providers, who also are minority investors and do sometimes provide debt, typically prefer to work in conjunction with an outside equity provider and also seek fairly high returns—in excess of 20 percent per annum—which is not quite as high as equity investors often seek but still hefty. When the mezzanines do take a form of equity, they often assign value to a company based largely on that firm's current and near-term expected cash flow. TPT wasn't a good fit for the mezzanine funds, and even if it were, their approach was not likely to motivate the three TPT founders.

The founders weren't thrilled with the idea of selling to a control investor. Having run their own business without outside interference for many years, they weren't excited with the idea of having bosses—a board of directors that could look over their shoulders; approve or disapprove budgets, veto investments or acquisition plans, and even fire them. We respected this point of view, but we pushed back. It is one thing to understand the vagaries of various categories of potential buyers, which they now did a little better, and quite another to understand the strengths, weaknesses, capabilities, constraints, and motivations of the specific people on the other side of the negotiating table.

I went back to my experience at Bridge, where I believed we had the right partner in WCAS. Bridge grew revenue from $40 million to $1.3 billion over a few years. And I also recounted my experience forming Telesphere—where I had picked the wrong partner, nice people but not the ones to help a high-growth tech company reach new heights. We told the TPT founders that you'll never know unless you investigate. Why not talk to a few PE firms as well as a few strategics and see what we learn? They agreed and engaged my firm to advise them on finding the right partner.

TPT Process

Over the next few weeks, as we prepared information materials on TPT—and helped them to know themselves too—we also began to identify and research potential strategic partners and potential control investors based on our understanding of the institutions' criteria as well as of the needs of our client. When we were ready, we solicited interest from a select group. Six firms responded enthusiastically. We had done some research on each firm before; now we did a ton more—including reference checking. We also encouraged TPT's founders to get to know personally the key decision-makers at each of the potential bidders, so they could better understand each before deciding which firm to negotiate with. We arranged meetings (both formal and informal) between principals, so that by the time bids were due, our knowledge of the other side was fairly extensive.

Initially, TPT's founders were still inclined to sell to one of the strategics. About twice the size of TPT, it was backed by a well-known private equity firm. While TPT primarily targeted corporate customers, and the other firm primarily targeted customers in the financial services arena, particularly in the technology area the firms overlapped. The problem was, the more the TPT founders got to know about that firm, the less inclined they were to work with them. References gave us concern about the company's leadership. (We called that a weakness.) The leaders of several companies that were acquired by this strategic had little good to say about the CEO or his team. And that CEO did little to ingratiate himself with the founders. His motivation was to build a company to take public in a few years. For him it seemed to be all about the price and opportunities to cut costs. Their technology appeared to be another weakness (customers complained that it was inferior to TPT's). So did opportunity for the TPT employees. The founders realized that even if they received a good payday personally, much of what they had built would be dismantled, and many of their employees would find themselves without jobs.

Meanwhile, one of the PE firms stood out: ABRY Partners of Boston. Their strengths were just the sort that TPT needed—helping their technology-based portfolio companies grow and prosper through encouragement and resources at the board level. ABRY's motivation was to find good, growing companies, with strong management teams, that operated in areas they knew well—and to help them grow. ABRY would encourage organic growth through internal investment as well as acquisitions. They would help with financing and financial expertise, and then in a few years help sell the company for a much higher price. Their record of successes with firms similar to TPT was outstanding. The people we and the founders talked to—people who had worked at ABRY portfolio companies, including references we sourced independently, not just those names provided to us by ABRY—were highly complimentary about the firm and about the individuals that we would be working with (very important). ABRY's strategic fit and desire to work with TPT was clearly strong. The ABRY partner went out of his way to help the founders get to know his firm as well as the portfolio companies in which ABRY was invested.

The two best bids we received were one from the strategic, offering to buy the entire company, and one from ABRY, offering to buy about 60 percent of the company. The founders could have taken much more money off the table at the closing had they sold to the strategic. Instead, they chose ABRY. It wouldn't have happened that way had we and the TPT founders not gotten to know the strengths, weaknesses, capabilities, constraints, and motivations of the people on the other side of the table. That's the Marine Corps Way.

Epilogue

We don't always get a lot of feedback on how our deals pan out. In the case of TPT, however, we kept in touch. We advised them as they looked at several potential acquisitions. With the help of ABRY, and financing provided via one of the bulge bracket investment banks, TPT acquired several companies that broadened their product line and added capabilities. In doing it, they also added debt to the company to pay themselves a dividend, which made sense.

Six years after TPT sold control to ABRY, ABRY decided it was time to test the market. The same bulge bracket investment bank that had helped them raise capital helped. But after several months, ABRY did not receive their desired price, so they ended the effort. A few months later, we were briefing the private equity firm Welsh, Carson, Anderson & Stowe and realized that WCAS had never been asked about their potential interest in acquiring control of TPT. I was surprised. This was the same PE firm that had backed Bridge. It was perfect for them: TPT was directly in their industry sweet spot, and it had the ideal size, growth, and profit profile. Further, it had the young, smart, expert leadership that WCAS covets. I also believed that WCAS would be perfect for TPT. They know how to help midsized information technology firms like this grow. They lead from the board level without micromanaging. They would get along perfectly with management. But no one had told them about it. I briefed WCAS on the company, and then with their approval, I talked with ABRY. Getting to know the strengths, weaknesses, capabilities, constraints, and motivations of the parties to this transaction was relatively easy. We knew both sides well and were able to communicate clearly with both. That made all the difference. ABRY and the founders sold the company to WCAS for a multiple of the valuation of six years earlier. Management and ABRY both considered the whole thing a home run, and we got paid. That's the kind of ending we like—everybody walks away happy—and that success would never have happened had we not fully understood the people on the other side of the negotiating table and done things the Marine Corps Way.

5

Know What the Objective Is Worth

WHEN I ENLISTED IN THE MARINES, THE WAR IN VIETNAM WAS STILL
hot, but by the spring of 1975, when I was on my second Far East
deployment aboard the USS *Tripoli,* it was clearly over—at least for
us. There was no sugarcoating it—the North had won. As we patrolled, Marines on my sister ships helped evacuate thousands of
desperate American citizens and refugees from the rooftops and
grounds of US embassies in Saigon, Vietnam—soon to be renamed
Ho Chi Minh City—and Phnom Penh, Cambodia. To many of my
colleagues the cost of this war was personal. More than fifty-eight
thousand Americans had died, including thirteen thousand Marines;
more than three hundred thousand Americans were wounded, including more than eighty-eight thousand Marines. We all knew
someone who was killed. We all knew many who were wounded.
And our losses paled when compared to the nearly 1 million Vietnamese that were killed on both sides and the over 2.5 million
Vietnamese wounded.

As we cruised the waters of the East China Sea, wondering which
domino might fall next, some of us asked, Was it worth it? Was the
failed war in Vietnam worth the price the United States had paid,
and the price our allies (the Australians, South Koreans, New Zea-
landers, and Filipinos) had paid? Was it worth the price that the
North Vietnamese paid, even in winning? Does winning justify any
price paid?

For that matter, what makes any war or any battle "worth it," other
than winning, and how can you know in advance? Over the years, I
have had a lot of time to contemplate what makes a battle (or a war)

worth the cost of fighting—and how can you justify the cost, in dollars or in lives—before you commit to fight it.

In chapter 1, "Take the Long View," I introduced the battle at Khe Sanh—a battle to defend a Marine base and airfield near a small village adjacent to a key North Vietnamese Army (NVA) supply route, a few miles from the Laotian border. There, in 1968, for seventy-seven days, Marines together with soldiers from the US Army, the South Vietnamese Army, and even some from Laos fought off a determined assault by forces of North Vietnam. Thousands were killed and wounded. Shortly after the NVA withdrew from the battle, the United States declared victory, withdrew from the base at Khe Sanh, and destroyed it. Shortly after that, the NVA returned and raised their flag above the airfield.

My Marine friends and I studied the battle at Khe Sanh as well as others, including the battle for control of Guadalcanal in World War II, where, for six months, Marines of the First Marine Division—my division—along with soldiers from the United States, UK, Australia, and New Zealand fought to dislodge the Japanese Army from a small mountainous and jungle-covered island in the western Pacific Ocean about one thousand miles north east of Australia. We debated the battles endlessly. While we "won" both battles, my friends and I concluded that the battle at Khe Sanh was not worth the price we paid; whereas, in spite of the much greater cost (seventy-one hundred American dead, mostly Marines; seventy-eight hundred casualties; and about thirty-one thousand Japanese killed), the strategic value of denying the Japanese the air base on Guadalcanal and establishing our own forward air base from which we could prosecute the war justified the cost. There has to be more to justifying the cost of a battle or a war than whether or not we won.

Four Factors of Valuation

The title of this chapter is "Know What the Objective Is Worth." Perhaps I should add . . . before you commit to the battle. When we look at the battles of Khe Sanh and Guadalcanal, we can learn important lessons about what those objectives were worth—and to whom. We can see what was known or could have been known before we paid the price for achieving victory—and how that knowledge should have affected our sense of what victory was worth. Looking at the battles, I have identified four important factors that, when taken together, help me to determine whether we should have engaged in those battles in the first place, and in addition the price that we should be willing to pay to win any particular future battle—and that's key. Any approach to valuation that doesn't allow you to put a price on some act that you are contemplating isn't worth a whole lot. You won't find those four factors in any Marne Corps manual. I've derived them from many teachings and my own observations. Interestingly, valuing companies or even valuing strategic political moves—such as bailing out a company or an industry—can be premised on these same four factors.

First, let's consider Guadalcanal. Capturing that small island was clearly *a strategic objective* for the United States. By this I mean that it was not simply a target of opportunity; this battle—if won—would materially advance the United States toward achieving our long-term strategic objective—defeating the forces of Imperial Japan. Note that I didn't say this was the only way to advance us toward achieving that objective, only that it was important in advancing us to that end— although in the specific case of Guadalcanal it was a critical strategic objective. It was an island that we had to take. Admiral Nimitz (who led all US forces in that part of the Pacific) was the master of "island hopping," skipping over islands and battles that did not need to be fought, leaving the Japanese stranded behind our lines. But had we not fought this battle, our march toward Japan would have been stymied, our supply lines at risk. Conversely, the Japanese had to defend the island for the same reasons. The airfield and Japanese aircraft based on that island allowed the Japanese to protect their supply lines, support their attacking forces, and deny the American military safe passage westward toward Japan. It also put their planes within striking distance of shipping lanes to the United States and Australia, a major US ally. The United States had to take this island and the Japanese had to defend it. It was that simple, and strategic.

For the North Vietnamese, Khe Sanh had strategic value in at least two ways: First, if they were successful in driving the Americans from Khe Sanh, it could deal a huge psychological blow to the United States and to the South Vietnamese. It may not have been the only way to achieve that goal, but it was the best opportunity they had at that time to re-create the victory that the North had recorded at

Dien Bien Phu—the battle that had driven the French out of Indo-china back in 1954. Second, whether or not they "won," this battle, it drew American forces away from the cities of South Vietnam, thus allowing the North Vietnamese Army to succeed in their larger Tet Offensive.

For the Americans and our South Vietnamese allies, the compelling strategic value of engaging in this large-scale battle was much less clear. Reportedly, General Westmoreland hoped that if the United States could draw the NVA into a large-scale battle and then crush their massed forces, it would break the North's will to fight on; it's more likely that having made the initial decision to reinforce and defend this remote combat outpost, Westmoreland was not willing to surrender it—and have it be our Dien Bien Phu. That's not strategy; it's hubris.

Second, the timing was right—for the Americans at Guadalcanal and for NVA at Khe Sanh. There's a whole chapter on the importance of timing later in this book, but for now I'll just note that the Americans waited to assault Guadalcanal until they had sufficient resources in place and then decided when and where to attack. We chose the timing. At Khe Sanh, the NVA chose the timing. Their assault on Khe Sanh was purposely timed to coincide with their Tet Offensive on the larger cities of South Vietnam. It tied up major elements of US forces while the rest of the NVA assaulted.

Third, the cost (equipment, money, and lives) was deemed to be both "affordable" and "reasonable." The Japanese poured more than thirty-five thousand soldiers onto Guadalcanal in an effort to hold that small island. More than thirty-one thousand of them died trying. I'm convinced that they would have poured more men and resources into the battle if they had been available. It was that important. The Americans knew that the Japanese had dug caves, tunnels, and fighting bunkers. They knew what it would take to dislodge them. The United States committed more than sixty thousand ground forces, an aircraft carrier, two battleships, two heavy cruisers, three light cruisers, and more than a dozen other ships of war. The likely cost of taking Guadalcanal was crystal clear to US military leaders well before the battle started, well before anyone could know who would win, and was deemed affordable.

The cost of fighting the battle at Khe Sanh was also deemed affordable—at least for the North Vietnamese. NVA general Giáp (who had led the assault on the French at Dien Bien Phu) concluded that he could tie up four NVA divisions—something on the order of thirty thousand men—and suffer casualties in furtherance of his goals. He may also have gambled that, while the cost in American lives to defend that remote base might be deemed "affordable" by some military commanders and politicians, many others who watched the five-month battle for Khe Sanh unfold on nightly news programs might come to a very different conclusion.

Fourth, the "risk/reward" trade-off in the event of failure was deemed acceptable for both sides. By this I mean that, in theory, they would only enter into the battle in the first place if failure would be a worse consequence than not fighting the battle at all. This can be a tricky part of the equation to assess for military commanders or politicians who are convinced that they will never lose.

In the case of Guadalcanal this part of the equation was straightforward. Losing simply wasn't an option. In the case of Khe Sanh it was more complex.

For General Westmoreland, the potential reward for engaging in the battle at Khe Sanh was crushing a large force of NVA, while the "risk" of not engaging in the battle was losing his perch near the NVA supply route. At least that was his risk until Westmoreland decided to defend the base "at all costs." Once he had committed, then the risk of losing this battle (which is different from the risk in not engaging in the first place) became personal humiliation—and possible national humiliation. That risk must have loomed large—large enough to cause Westmoreland to put thousands of American lives at risk. For General Giáp the potential reward for engaging in the battle was far more than simply chasing the Americans from a supply route. For him it was about diverting American forces from defending cities during the larger Tet Offensive and potentially winning the psychological war. Meanwhile, his risk of not winning the battle was relatively small. Few seriously expected the NVA to defeat the American Army—at least not militarily.

As you might have guessed, these four factors taken together drive the value equations of fighting battles in places that are far from Wall Street. They are also applicable to many business and political battles of consequence. We certainly mentally apply them to mergers and acquisitions and divestitures in our effort to know what the objective is worth. The rest of this chapter will discuss some of the ways that we do so. While the examples I cite will be m&a's, the approach is much more broadly applicable. Before joining any battle we all should ask, is this proposed battle (deal) strategic? Is the timing right? Is the price both affordable and reasonable? Are the risks of not entering the battle worse than the prospect of losing? Too often people don't take the time to think through this useful exercise.

AOL

The AOL merger with Time Warner is everyone's favorite really bad deal. The deal was negotiated in a hurry in late 1999 and announced in January of 2000—a heady time for the tech market. Essentially, AOL used its overvalued stock to buy Time Warner. The Time Warner shareholders effectively gave up 55 percent of their company in return. For a brief time it was hailed by many in the press as the "deal of the century" and a "mega marriage of earth and cyberspace." A few months later, as the Internet bubble burst and the value of the stock in the combined company eventually dropped by more than two-thirds, the media view shifted dramatically. For Time Warner shareholders it was a disaster.

That's easy to see—in hindsight. The interesting question for me is not how this disaster happened, or who was responsible, but rather, should this battle have been fought at all? And was the answer knowable before the battle was joined? It's a particularly interesting question when looked at from the perspective of Steve Case, AOL's CEO, because, from his perspective, every one of the four factors mentioned above was present and favorable. For AOL shareholders, it was a beautiful transaction. It was strategic: they held shares in a company with a huge market value and whose principal assets were subscribers who not only could flee at a whim, but were already beginning to do so, as access to the Internet rapidly changed. Microsoft, Yahoo!, Google, and others were increasingly competitive. AOL had no better way to survive than a merger with a content-rich firm to attach content to their distribution capabilities. For AOL, the timing was perfect, coming at the market peak and just months before the bursting of the Internet bubble. For AOL, it was totally affordable. For Steve Case and AOL, the biggest risk would have been to not enter into the Time Warner merger. I assume that after the deal was done, the shareholders quietly feted Case. They certainly should have.

For Jerry Levin, Time Warner's CEO, the deal with AOL was also clearly strategic—advancing his company toward an important long-term strategic objective, and there is no doubt that the timing seemed right. Time Warner did need to move its content onto the Internet, and a merger with AOL, the leading Internet service provider at the time, was a reasonable, perhaps exciting, potential solution—if the price was affordable and the risks of not entering into this battle were unacceptable. To me, it appears that these last two questions were not fully vetted at the time.

How Do We Get to Value?

A part of the flawed logic that drove the value of the AOL/Time Warner deal stemmed from them being publicly traded companies. Discussions about a company's value almost always start with the value implied by the public market for the company's shares. Investment bankers and corporate executives are taught that the public markets bake into a company's stock price the collective expectations of many experts for things such as future cash flows, risk, and the value of the company's assets and liabilities both on and off the balance sheet. That may be true sometimes, but frequently the collective expectations are wrong—just ask the shareholders of Time Warner. There has to be a better way.

StarMine

Joe Gatto, the founder and CEO of StarMine, had been hard at work for nine years building his San Francisco–based company when he approached us to advise him and his board of directors on selling it. Gatto understood the drivers of value—at least the financial ones. His company leveraged cutting-edge mathematically based analytics to deliver a "smarter" way to assess the value of public companies. His largest product focused on a smarter way to assess the collective expectations for quarterly earnings by public-company analysts. And he had other products that allowed analysts to better assess the "fundamental" value of a company. Much of the theory behind his firm was based on research Gatto had conducted while pursuing his MS at Stanford University. His genuinely novel concept had enabled Gatto to raise several rounds of capital from two well-known Silicon Valley venture capital firms. He'd designed successful products and built a business that in a few short years was serving scores of blue-chip firms from offices in Boston, Chicago, Denver, New York, Philadelphia, London, Hong Kong, Sydney, Tokyo—and San Francisco.

One of my senior colleagues, Michael Maxworthy, and I had been talking with Gatto on and off for over a year about his plans. The company he had built looked great on many dimensions: It was growing revenue at 35 percent annually, most of which was derived from recurring, subscription-based contracts, with renewal rates exceeding 110 percent a year—meaning that virtually all clients not only renewed but usually did so for more money than they had paid the prior year. It was a fabulous revenue model. Further, the company had just begun to expand internationally and had a lot of room to grow. They had a big market opportunity and only a few challengers. About the only downside was that the company had never made significant profit. Gatto and his board had purposely plowed back every dime they earned into growing the top line—a common tactic among fast-growing technology firms. That meant that Gatto and his team had little cash in their pockets to show for their years of effort. Their VC backers were patient, but Gatto and his team were ready to sell. That's why he came to me.

The problem was the value they sought. Because of the way the company had been financed, granting the investors so-called preference rights, Gatto and his management team would make little on a sale for less than $100 million, an amount that was five times the company's revenue—and an infinite multiple of its nonexistent profit. The tech and Internet bubbles had burst, and the investors understood that buyers had been burned in the past. They would be wary, and $100 million was a high hurdle for a company like this with zero profit. The investors also understood that there could be no sale without the active cooperation of Joe and his management team. Neither the investors nor Gatto had any interest in going through the pain of a sale process and having it fail. Before they began, they wanted our opinion on whether the company would fetch at least $100 million. That was the objective. And Joe had an idea.

Joe Gatto was a sophisticated client. Not only did he have his degree in financial engineering from Stanford, but also he ran a company that helped professional financial analysts to value companies. While at Stanford he had learned something I'd learned in my MBA program at UCLA, called discounted cash flow analysis or DCF. The theory is that the value of any business can be determined by taking its expected future cash flows and appropriately "discounting" those expected flows back to the present, using the time value of money (mostly expected inflation) plus a rate that reflects the risk to those gains going forward. Gatto had applied this DCF approach to StarMine and come up with a value of several hundred million dollars.

We Call It as We See It

Earlier, I've discussed the four factors that I use to determine what the objective is worth, and we'll come back to those four factors in a moment. But first, it's important to look at the approach as well as the assumptions Joe was making and how they might and might not mesh with those of potential buyers. Obviously a banker would always love to promise a client that he can get him not just what he expects but more, but in this case I wasn't so sure.

We agreed with Joe that $100 million (or more) could be the result of a DCF analysis, given his assumptions, but we were not so optimistic that buyers would agree to use DCF, much less agree with those assumptions. Buyers and sellers rarely agree on the assumed future cash flows, or on what specific value to assign to risk. DCF can help to explain a price already determined. But it is not a great predictor of price—the variables are too hard to pin down. A second problem with DCF is that it's hard to use on a company in growth mode that has little current profit or cash flow. How would you apply DCF to value a company such as Instagram which, when Facebook acquired it in a deal then valued at $1 billion, had thirteen employees, no revenue, and no profit? That was $300 million in cash at the time and about 23 million shares of Facebook stock, valued then at $30 per share. (As I write, Facebook is trading at $114 per share.)

DCF isn't useless; it can be used when the parties agree on the assumptions, which sometimes happen with stable, predictable financial instruments and firms. It can certainly be used to show prospective buyers that a given price for some companies or some securities is not foolish. But it's far from a perfect predictor of the value that someone will pay.

Comparables and Multiples

Joe also knew that his VC backers would look at financial metrics of "comparable" transactions and try to apply them to StarMine to predict value. It's common for people to tell me that if such and such a company sold for 6x its annual revenue, then my firm must be worth at least 5x revenue. (The most common multiple used by investors is that of earnings before interest and tax—EBIT—or earnings before interest, tax, depreciation, and amortization—EBITDA.) The multiple best known by the general public is probably the P/E multiple, or the ratio of the price for one share of a company's stock to the annual after-tax earnings attributable to that single share. A company that trades at, say, $200 per share and earns $10 per share (after tax) per year would be said to trade at a P/E of 20 (twenty times after-tax per-share earnings). Joe's VC backers were aware that a few high-flying publicly traded tech companies were trading at high multiples of revenue and wanted to know if they could expect the same revenue multiple for StarMine.

We noted that, like DCF analysis, valuation analysis using the multiples of sort-of-comparable companies can be a useful way to show a prospective buyer or seller that the price being discussed is "reasonable," or at least not foolish—as long as the companies are truly comparable. But again, the multiples can't be applied with any precision to predict a future value for a totally different seller—another company with four times the revenue, more profit, a different product set, management, growth rate, risk profile, etc. Further, buyers and sellers rarely agree on the set of comparable firms. They often like to shop for the comparable companies that support their arguments, and they only want to apply the metrics that they like best. I've met with CEOs of companies with strong profits but little top-line growth who believe that their company should be valued solely based on a multiple of those profits. I've met with managers at other companies without a lot of profit who believe that revenue multiples alone should be used to value their firm.

Prospective buyers tend to look at all of these metrics together, then combine this approach to valuation with other approaches. You can't just pick the one multiple you like best and believe it will be a predictor of value. It doesn't work.

Granted, these approaches have directional merit. They can help as a sanity check and we use them. But no Marine would say that because we paid for Guadalcanal with seventy-one hundred American lives (and seventy-eight hundred casualties) plus twenty-nine ships lost that this price can somehow be applied to the "value" (lives, casualties, ships) World War II leaders should have paid to take Iwo Jima—another heavily fortified Japanese-held island in the Pacific. How should we adjust for the fact that Iwo Jima (about two miles wide and four miles long) was far smaller than Guadalcanal (about ninety miles long and thirty miles wide)? It would be absurd. How are we supposed to factor into "value" the fact that Iwo Jima was only 660 miles south of Tokyo (well within range of the American B29 Superfortress bombers) or the fact that Iwo Jima had three Japanese airfields versus the one on Guadalcanal? These naïve approaches to valuation may have been how Yahoo! wound up paying $5.7 billion for Broadcast.com (and $3.6 billion for Geocities) and Time Warner agreeing to a $164 billion deal with AOL.

Yes, you can get some direction from looking at the values that others have paid for so-called "comparable" transactions. We did for StarMine—using the values of some publicly traded firms as well as twenty to thirty previous transactions among private companies that seemed somewhat analogous. We derived a directional sense for how others might value StarMine by adjusting the values of these so-called comparables to take into account a variety of characteristics, including StarMine's balance sheet and its unique intellectual property as well as its rapid growth and leadership position. We understood that none of these companies were really directly comparable to StarMine. They were all different. But we also understood that we could use them to help a prospective buyer see that a price of $100 million would not be out of line with the prices paid for at least some somewhat similarly situated companies. It wouldn't be dumb.

Again, we believed that we could justify a price of over $100 million—but it would be a stretch. And this certainly was no predictor of value.

The Marine Corps Way

Our four Marine Corps factors of value now helped us zero in on what the objective was really worth—or at least a reasonable range of value. We ask ourselves the same sorts of questions that we ask prospective clients: Were there firms that should find the need to acquire StarMine *strategically important*? Was the *timing* right for them? Did some of them have pockets deep enough that a $100 million price tag should be both "affordable *and* reasonable" given the firm's future? And were there some for whom the *risk* of not entering into this battle—losing the deal—was material and the reward worth $100 million or more?

Is There Strategic Fit?

Joe clearly understood the concept of strategic value. It is fairly simple: Does the objective of the battle (transaction) advance the parties toward their long-term strategic goals. (It's all about the future.) The more it advances the larger mission, the more it drives interest—and as economists will tell you, interest leads to "demand," which is one of the key drivers of price. (When I was in graduate school, my microeconomics professor taught that, in a world of perfect information, with no constraints on buyers and sellers, assuming there is demand by more than one party, the rarer an asset, the higher the price should be, and vice versa. Why is a large, perfectly clear, flawless diamond worth more than a slightly less perfect diamond of the same size? Because it's so rare—and many people want it. Joe Gatto must have taken the same courses.)

I like this concept—to a point. It fits with my sense that the ultimate valuation factor—the price that someone will pay for a diamond (or a house, car, suit, or business)—is not principally about financials. It's not about what it costs to mine the diamond, produce the car, build the house, or create the business. The problem is that strategic interest alone does not always result in demand—and it certainly does not determine price. We have had clients that assert that Google should want them and therefore pay some ludicrous price. The other three Marine Corps factors have to be present too (affordability and price reasonableness; timing; risk/reward, etc.).

Attacking Guadalcanal (for the Americans) or the American base at Khe Sanh (for the NVA) was all about strategic value. Buying Time Warner was strategic for Steve Case, the CEO of AOL. And as I will discuss below, buying Instagram was strategic for Facebook. In the case of StarMine, because we are industry experts, we knew several industry participants that we strongly believed should see Star-Mine as strategic in the sense that their ability to achieve their strategic objectives would materially be enhanced with the acquisition of StarMine.

Some potential buyers were obvious. Some were not. Bloomberg LP, for example, the large, privately held financial software, data, and media company headquartered a few blocks from our offices in midtown Manhattan was a natural from the perspective of strategic fit. We knew the company well, having talked to them about several other potential acquisitions. We also knew that Bloomberg was renowned for building everything in-house and for not making acquisitions. We had been talking to Bloomberg and understood that this attitude was under review. So talking to them about StarMine was worth a shot; but we could not count on them to be the buyer. (Bloomberg did take a hard look at StarMine, although they did not make an offer.) We also knew of several industry participants that a less knowledgeable adviser bank might assume would be interested but that we had a high degree of confidence would not.

This concept of strategic value can be applied to many potential battles and transactions. For example, for four years, a nice house next to mine sat vacant and for sale. The owners had moved to Florida, and they kept dropping the asking price until it was less than half of where it started. Did I offer to buy it? No, it didn't fit my needs. I was happy to let this house be someone else's good deal. If the prospective buyer doesn't see the strategic fit, then it doesn't matter how wonderful we say the business—or the house or car or suit—is. They won't buy. I once had a CEO say to me, "Surely, so-and-so would buy my company for a dollar." Nope. If it doesn't fit, not even for a dollar! They will let it be someone else's good deal.

However, if we can identify a prospective buyer that does (or we believe should) see the fit with our client, then we have the potential beginning of a deal.

Is the Timing Right?

We have an entire chapter coming up on the importance of controlling timing, but the important thing here is that Joe Gatto understood that there is a time to sell and a time to wait—and that the same is true for buyers. StarMine's owners were ready—they had been invested a long time; the company was ready—it had grown to a level where it was clearly salable; and Joe was ready to reap the rewards of many years of effort. I sometimes tell prospective sellers that while I can't always tell you the right time to sell a business, I can tell you the wrong time—right after the market drops or the sales growth curve slows. But other factors besides the market and revenue growth rates impact good timing.

In late 1999, the timing seemed perfect to both AOL and Time Warner to merge. Six months later that merger would not have happened. One week after Facebook's IPO, their interest in paying a billion dollars for Instagram may have waned. The question was not only was this the right time for Gatto and his partners to sell, but was it also the right time for the buyers? (It's not uncommon in this business to find potential buyers who might have a strong potential strategic fit and be able to afford the battle, but who are preoccupied with other things—e.g., management change, other deals, other challenges.) While we couldn't know for sure whether the timing was right for any specific potential buyer without actually putting the opportunity in front of them, we did know the general state of the market (strong) and, as a result of our frequent interactions with many of these firms, their general appetite for deals (also strong). From that perspective, the timing did seem propitious.

Is the Likely Price Both Affordable and Reasonable?

The third key factor that helps us to assess what the objective is worth is the combination of *price affordability and perceived reasonableness*.

Another home up the street from mine is absolutely lovely. It is significantly larger than mine with much better views. My wife loves the kitchen. I love the view—and the garage. About a year ago, the house was put up for sale. Did I buy it? Nope—it was too expensive for me. The hard truth is that strategic value and timing alone are not enough if the opportunity is not affordable. And even if it is affordable, the price must also be seen as *reasonable*. Clearly, Facebook was capable of paying $1 billion in cash and stock for Instagram. But was it reasonable to do so?

Warren Buffett might desire a glass of lemonade, and he can certainly afford to pay $100,000 for it. But I assume that he would decline to do so, unless, for example, he was dying of thirst in the desert and there was no alternative. Why not? He has the "strategic" desire, he's thirsty, and the timing seems right. He can certainly afford it. According to one report, Buffett's annual income amounts to about $23,000 per minute. There doesn't seem to be much risk. But, under most circumstances, $100,000 is not a reasonable price for a glass of lemonade. And no one likes to be taken advantage of. No one likes to look stupid.

We came to believe that a few firms (not many) could find $100 million to be both reasonable for StarMine and affordable. We believed it because we were able to quantify at least one aspect of that value by projecting the likely revenue and profit opportunities for each of them once they owned the company. We knew one potential buyer, for example, that had nearly a half million customers, of which we could identify seventeen thousand who should be logical users of the key StarMine product. It was reasonable to assume that virtually all of these seventeen thousand would eventually use the product, although it might take several years for them to migrate. It was also reasonable to assume that the buyer could get each user to pay at least $1,200 per year for the service, since StarMine charged several times that amount already. By our analysis, this alone amounted to over $20 million of incremental revenue per year, for many years, with little incremental cost to the buyer. (We also assessed cost savings, but these were minimal.) Still, the profit margin could be enormous, easily justifying a price well over $100 million—if the buyer accepted our analysis.

Risk and Reward

The final question for us in the case of StarMine was the perception of risk. What risks would buyers perceive if they were to acquire StarMine, and what was their risk in not engaging in this battle—not buying the company—and how would either impact their willingness to pay at least $100 million?

Frequently we hear prospective buyers and sellers worry about the risk associated with a transaction. Buyers worry that sellers may know something they don't. What if the future is not as bright as the seller portrays. Could competition take away market share or drive down price? What if new technology doesn't work as advertised? Is management up to the task of taking the company to the next level? Will they stick around? Sellers worry that the buyer might not cooperate in helping them to achieve an earn-out. What if the value of stock used as acquisition currency drops? What if I hate these people that I am locked in with? Sometimes people worry about their careers. No parties to a transaction like to believe (or find out after the fact) that they should have received more; and no buyers like to believe (or find out after the fact) that they should have paid less. For corporate managers as well as for many investment professionals, stupid moves can be career ending. And that's a risk most don't want to take. But sometimes not engaging in a battle has risks—or in this case, not buying a company—especially if the opportunity checks all of the four Marine Corps boxes and is unique, meaning that if this one gets away, an equivalent opportunity may not come along for a long time.

Lawyers will tell you that contracts can help mitigate risk. That's true—to a point. When working with buyers as well as sellers, part of our job is to work with the lawyers to help mitigate risk. We help sellers and buyers understand not only why they should transact (strategic value, affordability/reasonableness), but also why entering into the deal is less risky than might be perceived (and sometimes why not entering into a deal may be riskier yet). Also we may help them see that the price being discussed will not later look stupid. But there are few risk-free battles. Winning is never a sure thing. In most cases, at best, some of the larger risks are identified and apportioned. But unknown risks are a challenge to mitigate. Ask General Westmoreland: the future is always uncertain. Intelligence about the other side is rarely perfect.

StarMine

There were risks to an acquirer of StarMine. There always are. Joe was both the intellectual who had started the company as well as its leader. He was the glue that held it all together, and any buyer would want him to agree to stick around. He was ready to commit to work with the new owners—assuming the right set of circumstances. Two other firms also offered products roughly similar to those of StarMine. Both firms were much larger than StarMine, with significantly more resources. Could they squish StarMine like a bug? Maybe. But Gatto was convinced that only one of the potential buyers had a reasonable chance to replicate StarMine's products, and that was fraught with execution risk. And Gatto had an ace up his sleeve—StarMine's intellectual property, its IP.

StarMine had not only developed many proprietary algorithms for how to perform its analyses, it had also patented many and had applied for others. These patents gave the company some confidence that no one could attack it or cause it to lose product uniqueness. These patents also meant that the winning buyer would have lower competitive risk going forward than those firms that did not buy StarMine. That's right—there was risk in *not* buying the company, because those that did not would have to contend with the winner, who would have these patents and perhaps be able to use them to keep rivals from competing (at least for a time). Accountants may not be allowed to include the value of this intellectual property on the company's balance sheets. (The gods who define GAAP generally won't let them, unless the IP was acquired.) But we certainly could use it to show value (and mitigate risk) to prospective buyers.

Back to Instagram

In April 2012, Facebook acquired Instagram with its thirteen employees for a combination of stock and cash that was valued at $1 billion. (I hope the sellers held on to their stock; it would be worth much more now.) That's a lot of money for a two-year-old company with no revenue and no profit. Was it a smart deal for Facebook?

It certainly was strategic. Facebook had had a key objective of developing mobile applications for some time, but the results were not yet clear. They had also been trying to develop their own mobile photo-sharing application for some time, to little avail. Meanwhile photo sharing had become an important tool for Facebook's users, and Apple, Google, Microsoft, and Yahoo! were working on their own solutions. Instagram was the leader in the space. It had built up a community of 27 million users, mostly on mobile devices. It was becoming a mobile social-media destination Web site in its own right. Clearly this deal was strategic. But was the timing right?

The timing could not have been better. Facebook was planning its IPO, which it hoped would give it a lofty value of as much as $100 billion—one of the biggest IPOs in Internet history. One major question from potential investors was, could Facebook continue growing at an astounding rate without a viable photo-sharing application? Another was whether Facebook could continue growing at this rate without a better strategy for monetizing mobile applications; and a third was could they continue to attract younger users. Instagram checked all three boxes for them.

But was the deal affordable and the price reasonable? The $1 billion price tag Instagram sought was clearly affordable for Facebook. It was $300 million of cash, which Facebook's investors were more than willing to put up, plus the issuance of 23 million new shares that would dilute the value of all the other Facebook shares to the tune of less than 1 percent of Facebook's anticipated market value—and it might be key to achieving that lofty value to begin with. But was $1 billion reasonable for a company with thirteen employees and no revenue?

Instagram didn't have to sell; plenty of investors were out there eager to pour in more money, at valuations in excess of $500 million. Other companies, including Google and Yahoo!, were rumored to be circling and would be willing to pay a high price. Thus, the price to Facebook to buy the company right now—a month before Facebook's scheduled IPO—was $1 billion. Clearly the Facebook board decided that it was reasonable, and they likely did so after considering the risk of not buying the firm.

Was the Risk/Reward Trade-Off Acceptable?

The risk of not buying Instagram was significantly higher than the risk of the deal. Facebook could afford to "lose," could afford the financial loss if the acquisition was a bust. The cost of not engaging in the battle (not buying Instagram) was much higher. Not buying Instagram might have cost Facebook far more than $1 billion in the IPO and made them compete with the firm that did buy it.

It seems to have worked. Facebook was valued at over $104 billion on day one of its IPO, May 18, 2012. Four years later it surpassed $330 billion. Meanwhile the number of active Instagram users averaged nearly 400 million each month. In December 2014, an analyst from Citigroup valued Instagram alone at $35 billion! (It is now 25 percent larger.)

StarMine Resolution

We came to believe that while the pool of highly likely buyers for Star-Mine at $100 million or more was small, there should be at least three strategics for whom the strategic fit would be strong, the timing right, the $100 million affordable. We would have to show them that $100 million was reasonable and that the risk/reward trade-off acceptable.

We did not believe any demand was likely from pure financial investors at anything near the valuation that Gatto and his team were seeking. We know those firms and we know how they approach valuation. So, our focus would have to be on those three strategic buyers—plus a couple of outliers.

We managed the fairly complex sale process in our usual thorough manner. While all three strategics made bids, none offered anything even approaching $100 million. We needed to help these bidders see the light.

Because of our earlier homework we were able to go back to these three and reinforce the strategic fit, remind them why the timing was right, and show them why $100 million was reasonable, using many of the techniques we described above: DCF, comparable-company multiples, plus the one that matters most—imminent loss. As with Instagram, we helped them understand that they were about to lose

StarMine to a rival. One bidder declined to improve their offer, but the other two materially increased theirs, and StarMine was acquired for $100 million.

The sellers, including the VCs and management, were convinced that the price had been well vetted and fully stretched; the buyer was pleased to have a unique opportunity to add significant strategic value while generating substantial revenue and profit. Joe Gatto was happy to get the deal done and to be given a larger role in the new parent company; the employees were happy in a new environment with additional resources and opportunities to grow; and the customers were glad to have a more fully integrated support and service team and broader product offering.

The question of what an objective is worth comes up in my world nearly every day. It's not an easy question to answer, even though some on Wall Street can make it seem so. But it should be thoroughly vetted before committing to battle or entering into a transaction. One report I read said that 70 percent of acquisitions studied did not meet expected profit targets five years after the transaction was completed. That doesn't per se mean that the seventy percent were all miserable failures. Many still provided the buyer with much needed technology, talent, products, customers, and more. Many provided buyers with a return on invested capital that exceeded other alternative uses of that capital. But still 70 percent is a cautionary tale. For every successful Facebook/Instagram deal, there is the potential for a Time Warner/AOL fiasco.

Plenty of metrics give some broad directional sense of potential value: DCF, comparable multiples, etc. But if you apply the four Marine Corp concepts on top of those metrics, you'll vastly improve your odds of understanding the value of the objective before you enter into battle, and that greatly improves the chances that you will win. That's the Marine Corps Way.

6

Know Yourself

President Ronald Reagan once said, "Some people spend an entire lifetime wondering if they made a difference in the world. But, the Marines don't have that problem."

It's true. But my daughter once asked me why that is. Why do so many people believe that Marines are special? Why does the press make a bigger deal out of someone who was a Marine as opposed to someone who was in the Army, Navy, or Air Force? And for that matter, why do Marines seem more proud of their service than do many other military veterans not in the Corps? I get that boot camp is tough, she said to me, but there must be more to it than that.

One answer has to do with our reputation for being willing to go where no one else dares to go; for being "first to fight"; for facing seemingly insurmountable odds calmly and defeating the enemy through a combination of skill, discipline, toughness, and a refusal to quit; for being "always faithful." That reputation has been earned by the actions of Marines in nearly every battle, skirmish, and war they have fought in from the American Revolution to the latest wars in the Middle East. It is a testament to Marines that virtually every one of us feels personal embarrassment when some former Marine breaches our code of honor.

But a reputation is not what makes you special—it's the things you continue to do every day to deserve that reputation that do. For Marines, it starts with our people—the way they are recruited, selected, promoted, and retained. Every Marine is a rifleman. It's not exactly about our equipment, which, we like to point out, is highly specialized but often less modern than that of the Army. It's about how we use that equipment. It's about the Marines' unique ability to closely integrate air, sea, and ground forces. It's about the esprit de corps that Marines develop and their unbounded loyalty to one another. And, among other things, it's also about strong adherence to the eleven principles that I talk about in this book. It's not any one of these things, it's the combination of all these values, practices, and principles that make Marines uniquely ready to "fight our country's battles in the air, on land and sea," as the "Marine Corps Hymn" proclaims. It's why Marines are convinced that we're the best on the planet at doing what we're called on to do.

But Marines also are nothing if not realistic about our constraints and limitations. Marine general James Mattis—the leader of Marines in Iraq, once famously said, "You cannot allow any of your people to avoid the brutal facts. If they start living in a dream world, it's going to be bad." In battle and in business, self-delusion can lead to disaster.

Lieutenant Colonel Custer should have understood this concept before he sent five of his twelve Seventh Cavalry companies to battle the forces of three Native American tribes at the Little Bighorn. Legend has it that, when the smoke cleared, the only thing left alive from the five companies was a horse. The British Light Brigade should have understood their limitations before they charged and were wiped out by the Russians at Balaclava (the "Valley of Death"); the British and the French should have planned better at Gallipoli; Napoléon should never have invaded Russia and probably should have avoided Waterloo where his troops were outnumbered by the English together with the Prussians; the United States should never have supported the Bay of Pigs invasion—or the escalation of the war in Vietnam— without a better plan to win; the Egyptians and Syrians should have understood their vulnerabilities before they launched their ill-fated attack on Israel on Yom Kippur in 1973. HP shouldn't have bought Compaq (or Palm); eBay shouldn't have bought Skype; Google shouldn't have bought Motorola (although the patents certainly had high value). The list is long.

On Wall Street, on Main Street, and in the Marine Corps, before entering into battle, or a transaction, you must clearly understand your strengths, weaknesses, capabilities, and constraints. You must know what combination of skills and resources gives you a competitive advantage. You should know what it is that you do better than anyone else on the planet. Without that thorough understanding of your unique strengths and capabilities—and vulnerabilities—it is tough to know what actions are most likely to be successful.

Take Porsche, for example: In 2005, Porsche AG, the German auto manufacturer best known for its high-end sports cars, began buying shares in Volkswagen Group in an attempt to take over the much-larger carmaker. It was a battle between cousins: Wolfgang Porsche, who was the chairman of the Supervisory Board of Porsche, and Ferdinand Piëch, who was the chairman of Volkswagen. Both men were grandsons of Ferdinand Porsche, inventor of the original Volkswagen. By 2007 Porsche AG had accumulated more than 40 percent of VW's shares, borrowing billions and using complex derivatives to do so. Then they bought another 31.5 percent—all in an attempt to reach a 75 percent threshold that would give them control. Along the way they accumulated $20 billion of debt! When the global financial crisis hit in 2008, Porsche was hit with a double blow: sales plummeted, and the credit they needed to pay for the accumulated debt evaporated. Porsche's stock price dropped precipitously, and suddenly the company was in deep trouble. Piëch than turned the table on his cousin, as VW bought Porsche. Clearly, Mr. Porsche did not fully understand his own limitations and constraints—or perhaps he overestimated his strengths.

General Petraeus as well as Sun Tzu knew that the need to truly know yourself in depth—honestly—and to figure out what you can do better than others is a critical element to winning battles in war. It's the same on Wall Street as well as Main Street. You have to understand which of your strengths gives you an advantage you can leverage, before you can build on them, even before you engage in battle. Then, you must understand where you may be vulnerable—and be on guard.

We are in the business of helping people to buy and sell companies. It always surprises me when we talk with a CEO who cannot articulate how his or her company's strengths allow it to do something better than anyone else on the planet. I can for our firm. I simply don't understand the me-too company or the investment bank that is "almost" as good as the competition but less expensive. How do they differentiate themselves from the crowd? By their Rolodex? Bad idea. To be clear, most of them can talk about their strengths and weaknesses. Some say with pride that no one else does what their firm does in exactly the way that they do it—and that therefore their firm is unique. Okay, maybe that's true, in the same way that all children are unique. However, uniqueness alone doesn't confer strategic value, and it is strategic value that leads to demand. Your quarter-inch drills may be made of a different material from mine, for example. Maybe they have more or fewer twists. All of that may make my drill "unique" to me—and yours unique to you. It might be even more unique if mine were pink. But how do those attributes help you win battles?

"Chesty" Puller

In late November 1950, Colonel Lewis "Chesty" Puller, perhaps the most famous Marine ever, pulled off a feat that others had deemed "impossible." Days earlier, the armed forces of the United Nations—including units of the US Army and Marines—appeared to be on the verge of victory in Korea. Puller was the newly minted commanding officer (not yet a general) of the First Marine Division (the division in which I served decades later). He and his Marines had chased the North Korean forces deep into their homeland—closer and closer to Korea's border with the People's Republic of China. It looked as if there might be a chance to win the war quickly. Then, unbeknownst to Puller, the Chinese People's Liberation Army entered the war in support of the North. In quick succession, they attacked and overran South Korea's Army at the Battle of the Ch'ongch'on River, then decimated the US Army's Second Infantry Division on the UN forces' right flank. The UN Command retreated; the US Eighth Army retreated. On November 27, at the Chosin Reservoir on the Korean eastern front, Chesty Puller's First Marine Division, with about 12,000 to 15,000 men plus about another 2,000 to 3,000 soldiers of the US Army, found themselves fully encircled by more than 360,000 Chinese and North Korean soldiers. There was no one to rescue them. It was the depth of winter in North Korea with temperatures twenty-five degrees below zero. Puller's men were exhausted, cold, and vastly outnumbered. The rest of this story is Marine lore. Chesty refused to quit. On December 6, he led his men on a famous breakout. He maneuvered, took advantage of every opportunity, and fought his way to the sea. The battle lasted more than two weeks, in the freezing cold.

Puller knew that, as exhausted as his men were, they were better trained and better equipped—and their leaders had more relevant combat experience than their enemy. He used their superior skills, weapons, training, and experience to great effect. Along the way, the Marines and their UN allies effectively destroyed or crippled seven enemy divisions. Chinese casualties were estimated at 35,000 killed. Puller emerged at the port of Hungnam with his men, including all of his wounded, trucks, and equipment. The Marines lost 836 killed and around 12,000 wounded—mostly from frostbite. To reporters at the port he said, "Remember, whatever you write, this was no retreat. All that happened was we found more Chinese behind us than in front of us. So we about-faced and attacked." Puller was awarded his *fifth* Navy Cross.

Chesty Puller knew the strengths and weaknesses of his unit. He knew what they were capable of—and he knew where he was vulnerable. He knew which of his strengths could be leveraged and used that knowledge to lead his division to victory in a fight against an enemy that had defeated others—against odds some had called insurmountable, and in subzero temperatures. That kind of self-awareness of weaknesses and strengths that can be leveraged gives buyers and sellers a clear advantage on Wall Street and on Main Street. You must *know* yourself before you can act with confidence. You must know your which of your strengths and capabilities gives you that unique combat advantage—before you engage in battle. And then you must use them.

Tenfore

About a month after we formed Marlin & Associates, in early 2002, I had a conversation with Charles Jillings, an investor in European technology companies. He owned a piece of a UK-based company called Tenfore Systems, with which I'd had some dealings over the years.

Jillings was frustrated. He had been invested in Tenfore for years, but it was not paying off—the company was growing, but only slowly. It had entered into several conversations to sell, all to no avail. I offered to look into it further, but Jillings wasn't the principal shareholder, and those in charge had a banker that they liked.

Over the years we kept up with Jillings and with Tenfore as the company hired and fired several CEOs. Then, in 2008, six years after my initial contact with Jillings, and only a few months before the beginning of the global financial crisis, Jason Panzer, one of my partners, reached out to the latest Tenfore CEO. Panzer's timing was good because Tenfore's owners had recently concluded that they were ready to sell and were ready for a different banker. After some internal conversation, the owners of Tenfore asked the CEO to reach out to us.

The CEO, Gordon Bloor, was a smart, hardworking super salesman who had come up through the sales channels at a number of large European technology firms. He had been brought in four years earlier by the wealthy family that had funded Tenfore, with hopes of jump-starting a firm that had still shown more promise than growth. He had been enticed by stock options and his first shot at being the CEO of an independent company. He was at least the third CEO of Tenfore in less than a dozen years, however, and while progress had been made on some fronts, things still hadn't gone quite as well as Bloor or the owners had hoped. If the company was sold now at prices that Bloor believed reasonable, his stock options would likely be worthless and he himself would probably be out of a job soon after; that's often what happens to CEOs of acquired companies. Bloor's big career move in becoming a CEO looked as if it was about to become a bust, so as you can imagine, he wasn't exactly happy about having to deal with us.

Before we agreed to engage in this battle, we wanted to figure out Tenfore's biggest strengths and weaknesses. With that information, we could figure out what firms (if any) might find Tenfore to be *strategically important*—and why.

Tenfore's primary business was delivering real-time, enterprise-wide, desktop analytic software used by global traders of financial instruments. Most of its competitors were in Europe, a market in which it competed with much bigger companies such as IBM and SAP, and to some extent with the big providers of financial data such as Reuters and Bloomberg. Its principal customers were smaller banks, brokers, insurance companies, asset managers, and other financial services firms with limited budgets. Because of a prior CEO and a small acquisition, they had a number of customers in Germany, Luxembourg, Greece, and the UK. Even after spending millions of dollars on upgrading infrastructure, strengthening their research and development, improving operations, and building a better sales and marketing organization, they found their growth in revenue was still moderate. With so much money going into product improvements and infrastructure strengthening, virtually no improvement was made in profitability.

Bloor said to me, "Every year, we applaud ourselves for the four or five clear product enhancements that we introduced. We're pleased with ourselves—until we realize that the competition introduced forty product enhancements in the same year. It seems as if the further ahead we get, the further behind we are."

We asked Bloor about his strengths: What made his firm special or unique? Why did he believe that buyers would value that strength? Why did he believe that the company could in the future maintain whatever advantage it had?

We didn't particularly like the answers.

Know Yourself

Marines spend a lot of time ensuring that every Marine leader understands the strengths, weaknesses, capabilities, and constraints of his unit. Three of the eleven Marine Corps leadership principles embody this philosophy (know yourself and seek self-improvement; know your Marines and look out for their welfare; and employ your unit in accordance with its capabilities).

Bloor could articulate several aspects of his company that he considered to be strengths—reasons why customers bought Tenfore's products. But what convinces a customer to buy a product is often not the same thing that will cause someone to buy an entire company. Here were the four basic planks of his pitch:

First, Tenfore had a decade-long history in the industry. They'd learned what customers wanted (or at least some subset of customers).

Second, they had made significant investments in some pretty cool technology that gave them reasonably sophisticated desktop applications (although not the *most* sophisticated).

Third, they had several thousand end users who would attest to the product's roadworthiness. If you are selling a technology product to sophisticated customers, and they're using that product in production, it must work.

Finally, they were priced below the competition.

Bloor figured they could keep selling that unique combination for years to come—why not?

That approach sounded like potential trouble to me from a Marine's perspective. It didn't present any particular strength that could be leveraged—strong enough or unique enough to cause customers to come flocking, nor interesting enough to cause most potential buyers to be excited. Business graveyards are filled with the names of companies with long, illustrious histories that had made big investments and had many customers before disappearing: Pan Am, Eastern and TWA airlines; E. F. Hutton, Paine Webber, and Lehman Brothers; Amdahl, Atari, Compaq, DEC, Univac, and Wang computers; Blockbuster, and Wards; and dozens of auto companies—Studebaker, Nash, Checker . . . Oldsmobile, Saab . . . DeLorean . . . well, maybe not DeLorean—not that much history or many customers. But I could go on and on. Remember Zenith? How about Netscape?

The strengths that Bloor enunciated could be said of a number of other firms in the industry at the time: functionality that was "nearly as strong" as that offered by the larger vendors; "good enough" for some smaller customers; and less expensive. We didn't believe that it was enough to give them a sustainable advantage—not enough to make the firm strategically interesting enough for someone to pay a lot of money for it.

It wasn't unusual. We've realized many times that what management thinks makes their company cool (or not) doesn't match with our sense of what buyers would be interested in. We needed to look harder.

Bloor's explanation of the company's strengths also offered a potential explanation for why prospective acquirers had had so little interest in the company in the recent past. Bloor told us that he had once assumed that one of his direct competitors would buy the company just to cut out all the costs and retain the customers. A few years earlier he and one of his board members had approached several of these competitors. But they already had most of what Tenfore had and showed little interest in spending a lot of money to buy the company. For much less, they reasoned, they could just poach Tenfore's customers one at a time.

Strengths Only Confer Strategic Value
If They Help You Win Battles

Marines don't like to enter battles unless we believe that we can win. Similarly, I don't like to take on the sale of a company if I don't believe we are likely to be successful—we don't like to play Lotto: to take on an assignment and pray for good luck. It doesn't make sense for either us or the client. Once we are engaged, we work hard over many months. We stick with our clients through just about anything, but that means it's especially important that we choose our battles carefully. We don't think it's fair to ourselves or to clients to agree to guide them through a prospective sale if we don't believe that we have a high likelihood of success. I was now approaching an assignment to advise on a sale of Tenfore with skepticism.

Our one remaining hope with Tenfore was that we might be able to dig deep, ask questions, and see some strength that some set of buyers might find compelling—even if the company's management themselves didn't see it. It's happened before. When our clients have trouble seeing where unique strategic value lies within their firm, we believe that part of our job is to do our best to help them find it. It's the best way to prepare for the battle to come.

Not all bankers see this as part of their job. When I was at VS&A, for example, when advising a seller, we were told to present the company as it was. We'd never "look under rocks" and never offered forward revenue projections. It was deemed too risky for the bank and the client, and our job was to present the past and the present and let the prospective buyer assess the future after conversations with management.

But the Marine Corps Way is to be in control of the process. To gain control, we needed to help Tenfore know themselves better. We needed to help them find what we call their leverageable strengths; that is, strengths that can confer strategic value—strengths that may help some buyer to solve real problems that real customers have. (Being less expensive is just an added bonus.) If companies can't find that strength, we need to help them. So we set up a meeting and systematically drilled down at Tenfore.

We worked with the company to gain more insight into their market and market opportunity; their products and product plans; their intellectual property; their customer base; and their technology. We looked for nuggets of strength that they might have missed. For example, it'd be great news to hear that they had created relationships with a few big institutional clients that potential acquirers might covet. We've had that happen before. A company's products might be borderline to what an acquirer is interested in, but if the company is selling to big clients—the US Air Force or General Motors or Goldman Sachs—that can be enticing. Unfortunately, the situation at Tenfore wasn't encouraging.

We looked to see if their products incorporated some unusual and difficult-to-replicate features. We once had a Switzerland-based client called Brainpower that claimed such unique product capabilities as its key strength. They asked us to help them find a partner. When we asserted those product capabilities to a senior executive at Bloomberg LP, the large financial information and media company, he simply didn't believe us. He said that Bloomberg had been working on that capability for years and had been unsuccessful. He said that their team working on it was larger than the entire workforce of our client. He didn't believe that a midsize Swiss company he had never heard of could have succeeded. Once our client's technology team proved to Bloomberg that they had, indeed, solved the problem, Bloomberg quickly bought the company.

Unfortunately that did not seem to be the case here, either. We looked to see if Tenfore might have patents on their technology that would be of benefit to an industry participant. Again, no joy.

We asked about the owners' appetite to invest in new analytic tools that were in hot emerging areas. We didn't get a warm response. What about making a few acquisitions of their own first? Would they consider acquiring small companies with interesting technical capabilities, products, or geographic presence that could be added to those of Tenfore?

All these were nonstarters.

Tenfore's biggest strength seemed to be the combination of low price, reasonable functionality, and high switching costs. Once a client had bought Tenfore's product, it was expensive and time-consuming to switch to another vendor. For many clients that combination of low price and acceptable functionality was enough. Smaller competitors found the combination difficult to overcome—and larger ones largely ignored it.

We couldn't think of any potential buyer that would be excited to acquire Tenfore who could afford a reasonable price. A few smaller companies might possibly have an interest in taking over Tenfore's customer base if the purchase price was low enough or a part of a non-cash merger. But the small guys didn't have much money, and Tenfore's owners were not interested in a low price, much less a transaction that would require them to trade their illiquid control position in a relatively small company for an illiquid stake in some slightly larger but still small company. No thanks.

Not every company has strengths that can be leveraged. We wondered whether it made sense to try to help sell this company—we could see no way to position Tenfore as anything more than a commodity provider with an uncertain future. I was about to decline the Tenfore assignment, but then one of our people noted two interesting things about the company that had come out of our close look at the data they provided.

Finding the Pearls

The first thing that our people noted was that Tenfore was significantly more profitable than they had been reporting—at least from the perspective of a potential acquirer. That's because profit, by definition, is revenue minus expenses. Acquirers focus on the expense base that they will have going forward, not on the *past* expense base. Tenfore had incurred a series of expenses for the development and rollout of new technology, much of which was spent on third-party, outsourced software developers who were no longer being used. These projects were largely complete, and the company would not have those expenses going forward.

This was good news. Alone, it might not have been enough to make the company strategically interesting—but combined with the second thing we discovered, it could make a big difference in purchase price if we could find someone who was interested.

When we dug into their data, we found, second, that a fair portion of their top-line growth was coming from a product that Bloor and his team hadn't talked to us much about because the product had nothing to do with what they saw as their strength: their much-touted analytic desktop application software. Instead, this growth was from sales of real-time streaming market data that was collected from more than a hundred data sources from around the world. The purpose of the Tenfore "data service," as the company called it, was to pump data into Tenfore's core-enterprise analytic application. For them, it was like plumbing in a house—necessary, but nothing they'd ever thought of as a significant potential revenue source in and of itself. However, over the preceding five years, as the company had invested heavily in the technology behind this plumbing in an effort to gain a competitive advantage in analytics, a small but growing group of customers had asked to purchase just the data service—to power their own applications or applications developed by third parties. Revenue from the data service was several million dollars and was growing at 30 to 40 percent each year.

Tenfore had spent millions of dollars building state-of-the-art data centers to collect and distribute real-time data from major financial centers in Europe and the United States, and the company was opening similar data collection and distribution facilities in Asia. They had written their software code themselves, using the latest computer languages and approaches, all in an effort to bolster the speed and reliability of their analytic services. Apparently, along the way, Tenfore had assembled the infrastructure to create, distribute, and support a world-class real-time market-data product. Who knew?

Tenfore's data service was barely "productized." It had a price list, but scant sales literature and only a brief mention on the Tenfore Web site. And sales were not particularly large. But this product, while not unique, was unusual. Only a few firms in the world had assembled such a powerful network of data sources and could deliver the data as fast and reliably as Tenfore, and Tenfore's was the only one available for sale. It was a bright spot in an otherwise dull landscape. We started asking questions. The more we learned, the more excited we got. And the more excited we got, the more excited Bloor got.

We believed that we had at last found a strength within Tenfore that was strategically leverageable—something that we believed that multiple strategic buyers should find of value, if they understood it. Bloor realized that just maybe his stock options could be worth money after all.

Leverageable Strategic Value Is Not Always Obvious

As I mentioned, Bloor was nothing if not a good salesman, and he was smart enough to know that potential buyers, like the company itself, might not immediately recognize and value the attributes we were discussing. It was too easy for them to get lost in the weeds of past financial performance and the commodity nature of his principal products. He was right—even when we are dealing with potential buyers in the same industry, we always have to work hard to help them see how this opportunity may advance them toward their long-term strategic objective. Our job now was to work with Bloor to clearly communicate this leverageable strength—to help prospective partners see and appreciate Tenfore for what it was, as well as for what it could be. Otherwise, someone at the prospective partner may misunderstand or, worse, apply the Dilbert concept—anything I don't understand can't be all that difficult, and my internal IT guys can replicate it in six months.

It's All About the Future

Bloor now had more confidence in his company and its products. We had shown him that it was more profitable than he had realized, and that he had a unique, growing, and potentially strategically interesting product. Now we had to contemplate how a potential acquirer would see the opportunity.

In an earlier chapter we discussed the need to know the enemy—to understand the party on the other side of the table. One thing that sellers must know about buyers is that you are often asking them to trade certainty for risk—the certainty of staying in their safe home ports (conserving cash, stock, or debt capacity) for the risk of pursuit of an uncertain future. Before most sellers will commit to a transaction, they want a sense of what is likely to come in the future. They need to assess more than the past. They need to understand in detail where the journey is going and what they are likely to encounter along the way. They want more than conversations. They want to see detailed product plans, expansion plans, and management plans. They want to know where the technology is going and what the firm is doing to take advantage of it. They want to understand short-term objectives and long-term goals. They want to understand the size of the market opportunity and how competitors are likely to act. And they want to see bottom-up detailed financial forecasts that are logical and believable. To help buyers see those things requires that you know yourself—in detail.

We accepted the assignment to sell Tenfore, and for the next few weeks we worked with Bloor and his team to assemble the material that would show a prospective buyer what the leverageable strengths of the company were. The company developed projections for future products, markets, and potential revenue and expenses—that is always the company's responsibility, not ours—but we made sure that those projections made sense, and we challenged Bloor and his team to explain if they seemed too aggressive or too timid. (Could they really open up three new foreign markets in one calendar year? Had they fully accounted for the support costs?)

To get the best results, sellers must know themselves. They must have thought carefully about their sense of what that future can look like, so that they can share that vision with the potential buyers. It's not a guarantee; it's a projection—and we make that clear. But we know that it's a subject that every buyer wants to discuss. The projections for future product development, market penetration, or financial results of a company as a stand-alone may not always be rosy. Some companies have warts. Sometimes companies have capital or capacity constraints or other reasons why their growth will be limited—at least as a stand-alone. But to try to hide those warts or constraints is foolish, as most buyers will eventually discover them. Far better to identify the risks yourself and highlight the ways to mitigate them. Also, we didn't have to limit ourselves to portraying Tenfore's future only as a stand-alone; we could identify potential opportunities to increase revenue faster if it was combined with the right partner, as well as opportunities to reduce duplicated costs. It's all part of knowing yourself.

Resolution

Once we understood what particular strengths of Tenfore we wanted to emphasize, we needed to use that knowledge to identify potential acquirers. We looked for companies that were spending millions each year on buying similar real-time market data feeds from others—firms that might covet having their own captive proprietary global data service such as the one that Tenfore provided. Quickly we identified more than a dozen such firms around the world, in Australia, Canada, China, France, Germany, India, Ireland, Sweden, Switzerland, the UK, and the United States. We began reaching out. Several of the firms had built or were reselling desktop analytic systems that were conceptually similar to those that Tenfore had developed. Unfortunately, our timing coincided with the beginning of the global financial meltdown of 2008. Some bankers would have balked at taking a company such as Tenfore to market in this environment, and we discussed that formidable challenge with the owners. But they wanted to sell, and we now believed we had a company with leverageable strengths that would be of interest to some buyers no matter what the climate.

At first, it didn't look so good: more than half of the potential suitors dropped out almost immediately—either as a result of a retrenchment during the financial crisis or their inability to see the strategic value. A few of them told us that as a result of financial conditions, they weren't going to be buying anything in the near feature. But four firms continued to show strong interest. We worked with Bloor and his team to help each of them understand Tenfore's leverageable strengths and capabilities. Bloor tried to show each what made Tenfore unique in ways that would confer strategic value. We did our best to help each see why the long-term future would be bright (and the risks low) in spite of the current storm. We tried to show each how Tenfore might perform in *their* environment—as opposed to its old, independent one. That's the future we wanted the firms to be excited about.

Seven months after engaging us, in the heat of the global financial crisis, the owners of Tenfore completed its sale to Morningstar. The family investors behind Tenfore got the complete liquidity they sought, and Charles Jillings got to exit his investment at a profit. Further, the company's customers got a deep-pocketed new owner that wanted to enhance the service. Management and employees joined a company that valued their team and understood Tenfore's strengths, weaknesses, capabilities, and constraints. Bloor was thrilled.

Not only were his stock options now worth some money, but also the new owners needed him to join them and take on a larger role.

To win, among other things, you must know yourself well. And if you don't know yourself, find someone who can help you appreciate a different perspective. That's the Marine Corps Way.

7

Control the Timing

IMAGINE YOU FOUNDED A COMPANY, BUILT IT TO A VALUE OF MORE THAN $100 million, and then one day learned your partners had arranged to sell it out from under you. You had exactly three weeks to raise enough money to buy *them* out or lose your company—and to make matters worse, you had to do so over the Christmas holiday. Sound daunting? This extreme situation, which I'll describe, may not be an everyday occurrence, but on Wall Street and on Main Street we are often forced to address challenges in all walks of life in which "the timing couldn't be worse." From the perspective of the partners, however, the timing of this ambush was nearly perfect—they controlled it—and that's what this chapter is all about.

In chapter 1 I touched on the Tet Offensive—the massive, coordinated attack by the North Vietnamese on more than one hundred South Vietnamese cities, towns, and military bases, all while their assault on the Marine Corps base at Khe Sanh was simultaneously raging. During Tet, the NVA were able to seize several large cities—among them the ancient port city of Hue, which supported US Navy supply ships and sat on an important coastal-highway supply route. It was the beginning of the end of the war. The NVA had controlled the timing.

The US military controlled the timing in 1991, when the United States led a coalition of forces in an assault against the forces of Iraq in an effort to drive Saddam Hussein's troops from Kuwait—the country that they had invaded in August of 1990. Hussein could not have been surprised. He probably watched the buildup on CNN. The first American forces landed in Saudi Arabia shortly after Iraq's invasion of Kuwait in August 1990; British and French forces joined a month later. Naval bombardment and the air war didn't start until January 1991. The ground war didn't start until weeks after that. Unlike Syria's Bashar al-Assad who forestalled a US attack on his country in 2013 by working with Russia, Saddam had neither the political acumen nor the allies to forestall the US assault. And unlike Vietnam's General Nguyên Giáp who, in 1968, launched a preemptive strike against American forces, Saddam did not have the military capability to seize the initiative. Saddam couldn't prevent his rapid defeat.

Controlling timing also does not guarantee that you will win, as the Syrian- and Egyptian-led forces learned when they launched a surprise attack against the Israelis on Yom Kippur 1973—but lost the war. But it can materially improve your odds of success, especially when the battle is conducted in combination with the other principles I write about in this book.

Sometimes, controlling the timing is about anticipating the actions of others and not allowing yourself to be the victim of someone else's timing. (Some say that was the problem at Khe Sanh—where General Westmoreland waited for the NVA to mass for an assault and then paid for it in what was one of the bloodiest and costliest battles of the Vietnam War. We had let the NVA control the timing.)

Having someone else control the timing is also what happened to one of our clients, a Canadian firm called FMC.

FMC

On December 10, 2004, I received a phone call from the CEO of a publicly traded Canadian firm called Financial Models Company (FMC). The CEO, Stamos Katotakis, was locked in a struggle with his firm's cofounder, Bill Waters, and an affiliate of the Bank of New York. Stamos owned about 43 percent of the company; Waters owned around 23 percent; and BNY owned about 11 percent. The remaining 24 percent was in the hands of the general public. The company had been trading around C$9 per share when they were approached by a European company with an offer to acquire FMC for around C$12 per share. Waters and BNY wanted to sell; Stamos had a lot of plans for the company and wanted to run it for a few more years—at least— and then sell it for a much higher price. He was too young to retire and didn't relish the idea of working for some big foreign corporation. A discussion went on for weeks—with Stamos trying to convince his partners to stick with him for a few more years.

Under the shareholder agreement between the three partners, before any one of them could sell shares to a third party, that selling partner first had to offer to sell their shares to the other two at the same price and terms. The others then had three weeks to accept that price and terms and buy out the seller, or else the partners were free to sell.

The discussion had been going on for weeks, and Stamos should have been more prepared for what might come next. His partners served him with notice of their intention to sell their shares to the European strategic. That firm would then offer to buy out the public shareholders, and if successful, the combination would give the European firm control of FMC. To prevent this, Stamos would have to work fast. He wanted to know if we could help.

Normally it takes months to put in place a takeover of this magnitude. The financing itself usually takes sixty to ninety days. Then there are bureaucratic requirements. For example, under Canadian law if Stamos wanted to buy out his partners' shares, he also had to offer to buy out his public shareholders. That meant that he had three weeks to find around C$120 million (at the time, about US$92 million) and launch a public takeover offer, or he would lose his company. That was not only potentially expensive, it was also bureaucratically complex, as he had to line up financing and go through the legal challenges of the takeover. Among other things he would need to work with lawyers to prepare and send to shareholders a detailed legal description of his proposed deal—what the Canadians call a Take Over Bid (in English and French); he would have to obtain a recommendation from the company's board of directors; and wait for the shareholders to respond. Further, the law required that full financing be in place before the launch of the bid. Stamos had less than three weeks, over Christmas (when most banks or investment firms were not staffed for deals), to regain control of the situation or face the likelihood of being forced out of the company he'd founded. He had nothing lined up. He wasn't sure it could be done. His partners had controlled the timing.

The FMC situation brought out my combat instincts. I thought it was pretty clever of Stamos's "partners" (although not very friendly) to launch a war over Christmas. We worked nonstop over the weekend; prepared a summary of the opportunity; reached out to several parties that we knew; and somewhat miraculously actually found two private equity firms willing to work with us to consider financing the deal. We quickly answered a bunch of questions, provided documents, and negotiated terms with both—finally settling on one of them (ABRY Partners). Stamos found lawyers; everyone began working hard as the holidays approached. It was intense. We worked through Christmas. At the eleventh hour, Stamos was able to sign all the papers and accept the "offer" of Waters and BNY and launch the appropriate offer to the public shareholders. (The partners were surprised!)

I was pleased and proud and I wish that this were the end of this story, but it's not. The jilted European strategic sued to block our deal on a technicality; a judge temporarily halted our bid; and while we were waiting for legal resolution, a new US-based strategic, SS&C Corporation, took advantage of the timing, entered the fray, and upped the offer. With the court ruling uncertain, Stamos decided to capitulate. At least he would get a higher price for his shares. Waters and BNY liked the higher offer too. All three accepted the new deal. Did we win or lose?

Certainly Stamos's partners believed they had won. They had started this battle in an effort to sell their shares for a high price. By controlling the timing, they had put themselves in a strong position to achieve their objective in nearly all scenarios. Stamos's strategic objective had been to keep control of his company for another few years and then sell—and he lost, even though he was able to sell his shares for a higher price than he would have received had we not worked together. He was happier with that, at least. SS&C, the US company that masterfully took advantage of the tactical situation and made timing work in their favor, also was a clear winner. Stamos made money. We got to tout our involvement. But these other guys had been better masters of timing.

Taking Control Is Not About Waiting for Everything to Be Perfect

In the early phases of the American Civil War, General George McClellan led the Union forces. His troop strength was rarely less than twice that of the Confederate forces that opposed him, but McClellan was consistently reluctant to attack. He may have had his reasons:

avoiding unnecessary loss of life, seeking higher probability of success, etc. But his reluctance to commit to battle came across as indecisiveness and was frustrating to many, including President Lincoln. It seemed as if the timing was rarely right. Eventually, President Lincoln fired him. Controlling timing is not about waiting for the stars to perfectly align and having every single element in place. There are few guarantees in life; and there are no risk-free battles. Rather, winning the Marine Corps Way requires that you understand your strengths, weaknesses, capabilities, and constraints, and act decisively when the odds of success are sufficiently in your favor given your alternatives—and before you are overcome by events. You don't want to be a victim of timing; you want to be its master.

In an earlier chapter I noted two instances when I took control of timing: once when I launched my attempt to acquire from the Swiss company Telekurs AG, the assets that would form my tech company, Telesphere Corporation; and again when I decided to launch the effort to sell Telesphere—ultimately to Bridge Information Systems. In the first instance, I could clearly see what was likely to happen if I did not take control of the situation. Eventually, I would have been in a battle with my bosses in Zurich, and in all likelihood in a year or so I would have been out of a job—either because I quit in frustration or they fired me. I could see that I had a brief window, perhaps a year, to prepare; a year to figure out what transaction price, terms, and structure might make sense for me and for the sellers; a year to convince the Swiss to sell; a year to line up financing. But to make it all work, I had to act—to force an outcome. I could not wait passively for the Swiss—else I might wake up one day and find that they had sold my company to someone else.

You cannot assume the status quo will last forever. For me things worked. Had I done nothing—and wound up being the "victim" of the Swiss—I suppose I could have whined. But in reality I would have failed in a situation in which I could have controlled the timing.

In the Telesphere case, I could again see what was likely to come. If I did nothing, our financial backers weren't likely to be willing to finance the rapid growth that my partners and I wanted; the company would have stagnated; key people would have left; there would be another battle over strategy; and the value of my stock would slowly erode. I needed to take control of the timing; and again, I did. That's the Marine Corps Way.

In telling others the story of FMC, I sometimes contrast it with that of another Canadian client we had a few years later—where that CEO instead controlled the timing . . .

Subserveo

It started with a phone call from my colleague Tom Selby, who leads our office in Toronto. He had just talked with Shannon Byrne Susko, the CEO of a local software firm called Subserveo, who said that DST Systems, the big, Kansas City–based, multibillion-dollar-revenue, publicly traded (NYSE: DST) technology company, had come knocking on her door. They wanted to acquire her company, and they were not interested in participating in an auction. They insisted on a quick fill-or-kill process. Any auction would chase them away.

For her the timing was all wrong. It was too soon. Like Stamos, Shannon had big plans to grow her company and sell it in the future for a lot of money. Like Stamos, she was not ready to retire; and like him, she had little interest in working for a big corporation. But she had financial backers who controlled the firm, and they wanted to explore a deal. What should she do? Could we help?

In her mid-thirties, Shannon had been named one of Canada's top-forty people under the age of forty. She had been a CEO and cofounder of a company once before—Paradata Systems, which provided software allowing merchants to process credit card and e-check transactions securely. That firm had been sold to an industry participant, and Shannon had made some money from that sale, but not enough to make her independently wealthy. That's how she wound up at Subserveo, a fast-growing software company that had developed an innovative, automated way to help broker-dealers and investment advisers meet regulatory requirements for state and federal compliance and disclosure. This was to be her ticket to a bigger reward.

Unlike Stamos, Shannon very much expected to sell her company in the next four to five years. That was part of her long-term objective—and what her financial backers expected. She just felt that if she had a few more years to build the company, it would be worth much more than today.

What Are the Real-World Alternatives?

We talked to Shannon about alternatives. She told us that if she didn't sell to DST now, Subserveo's future was bright. The product was robust, and customer reception was strong. There were hurdles: competitive pressure was increasing from smaller firms as well as from a few larger software vendors that were introducing products with similar features. But she believed that Subserveo offered superior benefits, and they were nimble. Also, to keep growing at their rapid pace, the company would probably need to raise additional capital (shades of Telesphere). She had VCs knocking at her door, but she was in no rush. She wanted to get bigger before bringing in more capital, in an effort to minimize dilution of her equity—and to keep the new VCs from gaining control. (Her current financial backers controlled the company, but they were a pleasure to deal with. She was wary about other VCs.)

The list of entrepreneurs that in hindsight look brilliant for wisely waiting until the timing was right before they sold or took their company public is long. In July 2006, when Facebook was but two years old, Founder/CEO Mark Zuckerberg famously turned down a $1 billion acquisition offer from Yahoo! Less famous is how Zuckerberg carefully controlled the timing of when and how much money he did take from investors so as to minimize dilution of his equity; maximize value; and retain control of the company he founded. Starting in 2004, when he raised about half a million dollars by selling 10 percent of his company to angel investors ($5 million post-money valuation), Zuckerberg was careful to control each capital raise. Eight months later he raised another $12.7 million by selling about 12 percent of the company at a $100 million valuation; and then a year later he raised about $27.5 million—selling about 5 percent at a $550 million valuation—and so on and so on, carefully controlling the timing of each equity sale, always maintaining control of his firm.

And Yahoo! founders Jerry Yang and David Filo also famously turned down an offer from America Online—the giant of its era—for a million dollars each shortly after they had founded their firm. Again, less famous is their careful control of the timing of each step in their rise, starting with a decision four months after the company was launched to accept $1 million from Sequoia Capital for 25 percent of the company. They had not accepted the first offer of VC money to come along; instead, they interviewed dozens of firms. Yang and Filo believed that they had the leverageable strengths and capabilities to grow the company to be worth a multiple of whatever value they received—and they wanted to be sure that they remained in control of the company to realize the opportunity. Boy, were they right!

Of course, plenty of people take joy in pointing to firms they say should have taken advantage of timing to sell but didn't. But often these people are either referring to taking advantage of a strong market before it collapsed, or referring to people who simply bet wrong. Some people say that Groupon, the company that offers daily deals on the Web for such things as dining and retail, mistimed a market because they turned down a $6 billion offer from Google two years after they were founded. Today Groupon is worth significantly less than that, but hindsight is always twenty-twenty. For me, Groupon did take intelligent control of the timing of their battle. The company was young and growing at phenomenal rates when Google made its offer. Investment bankers had told the board that the company could, someday, be worth as much as $20 billion; and most important, lawyers had told them that the Google deal faced a significant chance of being blocked by the US Justice Department on antitrust grounds. The founders did evaluate their strengths and weaknesses and the risks of engaging with Google—and bet on themselves instead. That's okay. Their company is still worth nearly $2 billion—and it's still growing.

Perhaps a better example, or at least one that is more analogous to the situation that Shannon faced, is Friendster.

Friendster

About a year after I started Marlin & Associates, I heard about Jonathan Abrams, a thirty-three-year-old entrepreneur with one of the hottest companies in Silicon Valley. Before Facebook—before Myspace, before Google Plus or LinkedIn or any of a dozen other social media sites that fundamentally changed the way people interacted with each other—there was Abrams's company: Friendster. Its story has lessons for Shannon.

Friendster hit the market at exactly the right time. Four years after Pets.com and dozens of others like it had crashed, the Internet was back in vogue: eBay had revolutionized online auctions, Amazon was taking on the biggest retailers with online shopping; and Web sites such as Match.com and Yahoo! personals had reached new heights bringing people together.

As with a lot of great ideas, Abrams had built Friendster without thinking of it as a real business. One article claimed that he saw it primarily as a way to identify and organize his friends' attractive female contacts and improve his dating record. Whatever his motivation, Abrams was smart, and he got financial backing and guidance from three well-known angel investors—former Yahoo! chief executive Tim Koogle, former PayPal CEO Peter Thiel, and Google board member Ram Shriram—who collectively invested something like a million dollars in start-up funding.

Friendster was becoming huge—at least in terms of visibility. It had become the first social network to amass a million users, and then 3 million. Its popularity and impact seemed limitless. Abrams was profiled in dozens of top magazines and appeared on late-night talk shows. *Time* magazine called it one of the best inventions of 2003, and *Entertainment Weekly* named Abrams the Friendliest Man of the Year in its annual "Breakout Stars" issue. Friendster was the next big thing.

Success soon brought a fateful choice. Three months after he took in the million dollars from the angel investors, Google made an unsolicited offer to buy the entire company for $30 million—and at about the same time Kleiner Perkins Caufield & Byers and Benchmark Capital, two of the best-known venture capital firms in Silicon Valley, the same investors who had backed eBay, Yahoo!, and Amazon, offered Abrams $13 million in return for a minority piece of his firm—valuing his young company at more than $50 million. Further, in a fairly unusual tactic, they were willing to have almost $5 million of their money go directly into Abrams's pocket. (Usually VCs insist that their capital all go to help grow the firm.) But strings were attached to the offer. If he took the VC money, Abrams's ownership stake in Friendster would drop to about one-third; and the angel investors and VCs together would control his board of directors. Also, the VCs wanted Abrams to let a professional manager take over as CEO and bring in other professionals to address the company's technical issues. His angel investors advised Abrams to forget the quick payoff from Google. Instead, they told him, he should take the money from Kleiner and

Benchmark and let them help him build something amazing. It was all happening quickly. What should he do? "What now, Lieutenant?"

Take Control of the Timing

At this point Abrams had an opportunity to do what we were talking with Shannon about—take a Marine's approach to the situation: take control of the timing and evaluate your company's strengths, weaknesses, capabilities, and constraints in the cold, hard, uncompromising reality of the alternatives you have in front of you. And choose a direction before circumstances overwhelm you and the timing is taken out of your hands. But, to me, the choice of selling the whole company to Google versus taking $13 million from Kleiner and giving up control was false. There were alternatives, including taking less money from Kleiner—or from someone else— and retaining control.

It's true, as some have pointed out, that competition was rising in Friendster's space. A year after Friendster started, Myspace was launched, with music and other interesting features. But it was tiny. (Facebook didn't launch for another year after that.) And it's true that, as Friendster grew, its software needed to be modified to allow it to scale. But Abrams was a computer engineer by training. And he had time.

The mistake Abrams made was not in turning down Google or in taking money from VCs, it was letting others drive him into a false choice and a premature decision that resulted in his loss of control of his company. He could have controlled the timing of his capital raise better.

For Abrams and for most of us, $30 million is a lot of money to walk away from. If he was to do so, his downside risk was a lot higher than for the angels who had invested in his company. This was his life's work; whereas, for them, it was one of dozens of investments. They were risk-takers who could afford to lose. If he was to turn down Google, he needed to be in charge of the timing as to how much money the company took in and under what terms. The question was not only did Abrams believe in himself and his company to the degree that people such as Yang and Filo of Yahoo! had believed in themselves and their company, but also, could he control the timing of what was to come next?

Abrams turned down Google's offer and instead took the $13 million from Kleiner and Benchmark. In so doing, he lost control of his company.

It didn't take long for the wheels to come off the cart. Tim Koogle became interim CEO, soon replaced by Scott Sassa from NBC. Abrams found himself marginalized. The company hired several high-powered Silicon Valley professionals to spur growth and address the technical issues. Each of the new people had his own ideas on how to fix the company. Board meetings were reported to be acrimonious; management dysfunctional. The Web site experienced horrendous growing pains—it took as long as forty seconds for a page to load—an eternity on the Web. And it wasn't getting fixed.

In 2005 Abrams was replaced as chairman of the board. Two years later most of Friendster's users had quit in frustration or moved on to one of the other social media sites that were cropping up and doing a better job at meeting the challenges. Friendster was nearly dead. In a recapitalization, the company was valued at just $3 million. Abrams saw his equity stake diluted to about 4 percent.

Oh, what might have been! However, the lesson isn't that an entrepreneur shouldn't take risks, or that he or she must grab every possible opportunity to sell; and it's not that Abrams made a colossal mistake by not selling to Google. These are judgment calls that anyone can make in hindsight. They have little to do with controlling timing. (Although if Abrams had sold to Google for stock and held on to it, that stock would be worth something like a billion dollars today. I'm sure that hurts.) No, the lesson is about not being rushed prematurely into a battle on someone else's terms. It's about controlling the timing so that you can fight—and win—the battle that gives you the best chance to advance toward your long-term strategic objective. Abrams had alternatives. He could have sold less equity—raised less money now—held on to control of his company and been around to address the technical issues that eventually doomed the business. Perhaps Friendster would have been what Facebook is today. We will never know. Today, Abrams is no longer involved with Friendster, which rebooted as a small social gaming company focusing on the Asian market.

At Some Point You Have to Act

Shannon's situation was that DST's interest in acquiring Subserveo was on the table now (albeit without a specific offer or even indicated value). It was logical to assume that if Shannon did not sell now to DST, then DST would look for another way to meet their need, much as Google found another way to have a social media product after Friendster turned them down. Maybe some other buyers would be around in a few years, but Shannon could not assume that DST would be among them. And there wasn't time to run a full auction. Shannon had to act.

The timing may have been right for DST to buy Subserveo because they had a strategic need now and perceived that Subserveo could help them meet that need. But that was DST's reason to buy, not a reason for Shannon and her partners to sell. They had alternatives. Shannon could continue growing the company and go for a higher price in the future. She believed she was leading a company with great potential, and she was still having fun. But her resources were limited and there is always execution risk. Or she could try to sell small pieces of equity to raise capital as needed, much as Mark Zuckerberg did with Facebook. She did not have to sell to DST now—or ever. It's pretty easy for bankers to tell entrepreneurs that they should accept multimillion-dollar (or billion-dollar) offers. The reward for selling now is clear, whereas the probability of a significantly better payday is impossible to judge; and the downside risk relative to the reward is often high. But what should Shannon do?

The question for Shannon and for her investors was simply, is the timing right to sell now? Were Shannon and Subserveo in Jerry Yang's 1995 position with Yahoo!—with plenty of runway ahead of her? Or was she the CEO of the next Friendster—potentially heading for a cliff? Or something in between? There are no sure things. At some point you have to act.

Conclusion

In battles from Chapultepec (the "Halls of Montezuma") to the shores of Tripoli; from Belleau Wood to Iwo Jima; from Khe Sanh to Fallujah; from Ramadi to Helmand Province; and in many more, Marines have learned that controlling the timing of the battle can materially improve the odds of success. It's not about luck—good or bad. It's about recognizing and capitalizing on tactical opportunities when—and only when—you are ready, willing, and able to take advantage of those opportunities, and then actually pulling the trigger. It's also about not allowing yourself to be the victim of someone else's timing.

Shannon had told us that she and her investors always planned to sell the firm "in a few years." The market was strong now. Her firm was in a hot space and growing, and DST was here now. Her partners wanted her to explore a sale. But they were in no hurry. The price had to be right.

We advised Shannon to seize control of the timing of this battle. To start, we asked what price and terms would they be willing to sell the company for in a few years—assuming that the company continued successfully on pace. We asked them to be logical about the approach—not to pick a number out of thin air—and once they came up with a figure, we vetted it against several of the approaches that were discussed in the valuation chapter. We also asked them to be explicit about any other objectives beyond price, such as a continued role for management, employees, location, etc., as well as any constraints—and we asked, given that price and terms a few years from now, could they name a logical price at which they would sell now? We helped.

While this sounds like a reasonable approach, it is surprising how often it makes potential sellers uncomfortable to set price expectations without hearing from potential buyers. I get it. Sellers do not want to leave money on the table. But if you had a classic car or a home and were approached by some well-qualified buyer interested in purchasing that car or home, and you indicated a willingness to sell, the buyer would have a right to ask, how much? The same is true here. Further, if you insist that the buyer name a price first, you may trap the buyer and yourself in an untenable situation. They won't want to overpay. And with most corporate buyers, before they will put a figure on the table, that figure may have to be vetted by multiple senior people and possibly committees. Once that figure has been written down, it is often extremely difficult to get a buyer to double it. So, in situations like this, it is often to the seller's advantage to get your figure out there first. That's what I had to do in selling Telesphere. That's what Instagram did. And after much discussion, that's what Shannon did. It's all part of taking control of the timing.

Once we understood our client's desired price, terms, and other long-term objectives as well as their resources, strategic leverage, and the risk/reward trade-off of the alternatives, we telegraphed our expectations to DST, sent them some data on the company, and gave them a simple explanation for the price and other terms that Shannon and her investors desired. The owners were in no rush to sell. They believed that in a few years they could be worth materially more than our figure. They were willing to give up some of that future potential in trade for the certainty of cash now, assuming that they received their number. We told DST that if that price was too much for them, then we would part friends and see DST in a few years, when they would have an opportunity to participate in a more robust auction.

Shannon and her investors were not bluffing. They were willing to walk away from the table if they didn't get their price. The back-and-forth over the next few weeks was cordial, with negotiations and complications, but in short order the parties came to terms and the company was sold to DST.

Achieving objectives requires the ability and willingness to assess your leverageable strengths, understand the alternatives and the risks associated with each, and, most important, determine the course of action most likely to advance you toward your objective. Then if the time is right, act decisively. I don't know if the meek will inherit the earth eventually, but in the main, success does not come to the timid.

8

Negotiate from the High Ground

At about the same time that I enlisted in the Marine Corps, President Nixon's national security adviser, Dr. Henry Kissinger, was in Paris trying to negotiate an end to the war in Vietnam. He had been at it for almost two years. The United States had been prosecuting the war since 1962—trying to stop the march of communism in Southeast Asia and protect our South Vietnamese ally from their Soviet-backed North Vietnamese neighbor. There was little to show for the effort beyond fifty thousand American lives lost—and a lot more Vietnamese killed and wounded. The American people were fed up and wanted the United States to bring our soldiers home. Nixon had been elected in part on a promise to do just that—to get us "peace with honor." He and Kissinger were trying to find a way to get us out of the war without throwing our ally into the jaws of the North. After two years of negotiating, however, about the only thing the sides had agreed on was the shape of the table at which they would sit.

In October 1972 (just prior to the next presidential election), while I was at TBS, Kissinger and his counterpart, North Vietnamese Politburo member Le Duc Tho, reached a tentative agreement whereby the North would withdraw its troops from the South and allow free elections to take place; the United States would withdraw its troops from the country and cease bombing the cities and industrial sites of North Vietnam; and both sides would release prisoners of war. The tentative agreement didn't last. Talks broke off on December 13 and the United States resumed combat operations, including what was then called history's most concentrated period of bombing: American planes flew nearly twelve thousand sorties and dropped twenty-five thousand tons of bombs. In January 1973, Kissinger and Le again came to agreement. It looked a lot like the one I just described. Kissinger and Le were awarded the Nobel Peace Prize; although Le declined his—possibly because he knew that the North had no intention of withdrawing its forces from the South or permitting elections. They just wanted the United States to leave. Once the Americans withdrew, the North Vietnamese pounced and took control of the entire country.

The fact that negotiations with the North Vietnamese dragged on so long—and resulted in somewhat less than the "peace with honor" that President Nixon had promised the American people and a lot less than the victory that the South Vietnamese government wanted—has to do with an essential flaw that affects not just the grand chessboard of international relations but also your business.

My personal negotiating experience during my time as a Marine involved less consequential matters than those faced by Dr. Kissinger. I negotiated with battalion commanders who outranked me but whose cooperation I needed to get my job done; and with civil servants who ostensibly worked for me but over whom I had no power; and with civilian dockworkers and others whom we needed to help load and unload our equipment. What struck me about all of these negotiations was that they went well when you had an alternative and were therefore willing to walk from the table if you couldn't reach agreement. They failed when the other side perceived that they had you over a barrel and you couldn't walk away.

Nixon and Kissinger wanted the North Vietnamese to withdraw their troops from the South and to release our POWs. But America had limited negotiating leverage. (Without any, Kissinger would simply have been begging.)

Le Duc Tho had his objectives as well. He wanted the United States to stop the bombing. It was hurting his economy and killing his people. And he wanted to unify his country. For all that, he needed the United States to leave Vietnam. But Le had greater negotiating leverage than Kissinger, if for no other reason than that his political leaders, unlike those in the United States, were not in a hurry. They had been fighting the colonialists (first the French and now the Americans) for more than twenty-five years—since 1946—and were willing to continue fighting for another twenty-five years, if that's what it took to win. Le had what we called the high ground.

The *high ground* has two connotations in the Marine Corps. From a tactical perspective, it's the physical place you want to be in for combat, since it's a better place from which to both defend the low ground or to attack it. From the high ground, you can not only see the low ground and thus enemy movements better; you are also in a position to rain firepower down upon it. Mortars, artillery, naval gunfire, airpower, and more can all be used more effectively from the high ground. It's also more defensible than the low ground. Occupying the high ground puts you in a position to dominate the surrounding part of the battlefield.

Clearly, the *high ground* has a second, more ethical connotation too. It means to do the right thing. Ask any Marine about Marine Corps values, and several words will invariably come up: *honor, courage, competence, commitment, teamwork, and loyalty.* These combine to form an ethos that is also about the high ground. As the author Josh Rushing described in his book, *Mission Al Jazeera: Build a Bridge, Seek the Truth, Change the World*: "In the simple moral maxim the Marine Corps teaches: do the right thing, for the right reason. No exception exists that says: unless there's criticism or risk. Damn the consequences."

In Paris, where the Vietnam peace negotiations were being held, it appeared to me that Le Duc Tho held the negotiating high ground from multiple perspectives. First, he believed that the actions of the North were morally correct—he saw the United States as just another colonial power trying to extend its regional influence by propping up a corrupt government. Second, he saw the United States as acting immorally in killing noncombatants and burning villages in places such as My Lai; using the chemical defoliant Agent Orange; and bombing Hanoi. Third, he believed that the citizens of the South would fare better under the economic policies of the North than under the corrupt polices of the South, which he felt served only the wealthy and powerful. To some extent he must have seen his moral position as being buttressed by anti-American antiwar protests around the world—including in the United States itself. Le also undoubtedly knew that he had the high ground from another perspective: he had negotiating "leverage." He knew that Dr. Kissinger worked for President Nixon, who had won the election in part based on a campaign to end US involvement in the war; and he knew that the war was deeply unpopular in the United States.

What about Kissinger? He had a few bits of leverage too: Nixon wanted "peace with honor," but he also didn't want to be the first American president to lose a war since James Madison in 1812. He wanted a negotiated peace, not surrender. We had made security commitments to the South that President Nixon said he would honor; we were killing the NVA in the South at a much faster rate than they were killing Americans and South Vietnamese; and we were bombing the North's industrial capacity at an even more furious rate. Further, during this period Dr. Kissinger also pursued a policy of rapprochement and détente with the Soviet Union (principal backers of North Vietnam) as well as with China. If he was successful, it could, in theory, isolate North Vietnam.

All of the above factors gave Kissinger some negotiating leverage. But the North seemed patient.

I've told you to seize the high ground in any negotiation—when you can. But there may be times when the other person seems to hold a stronger hand. That's what this chapter is about. Over time, as my own negotiating experience increased, I looked back on Kissinger's negotiations and my own experiences and combined them with the Marines' values such as honor, courage, competence, commitment, teamwork, and loyalty and formulated a concept that I call negotiating from the high ground. It has nine rules:

Rule 1: Be Prepared to Walk Away from the Table

Early in my tenure as a company commander, a lieutenant colonel battalion commander (not mine, but one who clearly outranked me) ordered me to divert a convoy of six large cargo trucks under my command. It clearly conflicted with my orders—and my sense of what was morally right. I understood why he wanted my convoy. It was a Friday afternoon and he wanted to get his troops and himself back to base so that they could clean up and leave for the weekend. His own people had failed to schedule his transportation, and his Marines were stuck until something could be arranged. Taking my convoy was more convenient for him than waiting hours for alternative transportation. But we weren't in combat; we were in California. And I had other orders and other troops who had done the right thing and were waiting for those same vehicles. In a spirit of magnanimity, I offered to have two of my vehicles shuttle his people back to his base while the rest went on their assigned mission. (I was convinced that four trucks would be enough for the other job.) At first, the battalion commander thought that he had leverage over me because he outranked me. But I had the high ground. I was right; I knew it; and so did he. But whether he agreed or not, he soon realized that my offer was my only offer. If he declined, I was ready to pull the entire convoy and proceed as originally scheduled. I was willing to walk from the table.

It took him a while and he tried multiple tacks to negotiate with me: he wanted three trucks, not two. It didn't work. He soon realized that he still had no leverage. I was willing to take all my trucks and leave. At some point he realized that he was just begging. We agreed on the two trucks and all ended fine.

My Marine Corps peers and I understood, as did the North Vietnamese, that Dr. Kissinger was not willing to walk from the Paris negotiating table. His mandate may have been "peace with honor," but his marching orders were to get the United States out of the war—and everyone knew it. Le could walk from the table; Kissinger couldn't. Kissinger wasn't exactly begging, but his options were few.

I once took a course on negotiating at Harvard Law School, conducted by Roger Fisher and William Ury, authors of the megabestseller *Getting to Yes: Negotiating Agreement Without Giving In*. The thing I remember most about that course was the idea that you need to understand your "best alternative to a negotiated agreement" or BATNA, and, most important, that you need to manage the other side's perception of your BATNA. That was key. You have to be sure that the other side believes that at some reasonable, logical point you will walk from the table because some alternative is clearly superior to accepting their proposed solution. Then, they may come around to your way of thinking—or at least a compromise. But until they see that you are willing to walk, you are just begging. Kissinger understood Le's BATNA—it was continuation of the status quo until the North won. Kissinger's BATNA was less clear. That was a problem.

Rule 2: Know Where You Are Going

A few chapters back, I wrote about the need to keep your long-term strategic objectives in mind when doing business—and while pursuing deals. That concept is also essential for effective negotiating. Having clear objectives while negotiating allows you to know what lesser points you can give in on—and what you can't. I needed at least four trucks to accomplish my mission. I could give up two, but not three. The battalion commander needed to get his people back to base. He would have accepted one truck if that was all he could get. It was better than none. Between us we forged a compromise that allowed both of us to get what we needed most.

In chapter 6, I mentioned a software company called Brainpower, our Switzerland-based client that Bloomberg LP acquired. Brainpower's chairman, Rocco Pellegrinelli, knew exactly where he wanted to go: he wanted to sell the company; he knew that Bloomberg was the perfect acquirer for his people and his customers; and he knew what price and terms he needed to get approval from his shareholders. He knew what he could trade and what he couldn't. Bloomberg recognized that Brainpower had achieved mastery over a series of products that Bloomberg, for all their extensive efforts over many years, had failed to achieve. But they had their own constraints. They wanted to fold Brainpower's capabilities into their own. They wanted to keep some key people but not others, and they had a maximum price. Both sides knew exactly where they wanted to go. The deal was struck in days.

Conversely, some years back we had a client who was not sure what she wanted. She engaged us to help find a buyer for the company that she controlled. But when we brought several viable potential buyers to the table, she wouldn't give up on any detail of the negotiations. She wanted it all her way. She insisted on things that made no sense to me. (For example, she wanted an agreement that when she traveled, she would fly first-class, while the acquiring company only allowed business class and then only on flights longer than four hours.) You cannot complete negotiations satisfactorily if you insist on every single thing. Why would you even raise a point such as this if you really wanted to sell the company? I realized that selling her company was no longer her strategic objective; instead, she now wanted to remain independent. We discussed things, she agreed, and we moved on.

Like so many others, those conversations reminded me of the days when Dr. Kissinger was negotiating in Paris. The North Vietnamese knew precisely where they were going. They wanted to rule over a unified country, and as a start, they wanted the United States out of South Vietnam, and they were not going to settle for less. Initially, the US strategic objective was simply to stop Soviet influence and communist expansion in Southeast Asia and protect our ally. We also wanted South Vietnam to be allied with the United States; and we wanted air and naval bases in the region. To accomplish those objectives we entered into negotiations asking the North Vietnamese to withdraw their army from the South; release our prisoners of war; and be nice. We wanted "peace with honor"; they wanted total victory. They won.

Rule 3: Recognize When You Have Leverage—and When You Don't

When I negotiated to buy the assets that formed Telesphere, I had one key leverage point. I was the seller's best alternative, and I knew it. I was willing to buy the company at a reasonable price and provide the Swiss with continuing access to the data they needed, without asking for many representations or guarantees and without asking for a noncompete agreement. I had the high ground. I knew that if the Swiss didn't strike a deal with me, all their other options were worse. Meanwhile, I had viable alternatives. In fact, buying those assets entailed a risk that I was only willing to take so far. I used that knowledge and that negotiating leverage to my advantage when I could. Most bankers would agree with this concept. The trick is recognizing when you do have leverage and when you don't, and then looking for leverage points.

At the Paris peace negotiations, all of Dr. Kissinger's alternatives to a negotiated treaty were bad. If he failed to reach some sort of agreement with Le, it would mean either more years of a war that few in America wanted, or else a unilateral retreat. Both outcomes were untenable. But he couldn't say that. He had to make Le believe that continuing the war was preferable to the United States than complete surrender. Le had most of the leverage; but not all. And Kissinger wisely used the leverage that he had. When peace talks broke off in December of 1972, the United States sent a clear message to the North. We bombed North Vietnam with a vengeance. In about two weeks, over Christmas, the United States destroyed about 25 percent of North Vietnam's oil reserves and about 80 percent of its electrical capacity. That was Kissinger's leverage. Le quickly came back to the negotiating table. The United States wanted a deal. We wanted our prisoners back and we wanted a signed pledge that the North would withdraw from the South and allow free elections to take place. The agreement was signed within weeks.

Rule 4: Tell the Truth

This is a tough one—especially since, in retrospect, it's clear the North Vietnamese did not live up to the peace agreements that they signed in Paris, and fairly clear that they never intended to do so. For that matter, the United States told South Vietnam that we would come back into the war if the North violated the agreements. That didn't happen either. So, in spite of the way politicians would spin it, these accords were based on lies.

Let's start with a simple Marine definition of lying. Lying is when you assert something as fact or truth that you are pretty darn sure is not the case. If I say that I will be at your office at 8:00 a.m. when I know that I plan to be at another meeting at 8:00 a.m., it's a lie. If I say that our forces will pull out of your country once the peace accords are signed, when I know that my country has no intention of doing so, that's a lie. If I say that my country will reenter the war if the bad guys don't live up to their end of the bargain, knowing all the while that it will never happen, that's a lie. Too many horse traders, used-car salesmen, politicians, and bankers lie—or at least too many of them seem to have a different definition of truth from mine. For at least some of them, if some statement has any small probability of being true whatsoever—no matter how infinitesimally small—then it isn't a lie. It's something else. It's always possible that the other meeting will be canceled, in which case I may well be there at 8:00 a.m.—so it wasn't a lie, right? Wrong.

Marines aren't supposed to lie, most obviously because people who believe in honor, courage, competence, commitment, teamwork, and loyalty should have no need to lie. To some that's just naïve: "Everybody lies." But, from a negotiating standpoint, telling only the truth is also smart because the cost of getting caught lying during any negotiation can be devastating. Notwithstanding Vietnam, negotiations based on lies rarely work out well for the liar over the long run. The newspapers are filled with stories of banks paying hundreds of millions of dollars in fines as a result of lying about mortgage quality, interest rates, taxes, LIBOR rates, and a dozen other things. It amazes me that so few have gone to jail.

It's about trust.

A few years ago, we were advising Deutsche Börse, the big German stock exchange, as they were contemplating acquiring a European company. Negotiations were going quite well. We were the lead bidder and days away from completing the transaction when we started to suspect that someone on the other side of the transaction had fabricated financial projections. The more we probed, the less convincing the answers became. Finally Deutsche Börse walked away from the deal. It wasn't about the numbers; we could have adjusted those. It was about trust. Once Deutsche determined that they couldn't trust the people on the other side, they didn't trust anything they said. And without trust there would be no deal.

We once advised Standard and Poor's (S&P) on the sale of one of its divisions. We had a viable offer from a company that was backed by a private equity firm. The CEO told us that his company had no debt, could move fast, and had the backing of his PE firm for this deal. When those statements turned out to be untrue, and he also tried to lower the price on which we had agreed, we realized that the statements were just negotiating ploys. We were not only peeved; we lost all faith in anything he told us. We declined to move forward with him. S&P sold the unit to someone else.

Trust is key to negotiating—even among sworn enemies. Kissinger and Le should each have trusted what the other side would do after a peace accord was signed, before either would sign. Perhaps they did each know what the other side would in reality do—and signed anyway. I'll never know. The United States shouldn't sign a free trade agreement with another country without trusting that the other side will live up to its commitments. The trust between parties doesn't have to be absolute. It rarely is. We'll talk about the concept of "trust *and* verify" in a later chapter. But without some level of trust there can be no deal. And getting caught lying kills trust.

When I served with the Seventh Marines, the concept of trust was reinforced through "sea stories" officers told us about negotiating with villagers in Vietnam. Remember General Walt's desire that Marines in Vietnam live among the local villagers—protect them while searching for bad guys? The Marines had to negotiate everything from safe passage to information on the enemy's whereabouts to finding the best sources of water, and the officers imparted some basic wisdom to us—trust is everything. Any deal made on the basis of lies probably won't last and puts you at risk. For example, if you told a village leader that you would pay him some amount as restitution for accidentally killing his water buffalo, you had best show up the next day with the money, or you would lose his trust. And if that happened, you could wind up with poisoned water and ambushes.

Cheating is lying. Directly lying isn't the only way to ensure a failed negotiation—or at least a failed peace. Cheating or otherwise taking advantage of those you believe to be unwary or unsophisticated can be virtually the same. It's all too common among those few bankers, politicians, and horse traders who give the rest of us a bad name. It may work for a while, but it can ultimately come back to haunt you. Not long ago, the newspapers were filled with stories about an investment banker who was convicted of six counts of securities fraud by misleading investors about subprime mortgage securities that he knew were doomed to fail. There are too many examples like this.

Rule 5: Remember the Peace

The negotiations in Paris that ended the Vietnam War were not the first war-related negotiations to be held in Paris. After the end of World War I, representatives of more than twenty-five countries arrived in that city for a peace conference that among other things created the League of Nations—the predecessor to the United Nations. Another outcome of that conference was the Treaty of Versailles, which required the defeated countries to accept guilt for the war and to pay huge sums as "reparations." The Germans, whose country was already nearly destroyed, were assigned most of the blame and most of the burden. Many believe this national humiliation led to the rise of Nazism and then to World War II.

One key to successful negotiating is to recognize that the signing of the accords—whether peace treaties or transaction documents—usually marks the end of a phase, but not necessarily the end of a relationship between the parties. When the negotiations are over, life continues, and while the parties to the war or to the transaction may not necessarily have to live together, usually they don't want to reengage in combat (or litigation).

When I went to buy the assets that would form Telesphere, I knew that, when the deal was done, my former Swiss parent company would become my customer. We negotiated a deal that was fair for both sides, and we made commitments to each other that we knew we could keep. When I negotiated with my financial backers to get the best terms for management, both of us recognized that after the negotiations we were going to have to live with each other. In addition to the terms of the transaction, we structured an operating agreement that protected both sides—to the extent possible. Our reciprocal obligations were clear and reasonable.

When I went to sell Telesphere to Bridge, I knew that Bridge coveted what we had; but I also needed to be sure that my employees and customers would have a good home after the negotiations were done. Bridge made commitments to me that they kept—and vice versa.

When General Ulysses Grant, commander of Union forces during the Civil War, negotiated peace with Southern general Robert E. Lee, Grant agreed to let the Southern officers leave the battlefield with honor—allowing them to keep their horses, baggage, and sidearms—and return home.

The smart negotiating tactic (notwithstanding Dr. Kissinger and Mr. Le) is to follow four simple rules:

- Remember that as peace follows war, life will be better if you plan to live in harmony after the deal with your former adversary.
- Treat the other side with respect and let them leave the negotiating table with their honor intact—and insist that they treat you with the same respect.
- Don't make promises that will be challenging to keep.
- Don't accept promises or conditions that will be challenging for the other side to meet without some sort of fallback mechanism.

At the end of World War II, Americans and our allies understood all four of these concepts when accepting the surrender of the Japanese. We agreed to let them keep their emperor and "maintain such industries as will sustain [Japan's] economy." These commitments allowed the Japanese to retire from the battlefield with some honor intact; and also we promised that "the occupying forces of the Allies shall be withdrawn from Japan as soon as these objectives have been accomplished and there has been established, in accordance with the freely expressed will of the Japanese people, a peacefully inclined and responsible government."

Rule 6: Negotiate Big Things Before Little Things

A few years ago we were working with SWIFT, a big European financial services company, helping them to evaluate a potential acquisition. The seller was represented by a competent investment bank, but the CEO of the selling firm would regularly attempt to negotiate directly with the CEO of SWIFT. (Usually that's a bad idea.) Before the selling CEO was willing to discuss the big picture of whether the two companies would fit—or whether there was a common strategy, much less agreement on a purchase price—the selling CEO wanted to negotiate a host of other things. While these were certainly important to him, they were not on the critical path to determining if the basic framework of a deal could be reached. Included were such things as new offices to be opened if SWIFT was the acquirer, and the dollar (euro) amount of investments to be made in specific product lines, etc. I understand these things were very important to the CEO. Negotiating the location of new offices makes no sense if there isn't going to be a deal at all. First things first.

The more the CEO pushed for commitments on these other things, the more uncomfortable SWIFT became, until finally they backed away from the deal completely. (If I had been the CEO's banker, I would have been apoplectic.) We never got to a final price. It again brought me back to the negotiations in Paris.

For months, the Paris peace talks were stalled because the parties couldn't agree on what kind of table to be used at the conference. The

North wanted a round table at which all parties would be equal. The South Vietnamese wanted a rectangular table with the North Vietnamese government on one side (without the Vietcong, whom they refused to recognize), and the United States and the South Vietnamese on the other side. International diplomatic negotiations are tough and full of symbolism. I get it. But if parties really want to come to an agreement, they need to find ways to solve these issues and move forward to negotiate the big things first. In this case, the real message was that neither side was in a hurry to come to agreement. If they had been, the leaders would have sat in a room and hashed out an answer in a few hours—at most.

Negotiating small things first is a good way to stall agreement. (See Rule #2.) And sometimes it's a good way to kill deals. Negotiate the big things first.

Rule 7: Don't Bully

When I was first commissioned as a Marine officer, I observed that a few of my fellow second lieutenants seemed to believe that their new gold bars gave them the ability to force junior enlisted Marines to do things just because they'd issued an order. They tried to use bullying to get their way. Having spent some years as an enlisted Marine before becoming an officer, I was well aware that even in the Marine Corps getting willing cooperation is far more effective than bullying.

For eight years, the United States tried to bully North Vietnam into retreating to its borders. We had been bombing the country continuously since 1965, when President Johnson had approved Operation Rolling Thunder. By the time of the Paris talks nearly a million Vietnamese had been killed. It didn't work—just as the German attempt to bully the British into surrendering by bombing London during World War II didn't work.

We see buyers and sellers try to bully each other all the time. When the bullying negotiator has his bluff called, even if he doesn't lose the deal, he loses credibility and negotiating leverage. Bullying rarely works; it just makes people mad. Kissinger in Paris had to deal with that fact.

Rule 8: It Is Personal

In 1982, delegations from the United States and the Soviet Union were at an impasse over a nuclear arms reduction treaty. According to press reports, during a break, the two lead negotiators went for a walk in the woods, during which they talked about their personal deep, shared interests in peace and security. This mutual understanding allowed them to break the deadlock and move forward.

Throughout much of the past thirty years of negotiating, I can't tell you how many times I have heard someone on the other side of the negotiating table say some variant of "It's not personal, it's just business." It's a common philosophy on Wall Street, in corporate boardrooms, and at political caucuses. And I get it. The American and the Soviet negotiators weren't going to make or lose any money, prestige, or power based on the outcome of the negotiations—but then again, it was in their personal interest to reduce the threat of nuclear war. Mine too.

When negotiating, it is smart to be dispassionate—to keep your long-term strategic objectives in mind. However, in many cases, the outcome of negotiations may be extremely personal to some of the people at the table. Their livelihoods, careers, finances, reputations, and legacies, as well as those of people they are close to may be at stake. It can significantly increase the probability of successfully reaching agreement if you can also understand, appreciate, and take into account the human implications of what you are trying to achieve. It certainly helps if you keep in mind the wants, desires, and personalities of the individuals on the other side of the table. It may be business, but it's not always "just" business—often, it's also personal.

In Rule 4, "Tell the Truth," we talked about the need for trust. But this is different. It's not about telling the truth, it's not even exactly about trust; it's more about empathy. Some of the most poignant stories I heard in the Marine Corps were told by lieutenants and captains who had negotiated with village leaders in Vietnam. To them, each of those agreements required understanding the wants and needs of the other side.

When I was divesting D&B's three businesses in South Africa, emotions were running high, as the locals that we worked with and I negotiated with (all white) saw the rest of the world condemning and abandoning them. Their country was in turmoil. Many of them had seen the devastation that came to Rhodesia (now Zimbabwe) as it went through its own turmoil less than six years earlier. (Some of them had lived it.) The UN had passed resolutions condemning the minority white rule; economic sanctions applied on Rhodesia by Western countries combined with guerrilla warfare had led to the end of that minority rule and a transfer of power; many of those in Rhodesia with money or education fled; the economy collapsed; chaos ensued. Now, similar economic sanctions were being imposed on South Africa; the UN had passed resolutions condemning the minority white government; guerrillas were bombing government buildings; and many of the most educated and moneyed were leaving and so were American companies. I was representing one of those American companies, and sometimes I could feel the anger and frustration in the air. I was on one of the last South African Airways flight from South Africa that was permitted to fly into New York before sanctions banned them. It was the last flight for the crew on our plane. The flight attendants were in tears. To them, it was all very personal.

Saying that things are personal is not the same as saying that you must be best buddies with the people on the other side of the table. Usually that's not feasible. It's not even necessarily about establishing a direct personal connection—although that certainly can help—and it doesn't mean that all negotiations must be held in person. For many phases of a negotiation it is easier and smarter if the principals are not in the room. Often, underlings (such as we bankers) can negotiate in ways that principals can't. If we lose a point, the principals can always overrule us.

So what, ultimately, does it mean when I say it's personal?

When I negotiated with the Swiss to buy the assets to form Telesphere, none of the people with whom I was negotiating were my close friends. I had never been to their homes, and they had never been to mine. But I knew what their issues and concerns were. I knew that none of them personally would benefit or be harmed financially whether or not the deal happened. Their bonuses would not be one cent higher or lower no matter how much I paid. But failure or a bad deal would not be career enhancing for them. I understood that for them the outcome was personal. For me and for my managers, the negotiations were even more personal. If the negotiations failed, we might see our company sold to some large corporation, and that meant an uncertain future. And if we did buy the company, it could still result in a disaster that could leave us without jobs. It was business—and it was personal.

On Wall Street and in corporate boardrooms, while negotiators may represent their organizations, people negotiate, not their institutions. If we don't understand what motivates—and frightens—those people on the other side, it will be more difficult to reach agreement with them and vice versa

Rule 9: Take Reasonable, Defensible Positions

The high ground is defensible; it's a good place to be in war. Over the years I have figured out that taking reasonable, defensible positions is also a good negotiating tactic.

In the 1950s, North and South Vietnam were separated by an area known as the demilitarized zone (DMZ)—an area about two miles wide on either side of the Ben Hai River, which ran roughly east-west from the Laotian border, across Vietnam, to the South China Sea. Early in the peace negotiations with the North Vietnamese, the United States pushed for all sides to restore the DMZ as the "first practical move towards peace." It sounds good on paper, but in reality the move would have affected the North much more than it affected the United States. They had troops in the South; we didn't have any in the North—although we were bombing the North with some regularity. The position was one-sided—and was never going to happen. Then the talks stalled for months as the other party made its own one-sided demand—insisting that the United States must cease all bombing of the North before there could be peace negotiations. It was the biggest single piece of leverage the United States had, and that wasn't going to happen either—at least not then.

I am no longer surprised by negotiators who start out with unreasonable positions—those that the other side are not likely to accept—expecting a counteroffer that will be more shaded in their own direction than would otherwise be the case. I know too many horse traders, politicians, bankers, and lawyers who like to play this game. They demand that something to be done in three days, anticipating that the other side will ask for sixty and they will compromise at thirty; or they ask for a $1 million, expecting that the other side will offer $5,000 and they can compromise on $20,000. The request for three days or $1 million seldom has any real logic, other than the random extremeness of the position. It's not defensible and it rarely works with sophisticated negotiators.

I am well aware that in 2002 Daniel Kahneman won the Nobel Prize in Economics for his work with Amos Tversky (who had died before the prize was awarded) on a form of behavior theory called *anchoring* that argues that in the absence of other guideposts, people are significantly influenced by suggested reference points (the "anchor"). It's true. We regularly suggest value ranges to potential buyers of our clients' firms. But anchoring works best when the guidelines are reasonably fact based or in the absence of other guideposts. It also works great when both sides know the game. It may even work for a rug merchant in the bazaar who starts with an asking price that is six times too high—hoping that the unknowledgeable buyer will settle for half. For more educated negotiators, however, setting unreasonable anchors more often just causes the other side to respond in kind. They offer one-third of the true value of the rug. This form of gamesmanship can be fun in bazaars if you know what you are doing. But on Wall Street, in corporate boardrooms, and in politics, setting unreasonable anchors can harm your credibility. Even if you win this round and take advantage of some unwary soul, the tactic may well come back to bite you later. It isn't necessary.

Taking reasonable and defensible negotiating positions is the essence of negotiating from the high ground. It encompasses several of the principles listed above (don't bully; tell the truth; remember the peace) but goes further than any of them.

Earlier, I mentioned negotiating with Bloomberg LP, the big financial information and media company, on the sale of Brainpower, the Swiss software company. I liked Bloomberg's approach to negotiating. They didn't stake out unreasonable positions and wouldn't accept any. After a lot of discussion on other topics, their lead negotiator said, name your price. If it's reasonable, we'll agree; if not, we'll walk away. They told us not to expect them to present a counteroffer in an effort to meet someplace in the middle. The approach forced us to be reasonable. We got the deal done.

Lee's terms of surrender to General Grant were anything but random. Lee offered to provide Grant with lists of his officers and men and promised that the officers would "give their individual parole not to take up arms against the government of the United States," and that "each company or regimental commander [would] sign a like parole for the men of their commands." Lee offered to give up his "arms, artillery, and public property." But he insisted that his officers keep their sidearms, private horses, and baggage and be allowed to return to their homes. Lee knew that this was the least he could get that would convince his men to obey and go home. They were not likely to surrender if they were to become prisoners of the North. Lee's position was logical and defensible. Grant must have recognized that he could not ask for more. He was wise to accept.

What do you do if the other side starts with an unreasonable demand?

A Lesson Learned Again

I started my firm in early 2002, and the first few years were pretty lean. When I got married in September 2004, money was tight. My wife had to decide between keeping the wedding dishes and painting the house. (She chose to paint.) But by the end of 2004, things were looking brighter. We still hadn't made much money, but we did have a growing roster of clients. One of them was a London-based technology company called Beauchamp Financial Technology.

Beauchamp had developed a suite of products to meet the unique reporting and management needs of alternative investment managers (hedge funds) around the world. In only a few years the firm had garnered well over a hundred clients (mostly in London, New York, and Hong Kong), who managed close to 5 percent of all fund assets under management globally. The company had initially been funded by the two cofounders, Bruce Mennell and Stuart Farr, and later took in capital from Goldman Sachs and one of George Soros's investment funds. Stuart and Bruce had seen the company's fortunes rise sharply in the late 1990s, then nearly get crushed with the tech market crash. They both were young—in their early forties—and they were not looking to leave the business, but the crash had scared them. They had been at this for some time and had never been able to take out much cash, and now the company had come back strong over the past two years and they were ready to de-risk. Goldman and Soros were happy to sell if that's what the cofounders wanted. We were engaged to advise them.

After doing our homework, putting together materials, and preparing the principals for what was to come, Paul Friday and I reached out to about twenty prospective buyers in the United States and Europe: We talked with both financial sponsors who might invest in the company as well as to strategics. Ultimately ten firms indicated preliminary interest; eight of the ten came to management meetings in London and New York, and ultimately four strategics submitted nonbinding offers, two of which were clearly superior to the others. (For different reasons including value expectations, all of the pure financial investors dropped out.) We tried to get the other firms to increase their bids, but it wasn't going to happen. So we focused on these two.

The two highest offers were from publicly traded, multibillion-dollar technology firms. One was based in the United States and the other in France. Both were acceptable buyers to Stuart and Bruce as well as to their investors. Both offered cash up front plus the potential for additional cash over a few years based on future performance (earn-outs). Neither firm offered enough cash up front to excite the sellers, but the combination of upfront cash plus the earn-out brought the total price well into the range that the owners had previously defined as fully acceptable. And they wanted to sell. They knew their strategic objective.

For the next few weeks we allowed both firms to conduct due diligence reviews and refine their offers. Finally we picked one to negotiate final terms with—the American firm—and entered into exclusive negotiations with the intent of completing the transaction in about a month. A big part of the reason for selecting the American firm was that Bruce and Stuart had developed deep respect for that firm's UK country manager, with whom they had the most dealings. (It was personal.) The cofounders also weren't sure that they wanted to be owned by a French firm, although they did get along well with that firm's chief negotiator. Goldman and Soros were content to let the cofounders choose the buyer.

Trouble began almost immediately as it became clear that the American firm felt no urgency. A never-ending series of requests came for information. Each time we provided information or answered questions, long periods of silence followed, and then more requests would come. The process dragged on for two months before we got a draft purchase agreement, and it did not reflect our nonbinding agreement. (They were not taking reasonable positions.) We had agreed that our exclusive period to deal would automatically continue until one party notified the other of its intent to end it. The American firm made it clear that if we ended it, they would walk away. (Another extreme position.)

For another month we tried. On several occasions, we reached "tentative" agreement on some point with the UK country manager, only to later be told that "corporate" back in the United States had turned down the agreement. Sometimes they came back with a counterproposal (often unacceptable); sometimes they didn't even bother to make one. Unfortunately during this period, with Bruce and Stuart focused on the negotiations, several expected sales contracts slipped and Beauchamp missed its quarterly revenue forecast. The cofounders continued to believe that they would sign the clients and make the forecast numbers for the full year, and they believed that their prospects for the earn-out period looked quite good. However, "corporate" didn't like the miss.

A week later the American firm notified us that they were shifting about 20 percent more of the purchase price from the upfront amount to the earn-out. There was no discussion. Stuart and Bruce were not pleased. I've always believed in negotiating from the high ground, and in part that requires us to take reasonable positions too. So, about a week later we all flew to the US headquarters of the company for what we expected to be the final negotiation. The American CEO, who I can only assume thought of himself as a clever negotiator, started the meeting with a lecture on how lucky Stuart, Bruce, and their team would be to join such an august firm as his. Then he told us that the price, terms, and conditions that he and his team had put on the table were nonnegotiable. A few times Stuart and Bruce tried to interject their views, and the CEO totally ignored them. A couple of times I tried—with a similar result. It was insulting.

Maybe for the CEO this was "just business," but for Stuart and Bruce this negotiation was all quite personal. They had spent years building this business. This was quite possibly their one shot at getting a payback from all that time and effort. This would be the home of employees and customers that they had brought into the fold. After the deal was done, they and their employees and customers were going to have to live with the new owners. Yet, Bruce and Stuart faced real risks in ending the exclusive dealing period. Not only was this the best price received, it was the only deal on the table. We had not communicated with the French firm (or any other prospective purchaser) for more than three months. They had no idea that Beauchamp had missed their quarterly numbers. We had no idea if they remained interested in acquiring Beauchamp. And we had been clearly warned that if we pushed back, much less ended the exclusive dealing period, the American firm would walk. We could wind up with no deal at all.

I don't take well to being bullied, and this guy was a classic. Had this been my company, I would probably have taken his head off (metaphorically). I would have walked away on general principle. But this was not my company. I was the adviser here; I needed to remain calm until I could talk to my clients and see what they wanted to do. So we adjourned. Stuart and Bruce then asked for my advice.

Conclusion

I'm pretty sure that most bankers would have advised Bruce and Stuart to remain calm and let them try to work something out in private with the firm. I have given similar advice during moments of stress. Most bankers would have done what they could to preserve the deal. It's part of our job description. The American firm was a large and credible buyer and had every reason to make this acquisition into a success. The price was still fair, and as the American CEO pointed out, if Beauchamp achieved their full-year targets, they would receive the same money as previously agreed. Further, we had no credible backup buyer. If this deal blew up, there might well be no deal, and hence no fee for us. And we were hurting for money at this time.

I thought about those factors, and I also thought about my feelings when we were contemplating a second round of negotiations with Telesphere's financial backers to add capital to grow the business.

In my career, I have negotiated a lot of transactions, but no others were as intense or personal as the negotiations in my buying the core assets that formed Telesphere, my first company, and then negotiating with my financial backers, and later negotiating the sale of Telesphere to Bridge. Something about its being your own money concentrates the mind. Not too many bankers that I know have had that experience—negotiating representations, warranties, indemnification, price, and other terms that they would personally have to live with for years to come. I carry this powerful experience with me when advising others.

I told Stuart and Bruce that much as I had eventually come to distrust the financial backers of Telesphere, I now distrusted the CEO of the American firm trying to buy Beauchamp even more. I saw him as a bully. He acted as if he had all the leverage. I clearly saw that if he could take advantage of that leverage, he would, every time, regardless of the consequences to the peace that should inevitably follow this battle. While he may not have outright lied to us, if this CEO acted this cavalierly toward Stuart and Bruce before the deal was signed, how would he and his team act with them after the deal was done—when the cofounders needed some degree of cooperation to achieve the potential earn-out? There's an old expression: "Fool me once, shame on you; but fool me twice, shame on me." We had been fooled by this guy once. How could Stuart and Bruce trust his company to live up to any agreement we reached if there was any wiggle room whatsoever? I couldn't.

I told them that if it were up to me, I would walk from the table. They agreed. A few months later we got a deal done with the French company.

9

Seek Foreign
Entanglements

ABOUT A YEAR AFTER DR. KISSINGER AND LE DUC THO SIGNED THE PARIS
Peace Accords, I was in the Far East with the Marine Amphibious
Unit. The United States had largely withdrawn its military from Vietnam. But for the South Vietnamese, the war remained hot. The NVA
were marching toward Saigon. We cruised the South China Sea and
the Western Pacific in case we were needed. We also spent some time
in Okinawa, Hong Kong, Singapore, the Philippines, and several
other interesting places. In August, we headed to Japan. We dropped
anchor near the city of Yokosuka, about an hour by train from Tokyo.
It was my first visit to Japan. I was fascinated.

The area around Yokosuka reminded me of some parts of the US
Midwest, with patches of industrial centers interspersed among farms
and small villages. Some of the office buildings seemed as if they were
still rooted firmly in the 1950s, with cubbyhole offices, mounds of paper piled on desks, and old-fashioned methods—including abaci! But
Japan's capital city felt quite modern, with high-rise office buildings;
Frank Lloyd Wright–designed hotels; eight-lane superhighways; sleek
restaurants and fashionable shops; and leading-edge electronics. Tokyo
moved fast—much like New York City.

This was by no means my first international trip. I had traveled
throughout Western Europe, including a brief stint visiting the Royal
Marines in the UK, and of course many ports of Asia. But Japan was
different. Little English was spoken in Tokyo and virtually none outside the city's center. Certainly no one I met near Yokosuka spoke
English, other than a few workers on the base—very few.

We were in Japan on the anniversary of the US bombing of Nagasaki. Americans were not always welcome everywhere. The guidance we got from our ship's captain at the time was minimal: keep a low profile (no uniforms off base); respect their culture (take your shoes off when you enter temples); behave as you would expect a visitor to behave in your home—because you are a visitor in theirs. He suggested learning some key phrases and admonished that if we got in trouble with the law, we would be subject to Japanese justice and should not expect the United States to save us. That was about it. But it was enough to keep most of us out of trouble—most of the time. I had quite an enlightening experience and wound up going back to Japan several times while a Marine.

Marines spend a lot of time overseas for at least two reasons: first, because our role is often to project American military force overseas— whether to protect our country's own interests or to defend those of our allies; and second, because if we do have to fight, our country would prefer to take the fight to someone else's soil, rather than fight on our own. Whatever the rationale, since we don't know where the next adversary may be, we must be prepared to fight anywhere. That's why we refer to Marine air/ground units as expeditionary forces. In my ten years as a Marine I worked with military (and others) in a half dozen countries. When I was working on the First Marine Division G3 (Operations and Training) staff, the commanding general gave me the additional responsibility of official liaison to foreign military officers who visited and trained with us. As preparation for this role, the Marine Corps sent me to a school run by the Foreign Assistance Office of the State Department to learn a little about diplomacy.

When I left the Marine Corps for a job at D&B, I found another organization that believed strongly in foreign entanglements. D&B had developed a long-term strategic goal of becoming the world's foremost provider of business-to-business information. To accomplish that goal, D&B needed to establish itself in each of the world's major financial centers. My boss, Dave McBride, was charged with leading that effort operationally—I led strategy and m&a.

Dave was never a Marine, he never served in uniform at all, but he understood the ethos and he liked to hire former military officers. He was responsible for managing everything that D&B had in more than a dozen countries, which included at least a half dozen major business lines, including D&B's flagship credit information business, its Donnelley Marketing business, its credit collections business, and more. As Dave's Senior VP for strategy and m&a, I worked with case teams from the strategy consulting firm Bain & Company to formulate and implement a strategy that would get us to that leadership position globally. We made great progress in many countries, but Japan was the big one that eluded us. It was proving to be a challenge, primarily due to a culture that I was just beginning to understand.

TSR

D&B had a business arrangement in Japan with a company called Tokyo Shoko Research (TSR). If a D&B client needed a report on a Japanese firm, we would buy it from TSR. Similarly, if TSR had a client that needed a report on a firm from anywhere else in the world, they could buy one from D&B.

We liked and respected the people of TSR. But our business with them was fairly small and not growing. TSR wasn't selling many of our reports on non-Japanese businesses. And D&B clients didn't particularly like TSR's reports on Japanese firms. While the reports were lengthy and looked comprehensive on the surface, they often lacked the kind of hard financial data that our clients were looking for. Further, they were too expensive for many clients. Meanwhile, the market seemed to be huge. We believed that TSR's product and sales practices had not kept up with modern times, but they were not particularly receptive to our ideas on how to do things differently. I began to see that many Japanese companies were not as efficient as Sony and the auto companies—many clung to old hierarchical ways of doing business and were overstaffed and slow. From our perspective, TSR fell into that category. (I'm told that it has since modernized significantly.)

D&B had global aspirations that required us to have a strong Japanese presence, and we weren't getting there. So we tried to change the relationship with them. We approached them as an acquisition candidate, but there was no interest. Few m&a transactions occurred in Japan in those days. The exception was when one strong firm that had a long-term relationship with another firm that was weak took over the weaker firm and preserved jobs. To sell was often seen as a sign of failure. In those days, we were told, to sell to a gaijin (a non-Japanese person or entity, and not exactly a term of respect) would have brought shame to the owners. But we needed a solution.

The experts told us that the best we could hope for was a joint venture with a Japanese partner that wanted to do things a different way. Unlike mergers, JVs were common in Japan, and JVs with foreigners owning minority stakes were commonly accepted. Fuji had formed a successful joint company with Xerox in the 1960s that was going strong; Dow Jones had a joint venture with a Japanese partner to publish *The Wall Street Journal* in Japanese; Boeing, GM, and General Electric all had Japanese JVs. There were many others. But D&B was not convinced that TSR would be the best JV partner—not unless they were willing to change the way they did business, and that did not seem to be the case.

In 1987, Dave and I went to Japan to see if we could find another way to gain market leadership in that country. By that time I had been involved with quite a few international-deal negotiations. But this one turned out to be the toughest of all. It is still bright in my memory—and that's where this story really begins. It took place about fifteen years before I founded Marlin & Associates.

The Approach

When Dave and I arrived in Tokyo, I found a remarkably changed place from the city I had first visited a decade earlier. The entire country seemed to be in the midst of a manufacturing and export boom. Per capita earnings were among the highest in the world. Tokyo had become a major financial center, and foreigners were everywhere. I found a great Italian restaurant in the center of Tokyo. The music scene was bustling with jazz clubs, rock concerts, classical symphony orchestra performances, and more. They liked Dylan! (Me too.) The city was a sea of building cranes—new office complexes, shopping malls, and apartments were being built. The Japanese yen was much stronger than it had been the last time I was here. So my US dollar went only half as far. Inflation was low; unemployment and bankruptcies were unheard of. The Japanese were even healthier than most other countries (lower infant mortality rate, longer life expectancy, etc.). They still didn't like selling Japanese companies to anyone—

especially foreigners. The Japanese were feeling confident. A bit later, Shintaro Ishihara, a leading Japanese politician who had been a minister in the Japanese government and later became governor of Tokyo, wrote his book, *The Japan That Can Say No*, which implied that Japan had long been a lackey of the United States and should stand up for itself. Sony's CEO, Akio Morita, wrote another book asserting the superiority of Japanese business practices and criticized US practices as out-of-date.

Before this visit Dave and I got a lot more guidance than we Marines had ever gotten from the captain of the *Tripoli*. We were told how to dress; in Japan as in Vietnam (and in many other East Asian countries) people are generally modest about their appearance. They expected arms and legs to be covered when visiting temples, and people didn't like to stand out in crowds. Hence, conservative business suits every place I looked. (Adapting wasn't too difficult; D&B's culture was pretty conservative too.)

We were told how to address people: the Japanese were fairly formal when addressing each other at work, using honorific endings such as *-san* or *-sensei* ("Mr." or "teacher," respectively), the latter of which I often used with older lawyers or others who would teach me. If I called them by their first name, they might be insulted at the lack of respect. (Younger Japanese are often more Westernized.) I know a bunch of older Americans that are the same way. Dave McBride was that way; he and others I know feel disrespected when people call them by their first name without being invited to do so. (It should always be Mr. McBride, not Dave, until he tells you otherwise.) Essentially the same was true in Japan, plus some. At first, to some in our company it seemed odd that within companies the Japanese often addressed each other by their titles—chairman, president, manager, section manager, supervisor, etc.—rather than by name, but this was just like the Marines, where we call the battalion commander colonel and may call a company commander captain or even sometimes skipper.

We were told that many Japanese, especially older ones, were not comfortable shaking hands, and yet bowing was tricky, conferring status on bower and receiver of bow based on how low it went. We were told it was best to just nod.

We were told that we were dealing with a culture in which most businessmen were told to maintain an impassive expression when speaking, but that we could find nonverbal cues if we knew what to look for. For example, if we raised an issue and the other side inhaled through clenched teeth—that indicated that the issue was a problem. If we saw an important person frown as one of us was speaking, we understood that this was a clear sign of his unhappiness. We had to remember about gifts—to both give them and receive them, but not to be too extravagant. We were told that it was impolite to pour your own drink when eating with others: pour your companion's drink and allow your companion to pour yours. If you poured your own, you would probably insult your companion; if you allow his glass to become empty and fail to refill it, then it shows your ignorance or lack of respect.

There were so many rules . . .

I understood that we couldn't just waltz into a Japanese company and propose an acquisition, especially in those days. It would be like going on a first date and, before dinner, telling the girl that you are looking for a wife, she's among your top three choices, and you have a few questions before you decide. It's not romantic, and not likely to succeed. Japanese courtships are long, and negotiating an agreement such as we were discussing would be a slow, methodical process requiring buy-in from many people. I had also been told that the Japanese want to get to know the person they are dealing with—get a sense of his values: his honor, priorities, and sensibilities. If those don't work out, there won't ever be a deal. (I've since seen that this philosophy and approach is common in a number of East Asian and Middle Eastern cultures.) This can mean a lot of conversations over many months around personal subjects that seem to have no connection with the issues at hand. It can be frustrating for a Marine such as me who likes to get one deal done and then move to the next one and is not easy when you are based six thousand miles and twelve time zones away.

We were also told that we needed to be "well introduced," and that the quality of the introducer helps the other side understand where you stand in their hierarchy. So, in 1987 we asked our Japanese attorney, Toshiro Nishimura, to arrange an introduction to Teikoku Databank (TDB), the largest business information company in Japan and TSR's number one competitor. (TDB also had an interesting, thriving sideline, investigating prospective brides and bridegrooms for the betrothed, and those who wished they were.) Nishimura was one of the most senior attorneys in all of Japan—cofounder of Japan's largest law firm, adviser to the prime minister, and board member of large Japanese companies such as Hitachi. We would be well introduced.

TDB was a family-owned company, founded by the father of the current CEO, Yoshio Gotoh, who was approaching seventy. His son, Nobuo, was about thirty-five and a graduate of an American university (Oklahoma, as I recall.) Nobuo was quite active in the company but he wasn't in charge; day-to-day activities were handled by Hideo Gotoh, the COO, who was Nobuo's uncle (by marriage) and Yoshio's brother-in-law (married to Yoshio's sister). We were directed to work with Hideo Gotoh (he had adopted the family name).

TDB was just as hierarchical and overstaffed as TSR. Their reports were similar and, from our perspective, had similar shortcomings—too expensive for non-Japanese customers, long on subjective material, too short on the sort of hard financial facts that our US and European clients wanted. The big difference was that TDB seemed more than willing to work with us. It seemed that Yoshio and Hideo were both ready to retire but did not want to turn over all of the family's assets to the next generation. A JV was a face-saving way to take a lot of chips off the table and yet have the business continue.

Hideo Gotoh was the epitome of a Japanese gentleman of his generation. In his early sixties, he was tall, with slicked-back hair; he wore only dark suits, white shirts, and conservative ties. He smoked constantly, even in his office (which was jarring for me as a Westerner, even then). He exuded formality, which I always reciprocated. To me, he was always either "Mr. Gotoh" or, when we got to know each other, "Hideo-san."

I was still a Marine. I had a clear objective. Since I knew that majority control was not in the cards, our object was to buy 49 percent of Hideo-san's company as part of a joint venture and also—and most important—get explicit buy-in to work together to create a bigger, better, more efficient company. We would leveraging their market-leading position and brand-name awareness in Japan, their physical presence in cities throughout the country, and their knowledge of local customer needs with D&B's more efficient data-collection and data-processing capabilities. This would allow us to sell international reports to Japanese businesses and sell reports on Japanese businesses internationally. But I had been told to tread lightly—to let the process take its own time. It had the potential to be nearly a billion-dollar transaction.

So for a full eighteen months, I found myself in Japan constantly. I flew back and forth from New York to Tokyo an even dozen times getting to know Hideo-san better, met with the CEO Yoshio occasionally, and with Nobuo regularly. I'd spent so much time in Tokyo by now that I'd learned my way around some parts of the city. I had my favorite running paths. I had my favorite restaurants and jazz clubs. I found a fun Australian bar called Maggie's Revenge owned by a fortysomething Australian woman who had come to Tokyo twenty years earlier with a Japanese boyfriend. She now had a silent Japanese partner, and she served tempura and pizza, burgers and yakitori, cold Australian beer and sake.

In all this time, however, I had been to dinner with Hideo-san exactly twice. Both were formal affairs. (Have you ever eaten "drunken fish"?) Hideo-san spoke little English (we always had a translator in meetings), so we never spoke on the telephone. I never saw his home or met his family. I can't say that I knew him well. But we would sit in his small office for hours—"discussing" deal points. It was big for an office in Japan but small for our meetings, barely large enough to accommodate a small traditional sofa, coffee table, and four chairs. It seemed as if at least six of us were always in the room—including lawyers and translators. Paper was everywhere—on his desk, on the credenza, on the floor. The window offered only a dim view of a side street. His secretary would run in and out constantly, bringing tea, cookies—and memorandums. We weren't exactly negotiating, at least not for the first six months. It was more like exploring what life could be like if we were to come closer together. It was an agonizingly slow process.

For the first few half dozen visits or so, Dave McBride had come with me, as well as our head of Asian operations, Ray Paske—a former Army officer (a West Point graduate) who had been an executive with American Express in Asia. Dave was good with the Japanese—polite, respectful, always trying to advance the discussions. Ray wanted us to move faster. He would have operating authority once a deal was complete, so it was good to introduce him to Hideo's company and to have his expertise, but Ray wasn't a deal guy and had no interest in being one. He was an operator, busy running real operations elsewhere. As a result, more and more often it was just me—with the lawyers, consultants, accountants, translators, and myriad others on our team trying to push the ball forward a few inches at a time.

Our lawyers were the best in the Japan. In addition to Toshiro Nishimura, we had Ike Shapiro, a world-renowned international attorney and leader of the international practice at Skadden, Arps, one of the most prestigious m&a law firms in the world. Ike was all-American—or so he seemed until you realized that he had been born in Japan before World War II to parents who were Russian concert pianists, raised there and in Shanghai, and educated in France and the United States. He was fluent in Russian, Japanese, Chinese, French, and English (and probably conversant in a half dozen other languages too). The Japanese said he spoke their language like a native. Even our associate lawyers were top-notch too. We had lots of help. My role was to be the client and the "deal guy."

But I was on a short leash. I had no negotiating authority beyond that approved in advance by New York. It took a full year of small talk before we were finally truly "negotiating." After eighteen months, we had drafted reams of paper on how we might work together, detailed new, more efficient ways of collecting data, talked about sharing D&B's computer expertise, discussed the format of new reports and much more, but we never seemed to be getting any closer to signing an actual agreement. It's not that the Japanese were voicing skepticism or erecting roadblocks; it's just that there seemed to be a never-ending series of questions. We would address one set of issues just to have another set arise. I was starting to despair. I wasn't exactly sure whether we had a legal problem, a contractual problem, a tax problem, a cultural problem, or a personal one. I was frustrated.

The next day, as I sat on an airplane heading back to the United States, I talked about my frustrations with Ray Paske and one of our attorneys, Kelly Crabb (an American who had lived in Japan, was a fluent Japanese speaker, and was then working with our lead American attorney, Ike Shapiro). As we talked, I developed eight rules for ensuring successful international transactions. (Note that these are different from the nine rules for negotiating—although those nine remain relevant here as well.) Here they are:

Rule 1: Be Sensitive (but Not Too Sensitive) to Culture

One day after a meeting with Hideo-san, I walked out of the restaurant at the Imperial Hotel in Tokyo with Ray Paske and Masakazu Iwakura, one of our Japanese attorneys, and I observed a scene that sticks with me almost thirty years later. A Westerner in a business suit was being introduced to a Japanese gentleman and simultaneously bowed deeply and extended his hand for a handshake. He looked awkward. The Japanese gentleman looked confused, and those around him smirked and held their hands over their mouths to hide their expressions.

My Japanese colleague explained that the Westerner was going about it all wrong. Perhaps most important, his attempt to be culturally sensitive was backfiring. Instead of earning respect by showing respect, the American just looked foolish. Masakazu told me that foreigners should only bow the head slightly, if at all, since most Westerners don't understand the bowing etiquette rules and Japanese don't expect us to.

As I sat on that airplane and reflected on our lack of progress with Hideo-san, I wondered if we were behaving too much like the American, bowing and offering his hand at the same time. Maybe we were being too accommodating of the Japanese approach to negotiating, and looking awkward and foolish as a result. They must want to do a deal with us as well, I thought—otherwise, what was the point?

Perhaps it was time for us to be more direct. More *American*. Perhaps it was time for me to be more of a Marine—not rude, but more transparent and more clearly goal-oriented. That had to be a better approach than the long sessions we were enduring that seemed to get us nowhere.

I wondered if we should be coming at Hideo-san some other way.

Rule 2: Be Fully Aware of the Other Side's Objectives. It's Not Always about the Territory, or the Money

During the Vietnam War, it was common for the press to describe North Vietnam's objective as "to bring communism to the South," and the American goals as preventing a "domino effect," with communism spreading from the Soviet Union and China throughout Southeast Asia. (Never mind that the Chinese and the Russians were not exactly on the best terms, or that Vietnam and China were historical enemies—that was the line we read.) These geopolitical questions were above my pay grade, but my teachers at TBS, and later my commanders such as Joe O'Brien believed that the North Vietnamese objective was in fact much more complex and more patriotic. As I noted in the last chapter, much like the American revolutionaries, they wanted to throw out the colonialists. They understood that, as with the Americans of 1776, Ho Chi Minh's objective inspired fervor among the "patriots" of the North, while the Americans were painted as foreign usurpers who sought to replace the French. Meantime, the South Vietnamese government officials were painted as greedy and corrupt—which many of them were.

What I took away from this was the value of thinking about things from the other guy's perspective. For example, here in Japan we had been introduced to Hideo-san as the lead negotiator. We treated him as such, and he was clearly a strong proponent of a deal, so it was frustrating not to understand why we weren't getting there faster. It took a long time before I focused on *why* Hideo Gotoh was pushing this deal. What were his objectives? Could it be about something more than money? Why was the company negotiating and why was he anxious? The company was growing and profitable. Why sell 49 percent to D&B?

I had talked with Nishimura and his protégé Iwakura as well as with Ike Shapiro and Kelly Crabb about the Gotoh family's motives and concerns. But on that airplane in talking about it more, we realized that perhaps we had missed a nuance. If the deal with D&B did not go through, then Hideo-san would probably continue in his position for another few years until Yoshio retired—but then Nobuo, Yoshio's son, was likely to be the successor. That meant that in a few years, Hideo could be out, and since his pay was not high by Japanese standards (to say nothing of US standards), he was probably done. His retirement income would be small. But if the deal went through, then the tie-up with a large public American company would not only make TDB look good, but also Hideo-san's personal influence and prominence would be materially enhanced. Moreover, his close working relationship with D&B might position him for a better role in the combined firm. He might even make money on the deal.

So where did Nobuo—the son—stand? We realized that we didn't know. I liked Nobuo. We were around the same age, and he was educated in the United States. He kept quiet during meetings, but when he did speak, he showed real intelligence and a real sense of humor. He kept his cards close to his vest, but it was starting to feel as if perhaps Nobuo and Hideo-san were not on the same page—and perhaps not on the best terms. I began to realize that the objectives of one might not match the objectives of the other.

Rule 3: Know the Local Rules—and the Local Concerns

At the time that we were negotiating with the Gotoh family, the Japanese tax system was fairly complex, and my team was convinced that the biggest challenge to getting this deal done was that the family was fearful of having to pay 70 percent personal income tax on sale proceeds. We spent a lot of time trying to solve this, but I never believed that taxes were the overriding problem.

My Japanese mentors—Nishimura, Ike Shapiro, and others—had impressed on me that in Japan, as in many other places, it is important not to equate success with "winning," because that would imply that the other side had somehow "lost." Instead, they stressed that, in Japan, success means that all achieve their respective objectives. Often, *all* means more than just the people in the room. Japanese businessmen sometimes use the term *sampo-yoshi*, which literally means "trinity of bliss." Somehow that implies that all parties (buyer, seller, and the public) must be satisfied in a transaction.

As we talked and probed and asked questions that we should undoubtedly have asked eighteen months earlier, I began to see many intertwining objectives. D&B was a large and prestigious publicly traded American corporation, and a member of the Fortune 500. A tie-up with D&B would add prestige to the Gotoh family and the company. I realized that this was important to the patriarch, Yoshio Gotoh, although I was not so sure about its importance to his son, Nobuo. Also important to Yoshio was succession planning. He wanted to be sure that when he was gone, the firm would continue, with Nobuo in some kind of leadership role, just as he had taken over from his own father. I suspected that Yoshio had an additional motivation: to keep his sister—Hideo-san's wife—happy.

Rule 4: Figure Out Who Is Calling the Shots. It May Not Be Obvious

In the United States and many other Western countries it is reasonable to assume that the lead negotiator is empowered to negotiate—to give and take, to accept and reject. Not so everywhere. It had already become clear to us that Hideo-san, while positioned as the chief negotiator, had no authority whatsoever to accept or reject terms. His brother in-law Yoshio was CEO, and he wanted consensus. (In Japan, the most influential person often does not participate directly in the negotiations.)

In many ways we were lucky, since often initial business negotiations in Japan begin with middle managers. At least we were near the top with Hideo-san negotiating and with Nobuo involved. But since we had only two of the three main players in the room, and we couldn't read Nobuo, I was having trouble reading the odds of getting that consensus and getting a deal done anytime soon.

Rule 5: Set Deadlines (and Mean Them!)

Marines like deadlines. We like to know exactly when we need to be attacking the beach so that we can then plan backward. In most of the world, business negotiations are deliberate affairs. They take time. But to get across the finish line, they need deadlines. They can't be totally open-ended. Battle plans need to have a D-day—a time certain to launch the attack. Peace negotiators often don't. This is not exactly the same as being willing to walk from the table—but it does have similarities.

My Japanese mentors had warned me that in Japan, and in many other Asian (and other) cultures, businesspeople simply refuse to make big decisions quickly. They need time to contemplate—and to build consensus. But my mentors also helped me to see that decisions are rarely made without a real deadline. The question is how to make those deadlines real, not arbitrary, without scaring off the other party. And what do you do if deadlines are missed?

In Tokyo, I began to see a pattern dealing with Hideo-san and the others. The Japanese didn't make progress with us until they absolutely had to, usually defined as when I absolutely had to get on an airplane.

Something in their culture about not wanting me to lose face by going home empty-handed allowed them to come to consensus more quickly. (The Japanese try never to do anything to cause loss of face.)

It was probably time to change the dynamics. It was time to figure out who was under the most time pressure. Did they want a deal more than we? It was time to set real deadlines.

Rule 6: Seek Face Time; Build Trust

In chapter 8, my rule 8 in negotiating is "It is personal." It's doubly personal in dealing internationally. As noted in that chapter, and as my Japanese mentors kept reminding me, in Japan, as in many other places, successful negotiations require trust, and building trust takes time. But in Japan, and perhaps more broadly when dealing with people from another country, building that trust is easier with face-to-face discussions. With people whose native languages are different, communication is helped immensely when you understand the physical context in which something is said. Eye contact, body language, facial expression, tone, and even silence are all part of the dialogue. (Yes, silence. Too many Americans seem to abhor silence. When negotiating, I have learned to try not to interrupt a person's thinking, as the person may be on the verge of coming to agree with me.) Phone calls and e-mails just aren't the same.

Further, international negotiations often don't only happen "formally." Informal face-to-face time can be a critical component to coming to agreement. (In an earlier chapter, I noted the progress made during the famous "walk in the woods," when the US and Soviet representatives who were trying to negotiate a nuclear nonproliferation agreement had an informal conversation about their respective desires and fears.) Even the little bit of informal time before a meeting starts, and after a negotiating session is over, can be used to better understand the adversary.

One evening, after a long day of negotiating, my team had dinner with the Japanese. I was seated next to Nobuo and we began to talk—not of business, but of his experiences at schools in the United States, sports, hobbies, even of his wife and his young son. We found that we had a number of things in common.

It's probably not a good idea to drink too much alcohol when with the other side, as that can lead to all kinds of mistakes—unintended insults, a slip of the tongue, etc. However, I don't believe that either of us followed that rule that evening. Life can't be all business, all the time. Not only is it boring, but also it isn't normal. People have lives. We continued talking and drinking well after the others had retired. Nobuo and I started to build a relationship that would later help me understand the motivations and desires of the other side.

Rule 7: Don't Over-Lawyer

Our lawyers were not only corporate law experts, they were also experts on Japan. They were present at each negotiating session; so were TDB's lawyers. It was useful. Besides, we needed buy-in from our general counsel in New York, and the lawyers had their own channel back to him. But lawyers are lawyers. It is their job and their nature to protect their client against virtually any and all contingencies, and that can become counterproductive to getting a good deal done. Lawyers are needed to inform businesspeople of the risks of various courses of action. Businesspeople need to decide whether those risks are acceptable. But when lawyers get control of the process, it can get in the way of good deals being done. I began to realize that this was happening in Japan. There are no risk-free deals.

D&B's general counsel back in New York was nervous about the risks to D&B in a foreign joint venture that we didn't control. He was giving guidance to our lawyers; and they were guiding Dave and me. Essentially what the lawyers wanted was a detailed prenuptial agreement—a clear methodology to unwind the joint venture if it didn't work out as planned, with every detail in writing. Those were my marching orders, and at that time I was not experienced enough to know that I should have pushed back. Our draft agreement was up to two hundred pages long! This approach was anathema to the Japanese, who were more used to short, simple, and even ambiguous contracts in which each side promised to respect the other and to work out any differences in an honorable way. I despaired of this deal ever coming to conclusion.

Rule 8: Put Someone on the Ground
with Authority to Negotiate

In Tokyo, I was the deal expert, but not the chief negotiator. We had no chief negotiator on the ground. My boss, Dave McBride, was the CEO of D&B International and the one who would be responsible for the business once the deal was completed, but he had limited authority. Every move was scrutinized by corporate finance, by the corporate m&a team, by our general counsel in New York, and by the chairman/CEO. I was empowered to "negotiate" only within a strict set of guidelines. When I began to chafe at those guidelines, I had no place to go. We had a ton of cooks back in New York—and no one chief cook on the ground in Tokyo. In the end, more than any other factor, that was probably our undoing.

Conclusion (of Sorts)

Eighteen months after my first meeting in Hideo-san's small office, I found myself once again sitting on his same small traditional sofa, a coffee table in front of me with tea served by one of his assistants. My Japanese-speaking lawyer Kelly Crabb was sitting next to me, and Nishimura himself was present. Hideo-san sat in another chair across from us, next to his lawyer and Nobuo. They had to bring in extra chairs. It was crowded. Yoshio was in his office across the hall.

After much internal conversation, and at my urging, I had received permission from New York to bring our discussions to a head. I told Hideo-san that we had all talked long and negotiated hard, and that we each had what seemed to me to be acceptable terms. We had agreed on value, risk protections, and prenuptial agreements. We had an operational plan. We had a heavily negotiated purchase and sale agreement. We had a detailed plan for what we would do once the deal was completed. We had ambitious goals in Japan and very much wanted to move forward with TDB as our partner. But we also couldn't negotiate forever. There was no reason why we could not now agree, sign, announce, and move forward together. We wanted to come to agreement now—this week—or we should call it quits and move on separately.

Hideo-san listened and nodded; he and Nobuo exchanged glances.

But they were otherwise completely impassive. There was no look of concern, no sucking in of air between the teeth, no anger, and no agreement. They just said that they understood. I went back to my hotel. I had no idea what would come next. I was nervous. The next morning, I got a call from Nishimura. They had agreed. The lawyers would formalize the paperwork by the end of the next day, Thursday, and the official signing would be on Friday. We would have our joint venture. I was thrilled!

I was slated to return to New York on Friday morning, and we arranged to have signature pages left with the lawyers and held a celebratory dinner on Thursday night. Everyone came: Hideo-san, Yoshio, Nobuo, his son, Nishimura, and Iwakura. As I recall, Ray Paske was there—but Dave McBride was tied up in New York. Ike Shapiro couldn't make it, but Kelly Crabb did. We even invited the Bain consultants. The lawyers on the other side came. There were toasts all around. We had done it! It was a great feeling.

I wish I could end the story right there, but I can't. Friday evening, in New York, I got a call from Dave, who had received a call from Ike Shapiro and the Japanese lawyers. The deal was off. TDB had decided not to sign after all and would instead go forward on their own without D&B. No reason was given and no request made to renegotiate any provision. Soon after, we received a formal, hand-delivered, written letter from Hideo-san that said the same thing. There was no explanation. I was crushed.

My inclination was to return to Tokyo to see if the deal could be resolved, but after much internal discussion, we became convinced that this deal was indeed dead.

I never figured out for sure what had happened, but I suspect that Nobuo talked his father out of it. What I did hear was that soon after the deal collapsed, Hideo was out of the firm and Nobuo became COO. A year after that we learned that Hideo also was out of the Gotoh family, having divorced Yoshio Gotoh's sister. Nobuo later succeeded to CEO when his father retired. Had we waited, would things have been different? I don't believe so. I've talked to Nobuo several times since then. We still exchange holiday cards. He is happy and successful building TDB as an independent company. Perhaps someday his son will take over.

Postscript

Nearly ten years after my failed negotiations with the Gotoh family, I found myself in Japan again, negotiating a joint venture for my new company, Telesphere. This time the person on the other side of the table was Yoshiaki Akeda, the forty-year-old manager of a major division within Nomura Research Institute (NRI). Akeda was technically savvy and moved quickly. He spoke English fluently. He didn't smoke. I had known him for about four years, as he had been my customer at Telekurs, and I had visited with him in Japan several times over the previous three months. I also had spoken with him numerous times by phone.

I have no idea what Akeda's office looked like because we always met in one of NRI's modern conference rooms or at a restaurant. I liked him, and we had gotten to know and trust each other. He knew how to get things done within the NRI bureaucracy. Telesphere was pretty new, and I very much wanted to establish a joint venture with NRI and to work with them to help us to sell our products throughout Asia. My goal was to get it done in six months. I had the benefit of my eighteen-month sojourn with the Gotoh family. I knew that I couldn't just parachute in and expect to consummate a deal and march out, but I also knew that a deal could be done. I also knew my eight rules.

I was sensitive to Akeda's culture and would always respect it, but I also couldn't afford to allow the process to take too long. Meantime, I was aware of NRI's objectives and sure that we could help them meet their goals. I understood the local rules and customs, and I knew that Akeda would have to get consensus internally before there could be an agreement. All I could do was help to arm Akeda with the information he would need to convince the others. Negotiations take time, but I also knew that I had to have a presence in Japan and Asia or else my business model was at risk.

I promised my board that I would either have a deal in six months or else we would go it alone. I explained that situation to Akeda. I was willing to put in my face time in Tokyo. I knew to negotiate with discipline and competence and fairness, and I was clear on what I wanted and was willing to document it at the end. But until then, a few e-mails would suffice.

When we were ready, I told Akeda that I did not need a two-hundred-page document. I had learned not to over-lawyer it. We needed to cover the essential points for sure, and both sides would want liability limitations. But overall, this deal would rise or fail based on trust and goodwill—and not on legal documents.

Over the next two months, Akeda and I met four or five more times. It was enough, and in three months, we had the makings of a deal—a joint venture. It took another month to document and get approvals, but while that was happening, we were laying the groundwork to get started. After a total of four months we were live on the ground—two months ahead of my own aggressive schedule.

Others told me that it couldn't be done, but we made it happen—and things worked out great. Not only did we get a deal quickly, but also the relationship worked out extremely well afterward. It worked so well that it nearly doubled Telesphere's profitability and made a material difference to our value when I eventually sold the company to Bridge.

A common thread throughout my career has been the recognition that to build a world-class business requires foreign entanglements. My firm has now advised on transactions involving participants in at least twenty-six countries on four continents. The ability to manage these "cross-border" transactions has become one of our hallmarks. As we do so, I try to remember three simple concepts:

First, the skills, principles, and practices that I learned in the Marines are applicable everywhere—to be successful in business and on Wall Street you do need to know yourself, know the enemy, know where you are going, negotiate from the high ground, etc. Dealing with people of foreign cultures just requires that you focus on these elements a bit more.

Second, staying safely at your home port is narrow thinking. While cross-border deals can be challenging, they are also necessary to bring efficiency and effectiveness to world-class organizations. Increasingly, the companies with a competitive edge are those that no longer define themselves by geographic borders. It may be easier to only buy from and sell to people in your domestic market, but a big world is out there beyond your borders, and most smart competitors are trying to figure out how to take advantage of that. The United States generates about 16 percent of the world's GDP—down from almost 20 percent ten years ago. To keep up with the times as well as to serve clients in the best possible way, we need to seek foreign entanglements

Third, foreigners are foreign, and successfully winning battles in foreign lands requires sensitivity to the nuances of difference. But you can't go "native." It won't work; you'll just wind up looking like that foolish American trying to bow—or worse. Be sensitive, but remain true to yourself and your principles. It works.

Seeking foreign entanglements is advice that I give to buyers and sellers of companies today. Seek them—and remember that your odds of success are materially enhanced if you follow these eight rules. That's the Marine Corps Way.

IO

Trust *and* Verify

IN THE LATE 1980s, WHEN I WAS NEGOTIATING TO DIVEST D&B OUT OF South Africa and also working to find a way to establish the company in Japan, among other places, President Reagan was negotiating nuclear weapons treaties with his Soviet counterpart, Mikhail Gorbachev. Reagan was fond of repeating the mantra "trust but verify." Reagan didn't invent the phrase, but it's a good one—and a sentiment that I heard a lot in the Marines—although I prefer to say "trust *and* verify"—because that's exactly what we do. When my Marines stood sentry duty, they were told to trust *and* verify the permission of anyone entering secure areas. For a decade I conducted (and was subject to) countless trust-*and*-verify inspections. It's not that my superiors didn't trust me. It's that prudence and good discipline require that we also verify. That attitude describes a healthy relationship in which you respect the party you are dealing with, and also show respect for yourself and the need to verify all assumptions related to the task at hand. It's also a healthier approach than "shoot first and ask questions later."

One of those Marine Corps trust-but-verify inspections is indelibly imprinted on my memory. It wasn't combat, or even a particularly tough training exercise. Instead, it was the time that the inspector general of the Marine Corps, along with a particularly large inspection team, flew from Washington, DC, to my base in California to check to see if I'd been doing my job correctly.

I had recently been promoted from company commander to the S-4—the logistics officer—for Third Battalion, Seventh Marines, a unit of about seven hundred Marines and Navy corpsmen. I was responsible for keeping those Marines and corpsmen fed, clothed, armed, and warm while in the base camp and while on the move; to obtain, maintain, and distribute everything the battalion needed for war and for peace, including nearly a thousand weapons, dozens of trucks, trailers, radios, spare parts, tents, sleeping bags, cold-weather gear, desert-warfare gear, and many other items. Also, I had to get them where they needed to be—moving all seven hundred Marines by sea, air, and ground to far-off places under strict time pressure. It was a big job and I needed to do it all within budgets that were always a tad too tight. And I was supposed to keep detailed records.

I had been in the job for only a few months when I was told about the inspector general's upcoming weeklong detailed review. This was a big deal, and for good reasons neither our equipment nor our record keeping were fully up to inspection standards.

We never had all of the staff and equipment we were supposed to, and keeping things in good working order was a challenge when we spent at least twenty days a month in the field. Things get lost, damaged, and stolen. Sometimes we had to borrow from other units. Sometimes parts were not available. Sometimes we had no money left in our budget and we had to make do. We tried—but we were busy. Now, the inspector general and his team of inspectors were en route. Didn't he trust us? Did he really have to "verify" that we were doing everything the Marine Corps Way?

Something that was referred to as IG hysteria soon ensued. The division commanding general trusted us, but he wanted a pre-inspection to verify that all was well (just being helpful); the regimental commander also trusted us, of course, but he too wanted a pre-inspection before division's pre-inspection—just to verify; and my boss, a newly minted lieutenant colonel who had never before gone through an IG inspection as the commanding officer had panicked. He didn't know what to do. He left it to me, with the highly constructive suggestion and admonition "Don't mess it up."

I understood how detailed IG inspections could be and had been through several—but never as the battalion S-4. Fortunately, a couple of sergeants working for me had been through these sorts of IG inspections several times. They knew what to do. They knew, for example, that our armory would be a major focus of the inspection, and one of them worked with our armory personnel to ensure that everything was in order. They organized our small staff to work with the personnel in the motor pool, the communications center, the supply warehouse, and other areas in the same way. They also knew that the inspectors at each level would need to find a few things wrong or they would never leave, and so we purposely gave them a few minor blemishes to find.

We felt some tension, but no hysteria. We needed dozens of Marines from around the battalion to help prepare the vehicles in the motor pool, and dozens more to work in the supply warehouse. The battalion commander was so nervous that he gave me whatever help I asked for. In the middle of the night before one inspection, he had the battalion duty officer call me because the commander wanted changes in the barracks to be sure we would be in compliance. But we got through it.

The regimental inspectors came first. They spent a full day auditing a dozen areas, and they found discrepancies—not just the ones we had left for them to find. We fixed them, and then the division inspectors came—and they found several more discrepancies, not just our plants. We fixed those too. We were ready; and then the IG came—and it was painful. They inspected for three days. They went over everything in painstaking detail—especially our armory. They counted, inspected, reviewed records, and took weapons apart to see how well they were maintained. They went over every record; they even counted how many blankets we had. In spite of our best efforts, they found a few more "discrepancies"—but by that time it was all minor. We passed. My battalion commander was ecstatic.

I relay this Marine Corps inspection vignette in part because I am reminded of it nearly every time one of our clients is subject to a trust-and-verify inspection (aka a due diligence review) by some big, sophisticated party on the other side of a transaction. The clients often ask the same sorts of question: Don't they trust us? Why do they have to go through this huge, detailed inspection process? I feel their pain. I have experienced it personally (including when I sold Telesphere to Bridge).

InfoDyne

InfoDyne Corporation was led by its founder/CEO Guy Tagliavia, a talented, driven software developer who was way ahead of his time.

Long before people were touting "big data," Guy proclaimed the big information technology giants just didn't get it. They didn't understand how modern technology could enable them to assimilate, integrate, compile, and analyze massive amounts of fast-moving data quickly and accurately—and serve their customers better. Guy believed he could meet that need, and he built a company to do just that. Chicago born and raised, with no interest in wandering far, Guy set up his company in a suburb near O'Hare Airport. He delivered what he promised, and by the middle of the first decade of this century, InfoDyne counted some of the most prestigious and sophisticated financial services organizations in the world among its customers. But as InfoDyne grew larger, managing the company had become more of a challenge. Guy was a software developer, not an administrator or an accountant. He asked us to help him find the right partner.

We ran our customary thorough preparation and documented InfoDyne's strengths, weaknesses, capabilities, and constraints so that we could provide appropriate information about his company to prospective buyers. We worked with Guy to identify those parties and to tailor our message for each. Because I have been through these detailed inspections before, we thoroughly prepared for the due diligence inspections that would come once we had settled on a partner. Before we even met with a prospective buyer, we worked with Guy to establish a "virtual data room," a secure, online data repository inside which we could have all the documentation that we could think of that anyone would ask for—all organized in virtual file folders within virtual file drawers. At each step, my staff "pre-inspected" it, making sure that it would pass our muster before we released it to a third party. Only then did we reach out to prospective partners.

At least six firms expressed substantial interest. We got to know each and negotiated with several. After some fairly intense negotiating, Guy agreed on basic terms with IBM, which not only offered him a strong purchase price, but also planned to make Guy and his team the center of their effort to develop similar products. Guy was thrilled, and he thought we were done, but he didn't realize that the hard part was yet to come.

I'll never forget Guy's colorful description of IBM's detailed due diligence review: "proctologic."

We are used to the due diligence reviews of large corporations; we are accustomed to having ten to fifteen people poring over documents, each with a specialty area, but IBM asked for access for more than eighty people in about a dozen groups. It was an army of deal guys and executives, technical folks, product sales and marketing people, accounting and tax experts, and lawyers (lots of lawyers). We couldn't keep track of them all. Their due diligence information request list ran thirteen pages, roughly ten pages longer than most, and was so complete that I might have recognized it as beautiful were I not intimately involved in addressing it!

They asked extremely detailed questions and expected clear written answers for each. They wanted five years' worth of history for each customer; five years' worth of accounting detail; state sales tax filings and state and federal income tax returns; detail about past years' operating results by customer, by venue, and by expense category; detail to establish product-line profitability along with detailed forecasts for revenue and expenses for each and more. (Unfortunately, InfoDyne didn't track expenses this way.) They wanted to examine Guy's software code in detail from a half dozen angles—validity, reliability, potential copyright infringement, documentation, etc. (It was IBM and that part seemed reasonable.) They looked deeply into his people from a dozen angles—their job, compensation, benefits, prior experience, education—and of course everything related to customers (agreements, pricing history, commitments, etc.). They looked at InfoDyne's relationship with its vendors, and so much more. Then they asked for meetings. It was almost enough to make a seller throw up his hands and go home.

But I had been through Marine Corps IG inspections (and countless other trust-and-verify due diligence reviews) more than a few times and I know how they work—although IBM's was the most extensive we have experienced in civilian life. I knew that these experiences go best if you anticipate what the other side will be looking for and thoroughly prepare—and that is exactly what we had done (although we did not purposely leave small things for IBM to find). The work we had done—assembling documents into virtual folders in the virtual data room—saved us.

IBM found things—inspectors always do, it's their job. Like the Marine Corps inspectors, they couldn't possibly go through all that effort and not find anything to talk to us about. They questioned whether InfoDyne had paid all the sales tax that it was supposed to pay in every state in which it had clients; they questioned that some customers had the right to terminate their contract upon a change of control; a dozen issues were raised. But we were prepared and re-solved each one—fairly quickly. Ultimately, InfoDyne passed. IBM bought the company.

An Important Part of the Process

Marines conduct trust-and-verify inspections because of the possible serious risks if combat units are incorrectly assumed to be combat-ready. Marine general James Mattis, whom I have quoted before in this book, said when he led Marines in Iraq, "Be polite, be profes-sional, but have a plan to kill everybody you meet." A bit extreme for some, perhaps—but it reinforces the notion that when the conse-quences are serious, trust only goes so far. You must verify.

On Wall Street and in business, while the stakes may not be life-or-death, due diligence reviews are also important to increase the probability that a battle (or transaction) will be successful. And some-times it is a legal requirement.

Officers at public companies are under particular pressure to confirm (as best they can) that their plans and forecasts are reasonable and feasible, so they must examine potential m&a transactions thoroughly before they complete deals. If they don't, "surprises" can leave the company and its executives subject to shareholder lawsuits and gov-ernment enforcement action. That's no fun. But even for nonpublic companies, verifying the most important assumptions can be critical to ensuring that a business transaction is a success.

In the corporate world, buyers are often being asked to give up the certainty of cash or other valuable consideration (e.g., stock) for an uncertain promise of something to come (profits, for example). Buy-ers may worry that the people on the other side of the table know something that they don't. After all, people present themselves and the opportunities they offer in the best possible light, often ignoring or glossing over potential risks or shortcomings; it's human nature. And sometimes people lie. Corporate executives and some politicians are concerned that they might later look foolish if their basic assump-tions underlying the deal don't come to fruition. That may not be career enhancing. That's why most buyers and sellers—and for that matter most Marines—start out a bit wary, unsure if they can trust the person on the other side of the table. That's why we verify.

People on both sides of Wall Street transactions as well as most other business deals—and probably most political deals—know that they can't verify every single person, detail, and assumption. (The list of items to check can be exhausting for the kinds of technology companies that make up the lion's share of our client base.) But people can do their best to verify the assumptions that are most important. When the process works, the parties develop more confidence in each other, and that helps the process to go forward. When the process fails, people may take on more risk than they had expected. Deals may close and then blow up. Sometimes people lose jobs. It is serious business.

Contracts Can't Protect Against Everything

Lawyers tell us that you can mitigate many risks with well-written contracts, and it's true, but not totally comprehensive. No contract can guarantee the future. Macroeconomic conditions change, and forecasts miss the mark. Further, few parties are willing to accept allocation of all risk. (Contracts tend to allocate risk.) Besides, contracts are only worth what those backing those contracts are later able to deliver. When lives or careers or material amounts of money are at stake, it would be foolish to rely simply on contracts without some verification.

In my world, where buyers and sellers are often meeting for the first time, as well as in the business and political worlds, principals want to do more than review paperwork or rely on contracts. They want to personally evaluate how much they can trust the people on the other side. I don't just mean verify that the people on the other side aren't flat out lying or hiding material (that's pretty rare), but also that the people on the other side are the sort that they want to work with. We tend to assume that people are competent in their roles; that they know the things that you would expect them to know; and that they have disclosed the things that should be disclosed, and it's important to check. But it's also important to verify cultural fit. No lawyer can do that for you. Executives on each side need to look each other in the eye and see how they twitch, how they answer questions, and how they come across in competence, trustworthiness, and compatibility. An important part of due diligence reviews is each side figuring out if they can "trust" the people on the other side.

So What Do You Do?

This is not a how-to book on due diligence reviews for Wall Street transactions, and this chapter will not present due diligence checklists to be used in any of a wide variety of situations. There are plenty of books on the subject. The object of trust-but-verify inspections, such as those of the inspector general and IBM, is to verify the most important assumptions that underlie the existing or possible relationship. The IG wanted to be sure that my battalion was ready for combat. IBM wanted to be sure that InfoDyne was ready to join IBM's business—and that IBM wasn't buying it under false assumptions.

In the part of Wall Street in which I work, a review of a company's financial records, corporate legal documents, tax records, and past and current litigation are nearly always a part of the due diligence review. The buyer wants to make sure that it doesn't fall into any hidden traps after the deal is done. But dozens of other areas may be important in some instances and completely irrelevant in others. For example, for corporate acquirers of technology companies—my bread and butter—the most important areas of due diligence reviews are often not a company's financials, but its products, customers, and intellectual property (IP). That's where IBM focused most with Info-Dyne. Do the products work? Are the customers happy? Does the company own the software code that it uses in those products as well as patents, copyrights, trademarks, trade names, and other IP?

Some of this can be verified by reviewing paperwork (customer agreements, employee and freelancer agreements, patents, etc.), but in addition, confidence can come from actually talking with customers who use the products. IBM did that—and came away happy. IBM also needed to verify that InfoDyne had complied with the export control rules, data protection laws, and software licensing rules. Those don't apply in many other cases.

In my world, sellers may have similar concerns—especially when a purchase price includes something other than cash, such as stock or options, or promises of future employment, or expectations of future installment or contingent payments. Sellers worry about the value of those promises. They may also worry about nonfinancial matters such as promises about the impact of a transaction on customers or employees. Contracts can only help to a limited extent. To mitigate these fears, sellers too need to verify key assumptions.

Due Diligence Failures Can Be Painful

It can be easy to get frustrated with the due diligence process. It's often the least fun part. It's exciting and fun to figure out strategy, find promising partners, and get them to think hard about how each can further the other's goals better by working together, but due diligence reviews get down in the weeds. Stories are legion about the extent of some of these reviews, and about the cursory nature—or the failures—of others. If you open the pages of *The Wall Street Journal* or the *Financial Times*, you'll find many juicy stories of the impact of less than completely thorough due diligence reviews.

For example, Shamu, the captive killer whale, is a star of many shows at SeaWorld, the animal theme park. In 1989, after acquiring SeaWorld, Anheuser-Busch learned that the purchase did not come with the rights to trademark *Shamu* or to the cartoon and characters inspired by Shamu. Due diligence reviews should have discovered that those rights had been sold to a small company that had created the cartoon. Anheuser-Busch later bought those rights back for $6 million.

Or as another example, in 1990, the Clorox Company bought Pine-Sol from American Cyanamid, expecting to expand the product line. Apparently, Clorox's DD reviews didn't uncover that in 1967 Cyanamid had signed an agreement that restricted the use of the Pine-Sol brand/trademark for other products.

One of my favorite stories of this sort is what happened to VW when it bought Rolls-Royce Motor Cars Ltd.

Rolls-Royce produced only nineteen hundred cars or so a year at that time (1988) with 70 percent of them under the Bentley name, which Rolls owned. However, Rolls was a desirable luxury brand, and several other car companies coveted it. The front-runner in negotiations was BMW, which was a key Rolls-Royce supplier, providing the mammoth twelve-cylinder engines that powered both the Rolls and the Bentley. BMW did its homework, and in April 1998, Vickers PLC (the owner of Rolls-Royce) accepted BMW's offer of about $575 million for the company.

Then Volkswagen AG (VW), a German rival of BMW's, stepped in and started a bidding war. VW already owned Audi and Porsche and wanted to add Rolls-Royce to their collection of luxury brands. Eventually, Vickers accepted VW's higher offer of £430 million (about $712.7 million at the time).

BMW had lost—or so everyone believed. But VW would soon learn a powerful lesson in the value of due diligence. BMW knew that back in 1973 Rolls-Royce had split into two companies—an automotive company and an aircraft-engine company. The aircraft company had kept ownership of the best of Rolls-Royce's intellectual property and branding, including its trademarked Rolls-Royce grill, the RR trademark, its Spirit of Ecstasy hood ornament, and even the Rolls-Royce trade name. The two new companies had then entered into a deal whereby the automotive company licensed the Rolls-Royce trade names and trademarks from the aircraft company, but it did not own them. (It did, however, own the Bentley names and marks.)

So, after BMW "lost" to VW, BMW then approached the aircraft company and quickly, separately, and quietly bought the right to use the Rolls-Royce name and other related intellectual property going forward. BMW then served notice on VW of its intent to use the marks and also announced its intent to cancel VW's right to buy BMW engines, within a year. VW discovered that it had acquired the Bentley models, a factory in Crewe, England, where both cars were produced, and other assets needed to build and sell big British luxury cars—but it did not have a source of engines, nor did it have the right to the Rolls-Royce name and brands.

Ultimately, German politicians intervened to avoid a lengthy, expensive court battle between two of the country's large automobile manufacturers. They brokered a transition period: VW would continue to build and sell both Rolls-Royces and Bentleys with BMW engines, while BMW built its own factory in the UK to produce Rolls-Royce cars. After four years, the deal would be up, and the battle would be on: BMW would produce and sells Rolls-Royces, while VW would produce and sells Bentleys. VW learned an expensive lesson on the need to conduct thorough due diligence—and act on the results.

There are lots of other examples. The question for bankers is, simply, where do our responsibilities begin and end?

Dragon Systems

A few years ago, I read an article in *The New York Times* about the sale of a company called Dragon Systems, a pioneer in speech-recognition technology. If you have asked Siri on your iPhone to find the closest Thai restaurant or post office, you may have benefited from their legacy. The buyer of Dragon was Lernout & Hauspie. Few people had any reason to pay attention to the story; it wasn't a big transaction. But *The Times* called this transaction "the business deal from hell," and it seemed to me that better due diligence could have prevented the problem.

Dragon Systems was founded by a husband-and-wife team of PhDs. Their proprietary technology had its roots in research that the husband, James Baker, had done for his doctoral degree in the 1970s. The company was an entrepreneurial success story, and they were making millions and thinking about going public. Then they started getting unsolicited offers to buy their company from the likes of Sony and Intel. The Bakers had a clear long-term strategic objective: to sell the company for a lot of money so that they could move on to whatever they had in mind for happily ever after. To help them sort through it all they hired a prestigious investment bank: Goldman Sachs.

In the grand scheme, with around $70 million a year in revenue and four hundred employees, Dragon Systems was small potatoes to Goldman, which is one of the world's largest and most prestigious investment banks. However, this was a hot company in a hot space that should have commanded a big price. The short story (it is more complicated than this) is that Goldman and the Bakers reportedly agreed on a flat $5 million "success fee" to Goldman if a deal got done. Five million dollars is a reasonable fee on a percentage basis for a transaction of this size and would be a hefty fee for my firm, but it's not that big a deal for a giant investment bank. Goldman assigned a four-person team to help the Bakers achieve their long-term goal.

Goldman must have done a good job describing the firm and preparing the Bakers for the transaction because they received multiple offers to acquire their company. Working with their bankers, they evaluated each. Ultimately, Goldman advised the Bakers to negotiate with Lernout & Hauspie, a Belgian company whose stock was listed on the NASDAQ in the United States and in Europe. That was the battle the Bakers chose to fight and ultimately they "won." They sold their company to L&H in a $580 million, all-stock deal—a strong valuation by almost any standard. Goldman was paid its $5 million fee; the Bakers were happy: high fives all around.

Now, Goldman is a well-respected institution. They have advised on some of the world's biggest and boldest transactions. The ugly thing that happened next at Dragon Systems certainly is not an indictment of Goldman, but just a few months later L&H was exposed as a fraud.

According to *The New York Times*, L&H had pumped up its stated revenue and profits and thus its share price by inventing customers and reporting sales that didn't exist. Most of the Bakers' stock became worthless. The Bakers may have won the battle, but they were now further than ever from their long-term goal. They had lost their company and the proceeds. They sued Goldman Sachs (and others) essentially on the basis that Goldman had not properly helped them with performing due diligence on the buyer. They showed that another part of Goldman, its merchant banking division, had considered buying L&H stock and had rejected the idea. The Bakers alleged, in hindsight, that their advisers should have helped them conduct more thorough reviews and warned them of the dangers of accepting stock as payment from this particular party. Even if the Goldman bankers were not aware of the work done by their sister unit, the Bakers felt that Goldman should have investigated L&H on their behalf with the same level of diligence.

According to the *Times*, Goldman's bankers demurred, and one of them testified that he thought his team had done a "great job" because they had done what they had been hired to do: "We guided them to a completed transaction." A court ruled in Goldman's favor, saying in part that it was not Goldman's job to examine L&H closely enough to determine whether entering the deal was a good long-term decision for Dragon Systems, but instead only to make the deal happen. Ugh.

That's the law. Further, we bankers are not the only ones involved in a deal. There are accountants, lawyers, and a host of others—

including the client, who always has the ultimate decision-making responsibility. Further still, hindsight is always twenty-twenty. Information is rarely complete and fraud is tough to detect. (Ask the shareholders of MCI, whose shares lost nearly all of their value after the collapse of WorldCom.) So, I'm not saying that the bankers could have discovered the problem in advance—I don't know enough. But I am saying that better due diligence by the seller on the buyer might have caused the Bakers to choose one of the other offers for their firm.

Countless times our due diligence reviews have revealed some unexpected facet of a company. Earlier, I recounted the time when we advised the New York Stock Exchange not to buy a UK company, as well as the time we advised SWIFT not move forward with an acquisition that they had initially found attractive. We've had similar experiences with sellers. On one occasion, for example, we advised our client to walk away from a buyer despite their handshake on a deal, based mostly on our sense that the CEO of the acquiring firm couldn't be trusted to live up to promises he was making. It's part of our job.

Prior Preparation Prevents Poor Performance

The Marine Corps taught me both how to conduct inspections as well as how to prepare for inspections—to anticipate what's coming and to be ready long before the inspectors show up. When we work with clients, we take the same approach. We anticipate, we prepare, and we stick with the client through the process. This starts before we ever accept an assignment.

We often conduct our own limited due diligence review before agreeing to work with a new client. We interview the client and try to assess what we see; we look at our own extensive databases and for public records on the business and its key executives; we decide if an even more preliminary investigation is appropriate before we agree to advise the client. After we have accepted an assignment, our inspection ratchets up. That's when my team requests and then reviews material that we know that most counterparties will want to see before they agree to a transaction. We know that a company will be subject to great scrutiny. We want to question it, understand it, believe it, and anticipate questions before the other side sees it—before any material issues arise. Often we ask for more, or for backup documentation. Sometimes it takes weeks. For example, a client once asserted that it had over a thousand customers. When we asked to see contracts and records, this count was revealed to include clients who were currently testing the product but weren't yet paying, as well as customers for whom our client could show us copies of invoices that had been paid, but no supporting contracts.

We knew that buyers would want to see those customer contracts as part of their due diligence, so we set the company to finding or replacing them. It was a heck of an exercise, but obviously it's better for us to find and remedy the problem before the buyer even asks. By the time the prospective buyers got into their due diligence, we had found or replaced everything. The management looked more competent. Trust was maintained. To be clear, we don't review legal agreements the way a lawyer would; we don't call customers; we don't inspect software code; we don't opine on accounting treatment that has been approved by the company's auditors; etc. We're not trying to conduct a full-scale due diligence review. But we *are* trying to prepare our client for what we know will come, to anticipate what the other side may look for. (We've seen hundreds of due diligence request lists. They are remarkably similar.)

We work with the client to assemble all relevant documents and put them into an organized electronic repository. These virtual data rooms are a great tool to help us keep track of everything. When we are ready, we open up the VDR to those on the other side. It's all about being prepared, and we stick with the client through the detailed due diligence review.

At InfoDyne, we didn't like everything that we saw at first look. My team members discovered several inconsistencies in the materials. These weren't all negative; some items actually understated InfoDyne's recent financial performance. Others were more neutral but were confusing. We did not understand all the assumptions that had gone into the financial projections, and when we asked, we found that the CEO, Guy Tagliavia, didn't understand all of them either. (He hadn't prepared them himself.) It took us a few weeks of back-and-forth, but when we were done, we had materials that we felt comfortable that the client could stand behind. Then we were ready to show that material to potential partners—and not sooner.

Our approach helps reduce the number of questions and issues the other side will have, but it won't find them all. It can't. We're not lawyers or accountants or software-code experts. Further, just as neither my team nor the regiment's team nor the division's inspectors found all the discrepancies that the IG later found, our banker review of documents will never replace or replicate the deep-dive due diligence that the other side often conducts. And like the IG, it seems as if the inspectors always find something. It's their job.

As a final example, the PE firm that was investigating our client Triple Point Technology for a potential recapitalization had their auditors pore over TPT's books and records. The auditors concluded that TPT had been recording revenue currently that should have been spread over several years. This seemingly esoteric question had a significant potential impact on current-year revenue and profit—and on purchase price. Our process could not have discovered this kind of issue, especially since TPT's books and records were audited by a credible accounting firm that took a different approach. TPT's accountants reviewed the findings but did not agree. We did not want to lower the purchase price, so we needed to find another solution. In this case, we worked with the company to recast TPT's revenue and profit over the past three years, as well as the forward projections, using TPT's methods and separately using the PE firm's approach to revenue recognition. We showed that the ultimate differential between their approach and ours was relatively small, in part because to be consistent under their approach we would have to pull revenue forward from past periods. Eventually, we convinced the buyer that our approach was reasonable. We got the deal done, without reducing price.

Conclusion

Trust is a critically important factor to reaching agreement on Wall Street, on Main Street, and in political caucuses. It is built up over time through many actions. But trust alone is not enough to cause people to risk lives, businesses, careers, or significant amounts of money. Before accepting those risks, Marines—as well as most businesses and most people—need to trust *and* verify. It's not easy, and some verification processes can require long and detailed efforts—such as Marine

Corps IG inspections. The consequences of failure can be serious. Deals have died that should have lived. Deals have been consummated that should not have been. Like IG inspections, these reviews are usually unavoidable; and also, like them, in the main, in spite of the pain, they are good for all concerned. They can give both sides confidence that everything is combat-ready or they can ferret out potential issues before they become major ones and can help to avoid problems down the road—after agreement is reached. Sometimes, the reviews can help you discover facts about the other side, or about yourself, that can help you avoid costly battles that should not be fought and transactions that should not be completed.

Marines, as well as business leaders who are on the receiving end of trust-and-verify inspections—aka due diligence reviews—can materially improve the probability of a successful verification by following many of the principles in this book. Like any other battle, it requires knowing your long-term objective; understanding the strengths, weaknesses, capabilities, motivations, and constraints of the other side; and anticipating their process. It also requires knowing your own strengths and weaknesses. (We told IBM that InfoDyne didn't have the staff to accommodate the process that IBM envisioned, so they modified it. That didn't mean they reduced the eighty people looking at documents, but it meant we could handle a lot of it through the VDR and via e-mails and conference calls.) And the battle calls for detailed planning, careful preparation, attention to detail, and discipline in execution.

In the end, we were well prepared. We were able to respond quickly to most of IBM's document requests and questions and explain why we couldn't for those remaining few. Some questions we had not anticipated (there always are), and IBM found a few issues. (How could they not, with eighty people looking?) There were potential tax issues (sales tax, mostly) and questions about incomplete software documentation (shades of my Marine Corps IG inspections) and issues about up-to-date third-party software licenses and more. But we helped the company work them through to satisfactory conclusions, maintained trust, and got the deal done. IBM became convinced that they knew exactly what they were buying. Guy became convinced that he would be getting just what he wanted: the right partner for his employees, his customers, and himself. He stayed with IBM after the acquisition long enough to smooth the transition, before leaving it in good hands to go on to new adventures (and to find new ways to increase his life's volume).

When you anticipate the trust-and-verify process and prepare properly, battles have an increased probability of working out the way you want them to—and that's what this book is all about. I survived the IG's inspection of my battalion, and we were more combat-ready as a result. Likewise, we helped Guy survive IBM's detailed due diligence reviews of his company and along the way helped IBM see that InfoDyne was combat-ready. That, in turn, helped Guy to accomplish his long-term strategic objective; and that's what we are here for.

Be Disciplined

TECHNICALLY, NORTH AND SOUTH KOREA REMAIN AT WAR TODAY. THE armistice agreement they signed in 1953 temporarily suspended hostilities; it was not a peace treaty. As I write, something like two million soldiers on that peninsula face each other daily, knowing that at any time some provocation could send them back to war. Regularly, some incident causes real bullets to be fired. Periodically, someone gets killed.

Two years before I enlisted, as the battle at Khe Sanh raged in Vietnam, North Korean forces sent a group of thirty-one specially trained soldiers into South Korea in an attempt to assassinate the South Korean president. It failed, but not before twenty-six South Korean soldiers and four US Army soldiers were killed. (At least twenty-eight members of the North Korean unit also were killed.) Days later, North Korean Navy patrol boats with support from MiG fighter jets captured the USS *Pueblo,* an American spy ship based out of Yokosuka, Japan—a port that I know well. The Americans said that the ship was in international waters at the time; the North Koreans disagreed. During the capture, one American crew member was killed and the other eighty-two were taken prisoner. They were then sent to POW camps, where they were starved and tortured. President Johnson ordered a massive response—sending six aircraft carriers plus support ships and aircraft to the region and calling up Army reserves for the first time since the Cuban missile crisis. This crisis played out for eleven months before the *Pueblo*'s crew was released. The North Koreans continue to hold the ship to this day. And that was not an isolated incident. Tensions run high in Korea.

A few years before I left the Marines, in my last deployment to the Far East, I took part in a massive joint-military training exercise off the coast of Korea with more than one hundred thousand troops from the US Army, Navy, Air Force (and the Marines), along with members of the South Korean military. They told us this was the largest joint-military exercise by far since the end of the Korean War. The stated objective was to improve the many ways in which the forces of each country worked with each other. It was clearly also meant to show the North that the United States stood together with the South and was prepared to defend that country. The North Koreans took it as preparation for war. We took it seriously.

The exercise was complex—requiring close and constant coordination and communication among the US Navy, Air Force, Army, and Marines as well as with units of the South Korean armed forces, ships, and aircraft. We also had to ensure close cooperation and coordination among the infantry, artillery, aviation, engineer, tank, and other support units that constituted our Marine Amphibious Unit (MAU). All this required a lot of disciplined and detailed planning.

About twelve hundred Marines were aboard our ship, including most of an infantry battalion and a Marine helicopter unit, and my job was to coordinate the ship's end of the MAU's ship-to-shore movement as part of a mock amphibious assault. The planning for the larger exercise had gone on for months before I became involved, and then our planning for our part in the exercise went on for weeks. Every detail of every movement of gear and people from various parts of the ship to various pre-embarkation staging areas had to be planned in coordination with the expected order of launch of helicopters to the beaches; embarkation then had to be planned as well as recovery, resupply, and rescue operations—and we had to have contingency plans. For this to be successful, all had to know their job well; everyone had to execute well. It took discipline.

The whole exercise reminded many of us—and probably the North Koreans—of the Marine Corps–led amphibious assault at Inchon in 1950. It too required huge amounts of disciplined, detailed planning and execution. That battle, which was spearheaded by the First Marine Division, involved more than 250 ships and something like 75,000 troops from several nations. The audacious move caught the North Koreans by surprise and cut off their supply lines. Two weeks later the United Nations' forces, led by General Douglas MacArthur, with generous help from the Marines, recaptured Seoul and the momentum of the war was changed.

Discipline Is Critical to Proper Preparation

Marines like winning. We don't like drama. As a result, we try to remove as many variables as possible before heading into action. We prepare—thoroughly. Among other things, we take the long view; we establish long-term strategic objectives and then we use disciplined planning and preparation to increase the probability of success. We try to think three steps ahead; we think about our strengths and weaknesses—where we need to be, with what expert resources, when, and what we are going to do when we get there. We try to know the enemy's strengths and weaknesses and anticipate where they will be, what they will do, and what could go wrong (from our perspective); we have contingency plans. We try to know what the objective is worth before we commit. We assemble the right team, obtain and stage the right equipment, train and rehearse. We ingrain repeatable processes on how we will act and react in different circumstances. Then we act. Planning is not accidental and discipline is not a separate step; it's the glue that holds all the rest together.

The benefits of good preparation are multiple. Processes generally go more smoothly; fewer people get hurt. There is no drama, and we achieve our strategic objectives: we win. MacArthur could not have captured Inchon and we could not have pulled off our exercise without a disciplined approach. Bankers take note. Politicians too.

Luck Has Nothing to Do With It

A few years ago, a colleague sent me an article from one of the entrepreneurship Web sites. Written by an investment banker, it was entitled "Six Key Rules for Selling Your Company." I'm always curious to find out what others in my industry are thinking, so of course I skimmed through it.

The first four "key rules" basically had to do with having a good company to start with. *(Agreed.)* The fifth rule was about having a good adviser. *(Of course.)* But the final rule struck me as odd. It said that the most important rule in selling a company is that you have to "be lucky," which the article didn't particularly elaborate on.

I understand the general philosophy that in any situation you can only control so much, and sometimes you get unlucky. In an earlier chapter, I told the story of the Navy Cross won by my former boss, Joe O'Brien, who ran into bad luck when his company of Marines was attacked by a force of North Vietnamese five times the size of his unit. The salient factor is that he used the highly trained, disciplined team at his disposal to survive and get his men to safety. He had a backup plan, stayed disciplined, and implemented it. In another earlier chapter, I noted that Chesty Puller had bad luck in Korea at the Chosin Reservoir, when the Chinese Army entered the war and had Puller's First Marine Division completely surrounded. Again, Puller didn't use bad luck as an excuse to fail. He employed the disciplined training of his Marines and fought his way to the sea.

The Marine in me recoils at the notion of relying on luck to succeed, and especially at the idea of advising business leaders that luck constitutes some kind of important element to a plan. Too much is at stake to rely on luck, whether we're talking about combat missions, training exercises, or the fate of a business that represents people's dreams and livelihoods. Sure, sometimes I've gotten lucky, and sometimes bad luck has intervened in ways that could not have been anticipated—such as when the global financial crisis hit and caused so many buyers to flee the market. But mostly, in my experience, the Marine Corps as well as most successful businesses owe their successes to a culture that eschews luck as a factor as much as possible. We use the eleven principles that I write about in this book, including taking the long view; employing experts; understanding our strengths and weaknesses as well as those of the enemy; controlling the timing where we can; trusting and verifying; and using disciplined, repeatable processes to try to take luck out of the equation. I carried these lessons into the business world, and it works. Marines make their own luck. So do good business leaders, political leaders, and investment bankers.

Sometimes Discipline Is About What You Don't Do

One part of discipline involves careful planning, training, preparation, and execution. But also, sometimes, discipline is about having the courage to *not* engage in battle at all. We don't have to fight at every opportunity. We don't have to transact each time we could—and bankers don't have to accept every potential assignment. Just as Admiral Nimitz skipped islands in the Central Pacific and MacArthur did in the Southern Pacific, we try hard to pick our battles—always bearing in mind the ultimate prize. When we lose the discipline of choosing when we fight, it can bite us.

We had been in business as Marlin & Associates for about a year when a CEO approached us with a request to help him sell his company. At face value, the deal violated several of my rules: His company was smaller than I normally like, had not grown the top line in several years, and was not profitable. All of these things militated against the likelihood of success. Moreover, the industry he served wasn't growing; in fact, it was contracting. But I managed to find some reasons to say yes. Even though the company had not been growing in prior years, the CEO told us that he expected substantial growth in the coming year. I saw a small but viable set of potential prospective buyers—maybe six to ten. The company had some proprietary intellectual property that these buyers might value, and I liked the product line and the CEO. He told us that he was willing to accept any rational price. But above all, my firm was young, we had not closed many deals, and I was hungry. I accepted the assignment. I shouldn't have.

For the next six months we worked extremely hard to get a deal done for this company. We applied our Marine Corps–inspired processes: we planned, we prepared, and we attacked. We were disciplined. And as were doing all the right things, the business continued to suffer. The promised growth did not materialize. In spite of that, we brought in offers from three credible buyers. Then, to add insult to injury, the CEO deemed all three of the offers to be well below what he was willing to accept. He chose not to deal and instead to continue running the company. Given his alternatives, and given his outlook for the future, I probably wouldn't have sold either. It was a legitimate client decision. Nevertheless, after all that work, it was a disappointing outcome for me and my team.

Was that bad luck? Not to me. I lost discipline when I agreed to take on an assignment that I shouldn't have. I knew what the situation was from the outset. We worked hard, and we gave ourselves the best probability of success that we could have. But the odds were stacked against us from the outset. In my world, we don't get paid for hard work. We get paid for results. I was reminded that sometimes it's okay to skip islands (battles). Sometimes, discipline is about what you don't do.

In another early disappointing assignment, we agreed to advise the owners on the sale of a company that was owned fifty-fifty by a son and a father. I say it that way because the son had started the company (he was the CEO) and only later brought in his father. The son signed the engagement agreement with us, ostensibly with the father's blessing—but oddly we weren't allowed to talk to the father. This should have been a warning signal!

The company had much to offer. It had great products, blue-chip customers, a strong international presence, and growing revenue and was quite profitable. It was growing fast in a desirable market. The management team was strong. We ran our normal thorough and disciplined process and received strong offers from several well-qualified strategics and investors. Unfortunately, only then did we learn that the father had no interest in selling, and he had blocking rights. There was no shareholder agreement, no "drag along" rights, and no one could change his mind. The son threw the father out of the company and off the board. That must have made for some interesting Thanksgiving dinners, but the deal never went any further. I don't chalk that one up to bad luck either. Instead, I relearned another lesson. We should have done better preparation before we took on the assignment and during it. We weren't disciplined enough.

Discipline Can Help Ensure Successful Execution—Especially When the Going Gets Rough

In early 2008, S&P asked us to advise management on the sale of its Vista Research unit. The catalyst to the sale was an investigation by Eliot Spitzer, the New York State Attorney General at the time, who was looking to see if some firms in the industry in which Vista operated were aiding insider trading. (Bad luck?) Vista was never accused of wrongdoing, and the company ultimately escaped the investigation quite clean. Nevertheless S&P worried about potential "reputational risk." They wanted to sell. We agreed to help. My colleague Jason Panzer led the effort.

We had done our homework: Vista was a strong company, growing and profitable. S&P was a committed seller. We had none of the issues of the other two firms that I described above. This one should have been easy. We prepared well including identifying a wide range of potential buyers. The most likely buyers and the ones that were proving to be the most interested were the big bulge bracket investment banks such as Bear Stearns, Goldman Sachs, Lehman Brothers, JP Morgan, and Merrill Lynch. Then came the global economic meltdown. (More bad luck?)

The combination of customer reluctance as a result of the AG's investigation and the bad economy caused Vista's revenue and profit to drop more, and that in turn made their financial projections suspect. I suppose this all falls under the heading of bad luck. And it got worse. As the global financial crisis deepened, our lead buyers (the big investment banks) all stopped returning our calls. They had more important things to worry about. Quickly, Bear Stearns got subsumed into JP Morgan and Merrill Lynch into Bank of America. Lehman disappeared completely. No investment bank was focused on buying our client's firm. More bad luck? Maybe, but we were prepared. Our list of potential buyers with strategic fit who could afford the transaction went beyond investment banks. We just needed to give them confidence in Vista's future. With S&P's blessing, we persevered. It wasn't easy. The economic environment had made many prospective buyers nervous, and that rarely leads them to take risks. But our disciplined process, and dogged determination, eventually paid off. It took another few months but we got the deal done. Luck had nothing to do with it.

Repeatable Processes Combined with Discipline Can Sometimes Work Wonders

Discipline in Marine operations begins with a clear sense of mission and then rapidly moves to having well-trained troops who are expert at their jobs so that they know exactly what do in a wide variety of circumstances. As strange as it may seem to some, it all requires developing good habits—repeatable processes that are so ingrained that they become natural.

When I enlisted in the Marine Corps, I was subject to the sorts of initiation rituals we've all probably seen in movies such as *Full Metal Jacket*: the thirty-second head shave (my hair was pretty long in the days before I enlisted), screaming drill instructors, merciless constant physical exercising, and a thousand rules that had to be followed to the letter. Among other things, we were instructed on exactly how to shower (what to wash, in what order), how to brush our teeth, how to shave (first shaving with the grain in down strokes; then up against the grain), how to make our bed (hospital corners, sheets tight enough to bounce a quarter on), hang our clothes, pack our footlockers, and dress ("blousing" our trousers over our boots) and undress (placing our clothing in appropriate places). We took barber shears to the field to give haircuts. Every morning, regardless of circumstances, we were expected to wash, shave, and brush our teeth and, if appropriate, wash our socks and underwear. We learned to take field baths in the field using water in our helmets.

At first, all this attention to small things didn't make a lot of sense beyond that. After all, I already knew how take a shower, shave, brush my teeth, make my bed, and get dressed. And who cared if my boots were shined or if I could bounce a quarter off my sheets? But as the months wore on, especially after boot camp, I began to see the logic behind the approach. When you're operating in the field, you're going to be a lot healthier if you've got short hair and do your best to keep yourself clean (and clean-shaven). The field is a lousy place to get sick, get lice, or have problems with your teeth or your feet, and the best way to avoid that is to keep hair short, bodies clean, and teeth regularly brushed. Blousing your trousers over your boots keeps bugs, dirt, and other stuff out. Putting your clothes away when you sleep keeps critters out of them too. When taking care of yourself and your equipment (including your boots) just becomes a repeatable daily routine, it avoids drama later.

These kinds of details also give supervisors (sergeants and officers) a quick (if imperfect) way to assess the readiness of their troops. The theory is that if a Marine has taken the time to make sure his hair, boots, and clothes meet the grooming standard, he probably has paid proper attention to other, more important details.

A lot of Wall Street bankers, just like a lot of business leaders and way too many politicians, don't give a lot of thought to establishing or monitoring repeatable processes—much less the discipline to make sure these processes are employed *all* the time. There's a fair amount of "winging it." In many cases, including my time at Veronis, Suhler, each partner, each managing director, each business unit head, and each congressman is left to find his or her own way to approach complex issues.

At my firm, we like allowing plenty of room for creativity; we encourage out-of-the-box thinking. But at the same time, we want to employ a disciplined, repeatable Marine Corps–inspired approach to solving the challenges that we know we will encounter. We need to be well organized and be sure that we cover all the bases if we are going to help clients win battles.

Disciplined Planning Runs Backward

As young Marine officers at The Basic School, we were taught to employ discipline in many facets of our lives (not just daily hygiene), including operational planning. Again, it's about having a repeatable process that works—and in this case, it starts with a "backward planning" rubric. The concept is that a smart tactical goal is an end point—or at least a phase point—and planning is about how you achieve that goal whether it's "Seize, occupy, and defend that hill by eight tomorrow morning and be prepared to hold it for at least a week" or else "Get us out of South Africa by December 31st, at a reasonable price and with a plan that allows us to reenter the country later." To get there, you can create a detailed action plan by methodically working backward from that goal step-by-step to figure out what you need to accomplish to attain that objective. At each turn, you need to anticipate what the opposing force might do and be sure that you have prepared adequate main and contingent plans.

For example, in an effort to take the hill by eight tomorrow morning given available resources, a platoon commander might decide that the attack should begin with mortar fire followed by a two-pronged attack, and he might estimate that the mission will take two hours. As he contemplates each step, he would think about the opposing force: How would they defend the hill? And then plan accordingly. He would work backward and decide where and when he would have to position his men to be ready to start the attack. From there, he would work backward further to determine when they would depart their encampment and with what food, ammunition, equipment, etc. Then backward again: What time will you feed the Marines, issue ammunition, and brief the platoon leaders? Step back: What time do the Marines need be awake? You keep moving your plan backward—carefully, methodically, making sure that all bases are covered, always contemplating how the opposing force might react—and always trying to have a plan B, just in case plan A falters.

Backward planning for the amphibious landings such as the ones that I helped plan for as a Marine were a tad more complex, and those on Guadalcanal and Inchon infinitely more complex yet, but the basic concept still holds. It is a great approach, and we employ exactly the same technique in trying to advise clients. We start with the end game and work backward, piece-by-piece, step-by-step, to figure out what we need to accomplish to achieve our client's strategic objective. And then we prepare.

Disciplined Communicating Requires Structure and Clarity

Discipline extends beyond the planning and preparation phases to the conduct of the operation itself, and it's the same for Wall Street, Main Street, and political centers. Marine officers are taught to use five clearly defined paragraphs when conveying directions to the troops. The five paragraphs carry the acronym SMEAC, for situation; mission; execution; administration and logistics; and command and signal. The point is to be sure that Marine leaders give their people all the relevant information they need in a concise, easy-to-follow method.

We start with explaining the *situation* in which we find ourselves. What is happening around us? Where is the enemy? What are their strengths, weaknesses, and capabilities? What do we believe they want? What are they likely to do? What resources do we have? What are our higher and adjacent units around us doing? What is their mission?

Then we move to our *mission*. What are our specific objectives today, tomorrow, and the next day, and why? How do we fit that into the big picture?

Next, we get to the meat: How are we going to *execute*? What is the assignment of each subunit within our organization? What resources will each have? How will we coordinate?

Administration and logistics are important. How will we get to where we need to be? And how will we get back? Where are the hospitals? What is the situation with food, fuel, ammunition, medicine, bandages, spare parts, and more? What are the rules of engagement?

And *command and signal.* We must know how to communicate during times of high stress. What radio frequencies should we use to to to call the bosses? To call for artillery support or air support? Or for medical evacuation? How to signal to friendlies that we are on their side? How to signal that we need help? What passwords and codes to employ?

I'm simplifying, but you get the gist.

Giving that information to people in a disciplined manner does two important things: (1) It helps your people succeed: the listeners know what is coming next and are better able to understand and retain what is being communicated; and it also reassures them that you understand that keeping them informed is important. (2) It means that you are explaining everything that needs explaining: By communicating in the same five paragraphs every time, in the same order, you can be relatively confident that you have covered all the important topics. The key is discipline: you can't skip steps.

SMEAC is by no means the only disciplined way to communicate direction. When I was at D&B, Dick Schmidt had his own version of SMEAC, using techniques that he had learned at McKinsey including something called the Pyramid Principle* to create well-thought-out presentations that were cleanly prepared and purposefully crafted to convince the audience to take some view or some action (or to be confident in actions that were about to be taken), which is quite different from the purpose of a Marine Corps five-paragraph order. Dick was just as disciplined as any Marine in his approach. What he presented had a clear order, and it worked. At my company we have developed our disciplined approach to use when communicating the strengths, weaknesses, capabilities, and constraints of our clients. But our approach wouldn't work for a bond trader, for example. There is no single right way to structure these communications—

---

* The Pyramid Principle is a concept developed by Barbara Minto from McKinsey and used by McKinsey to this day to structure their advice and reports.

what's important is that you develop repeatable processes that ensure clear comprehensive communicating—and then have the discipline to use that approach *all* the time, without cutting corners. It's all about discipline.

Disciplined Execution Requires a Disciplined Team Working Together

Having clear long-term strategic objectives, smart, clear intermediate goals, a solid plan to achieve those goals, thorough preparation, and clear communication still isn't enough to win battles. You also need a well-trained, disciplined team of domain experts to work together to execute that plan.

Marines, when on the line in a defensive perimeter, are assigned to pay close attention to a particular zone or "field of fire"—say from the tree that is fifteen degrees to your left to the boulder that is fifteen degrees to your right. The Marine to your left may be assigned to focus on a zone to your left, and another Marine to a zone on your right, and some other Marines will have your back. This system works extremely well—as long as each Marine trusts his buddies to perform their roles well. Otherwise every Marine would be looking everywhere.

At our firm, as in the Marines, it's all about having a team of experts that are not only individual experts, competent in their assigned roles, but who also trust one another to do their part well as part of a team that works together to attain a common long-term strategic objective. That's what we create for each client—S&P, for example—a dedicated deal team integrated with members of the client's staff. It's easy to say and hard to achieve. It takes discipline.

Selecting the right team members is crucial. Most Wall Street firms—as well as most well-run businesses—spend considerable time trying to do just that. The Marine Corps benefits because so many people want to be a Marine. That allows the Corps to be selective as well as to remove those who can't make the grade. It also helps that Marines are not a particularly large force. (As I write, there are about 220,000 Marines, including about 182,000 on active duty and about 40,000 reservists; compare that to more than 1 million soldiers in the US Army, including about 580,000 on active duty and nearly

500,000 in the Army Reserve and National Guard. The numbers are all drawing down a bit as I write, but the proportions remain about the same.) So, as a relatively small service, Marines often are able to pick the cream of the crop. But I believe that one of the many other advantages that the Marine Corps has in assembling the best team members is that it is a good meritocracy. Marines try hard to recognize talent and promote it no matter what school someone went to or what his or her parents once did.

My firm is a relatively small compared to the bulge bracket banks. Like the Marine Corps, we have no problem recruiting smart, hard-working people, and I recognize that this gives us an opportunity to select and shape the team and the approach in way that allows us to stay small and elite—we want to be the best. None of my other current team members is a Marine, but they are good. As in the Marines, we don't care where someone went to school or who their parents are. We hire and promote from within. This approach has given us a group of professionals in New York, San Francisco, Washington, DC, and Toronto that together form a team that any Marine would be proud of. They comprise a mix of professionals who bring to our clients long-term expertise in investment banking, private equity, and management. Some of them have traditional investment banking experience. Others come from corporate environments. One is a "recovering" m&a attorney. What they all have in common is that they are domain experts who respect the need to plan carefully and prepare thoroughly and have an ability to work well together in teams.

Leadership Requires Discipline

Marine officers all carry a weapon—a pistol or a rifle. And as we discussed in an earlier chapter, Marines are all riflemen—all professional war fighters. But a heck of a lot of things have to go badly before an officer ever fires a round. That's because a Marine officer's real weapon is supposed to be the team that he's leading—his platoon, his company, his battalion, etc. It's not just about having a gaggle of independently operating experts; it's about assembling those experts into a cohesive unit all focused on the same goals—each understanding his or her role within that team. And that takes disciplined leadership.

I learned from fantastic leaders that a well-led and disciplined team can do things together that no one thought possible—leaders such as Marine Corps colonel Joe O'Brien and D&B leaders Dick Schmidt, Dave McBride, and Bill Jacobi; and John Veronis and John Suhler—who started their own boutique investment bank thirty years before mine. To have an effective strategy, you need leaders who know how to lead.

What these leaders had in common was an understanding of the eleven principles that I describe in this book and a disciplined dedication to insisting on following all the steps—skipping none. They were nothing if not disciplined.

The same attributes should be true of leaders at Wall Street firms as well as those in government and at well-run businesses. But too often it isn't. If it's not every man for himself, it can turn into every small team within the organization for themselves. Too often there isn't enough sense of the entire organization's being behind the achievement of any given objective. As we saw in the Dragon Systems example, it's all too common for one part of a big Wall Street investment bank to have no clue that another part is working (or has worked) on a related deal.

Conclusion

If you ever visit Washington, DC, in the summer and you have some free time on a Tuesday evening, I suggest you check out the Marine Corps Silent Drill Team's performance. It is part of the weekly sunset parade at the Iwo Jima Memorial. Their synchronized movements are amazing—even more so when you realize that they do the entire thing silently, without uttering a word. It's kind of like Cirque du Soleil, only with rifles and bayonets, and it's a testament to the planning, practice, expertise, communication, teamwork, leadership, and disciplined execution described in this book.

Over the years, I have come to appreciate these traits as not only what it takes for that silent drill team to continue to impress, but also as the same traits that are required for Marines to continue successfully executing their missions with honor, courage, competence, commitment teamwork and loyalty. It leads to success on the battlefield and on Wall Street and Main Street.

For the past several decades, I have seen firsthand that those who pursue their goals without applying the principles that I write about in this book succeed far less often than those who do. I won't call them doomed to fail—some people do just fine. Some people win Lotto. But I have seen that those that do apply these principles with honor, courage, competence, commitment, and loyalty have a much higher likelihood of successfully achieving their long-term strategic objectives—and along the way they have less drama and feel good about how they got there too. I like that. It's the Marine Corps Way.

Acknowledgments

This book started in earnest when I was introduced to Bill Murphy Jr., a former reporter for *The Washington Post* and assistant to Bob Woodward. Bill is now a columnist for Inc.com and an author in his own right. I had put together more than one hundred thousand words in rough notes that were loosely divided into eleven chapters. Bill offered to walk me through all eleven—one at a time. Over more than a year, usually on weekends (we both have day jobs), he did so in painstaking detail—forcing me to be sharper, clearer, and more complete. We would talk about a chapter; I would send him a draft; he would send me his comments; I would revise; and we would start again. There would be no book without Bill.

Larry Kramer, publisher of *USA Today*, introduced me to a legend—Fredrica "Fredi" Friedman—the literary agent-supreme and fearless leader of Fredrica S. Friedman & Co. I thank Larry. Fredi is more than an agent. She is a mentor who knows her business. She has a roster of boldfaced names that she guides and represents. I am honored that she had faith in me and my book, even if she did make me rewrite parts of the proposal (several times) until it passed her muster. Fredi became my guide to the world of publishing—a world that is still totally unfathomable to me.

Eventually, Fredi led me to Tim Bartlett—the tireless editor from St. Martin's Press, who also had faith in me and the premise of this book and gently guided me to make each chapter even more sharply focused. Many others chimed in with their helpful comments and suggestions. Too many to name and thank. But I could not have completed this journey without them.

Throughout this journey, it has been my good fortune to be married to Jacqueline Barnathan, an editor in her own right, and to be the father of Victoria, now pursuing her own dreams in Paris—both of whom put up with me while I was cranky, preoccupied, and consumed with writing, rewriting, and rewriting again during times that I should rightfully have been spending with them. Family isn't just important; it's everything.

Index